Cyber Security
and
Network Security

Scrivener Publishing
100 Cummings Center, Suite 541J
Beverly, MA 01915-6106

Advances in Cyber Security

Series Editors: Rashmi Agrawal and D. Ganesh Gopal

Scope: The purpose of this book series is to present books that are specifically designed to address the critical security challenges in today's computing world including cloud and mobile environments and to discuss mechanisms for defending against those attacks by using classical and modern approaches of cryptography, blockchain and other defense mechanisms. The book series presents some of the state-of-the-art research work in the field of blockchain, cryptography and security in computing and communications. It is a valuable source of knowledge for researchers, engineers, practitioners, graduates, and doctoral students who are working in the field of blockchain, cryptography, network security, and security and privacy issues in the Internet of Things (IoT). It will also be useful for faculty members of graduate schools and universities. The book series provides a comprehensive look at the various facets of cloud security: infrastructure, network, services, compliance and users. It will provide real-world case studies to articulate the real and perceived risks and challenges in deploying and managing services in a cloud infrastructure from a security perspective. The book series will serve as a platform for books dealing with security concerns of decentralized applications (DApps) and smart contracts that operate on an open blockchain. The book series will be a comprehensive and up-to-date reference on information security and assurance. Bringing together the knowledge, skills, techniques, and tools required of IT security professionals, it facilitates the up-to-date understanding required to stay one step ahead of evolving threats, standards, and regulations.

Publishers at Scrivener
Martin Scrivener (martin@scrivenerpublishing.com)
Phillip Carmical (pcarmical@scrivenerpublishing.com)

Cyber Security
and
Network Security

Edited by

Sabyasachi Pramanik
Debabrata Samanta
M. Vinay
and
Abhijit Guha

Scrivener
Publishing

WILEY

This edition first published 2022 by John Wiley & Sons, Inc., 111 River Street, Hoboken, NJ 07030, USA and Scrivener Publishing LLC, 100 Cummings Center, Suite 541J, Beverly, MA 01915, USA
© 2022 Scrivener Publishing LLC
For more information about Scrivener publications please visit www.scrivenerpublishing.com.

Wiley Global Headquarters
111 River Street, Hoboken, NJ 07030, USA

For details of our global editorial offices, customer services, and more information about Wiley products visit us at www.wiley.com.

Limit of Liability/Disclaimer of Warranty
While the publisher and authors have used their best efforts in preparing this work, they make no representations or warranties with respect to the accuracy or completeness of the contents of this work and specifically disclaim all warranties, including without limitation any implied warranties of merchantability or fitness for a particular purpose. No warranty may be created or extended by sales representatives, written sales materials, or promotional statements for this work. The fact that an organization, website, or product is referred to in this work as a citation and/or potential source of further information does not mean that the publisher and authors endorse the information or services the organization, website, or product may provide or recommendations it may make. This work is sold with the understanding that the publisher is not engaged in rendering professional services. The advice and strategies contained herein may not be suitable for your situation. You should consult with a specialist where appropriate. Neither the publisher nor authors shall be liable for any loss of profit or any other commercial damages, including but not limited to special, incidental, consequential, or other damages. Further, readers should be aware that websites listed in this work may have changed or disappeared between when this work was written and when it is read.

Library of Congress Cataloging-in-Publication Data

ISBN 9781119812494

Cover image: Pixabay.com
Cover design by Russell Richardson

Set in size of 11pt and Minion Pro by Manila Typesetting Company, Makati, Philippines

10 9 8 7 6 5 4 3 2 1

Dedication

This book is dedicated to my parents, my spouse, my elder sister and my son Arnab Pramanik.

Dr. Sabyasachi Pramanik

To my parents Mr. Dulal Chandra Samanta, Mrs. Ambujini Samanta, my elder sister Mrs. Tanusree Samanta and daughter Ms. Aditri Samanta.

Dr. Debabrata Samanta

To my parents Mr. Madhava Rao R, Mrs. Padma M Rao from whom I learnt the Intonation.

Dr. M. Vinay

To my parents Mr. Nilay Guha, Mrs. Shila Guha; my uncles Mr. Malay Guha and Mr. Pralay Guha; My wife Mrs. Gargee Chakraborty and daughter Ms. Arohi Guha.

Abhijit Guha

Contents

Preface

This book focuses on the "interdisciplinarity" of cyber security and network security which contributes to the emerging dialogue on the direction, content and techniques involved in the growth and development of cyber security and network security education and training. The book "Cyber Security and Network Security: Advances, Applications and Emerging Trends" presents the latest methodologies and trends in detecting and preventing cyber and network threats. Investigating the potential of current and emerging security technologies, this publication is an all-inclusive reference source for academicians, researchers, students, professionals, practitioners, network analysts, and technology specialists interested in the simulation and application of cyber and computer network protection. It presents theoretical frameworks and the latest research findings in cyber security and network security technologies while analyzing malicious threats which can compromise cyber and network integrity. It discusses the security and optimization of cyber and computer networks for use in a variety of disciplines and fields. Touching on such matters as mobile and VPN security, IP spoofing, and intrusion detection, this edited collection emboldens the efforts of researchers, academics, and network administrators working in both the public and private sectors. This edited compilation includes chapters covering topics such as attacks and countermeasures, mobile wireless networking, intrusion detection systems, next-generation firewalls, and more. Information and communication systems are an essential component of our society, forcing us to become dependent on these infrastructures. At the same time, these systems are undergoing a convergence and interconnection process that, besides its benefits, raises specific threats to user interests. Citizens and organizations must feel safe when using cyberspace facilities in order to benefit from its advantages.

The current trends and future directions of diverse Cyber security and Network Security Research with applications in various domains are covered in this book. Assaults on computers are gradually becoming one of the most common problems on the planet. As the scope of digital misbehavior grows, it is critical to look into fresh techniques and advancements that can aid ensure the internet network's security. Continuous technological advancements have necessitated a deliberate approach to security challenges.

Chapter 1 explores that data security, both inside and outside client devices, is a very important problem in today's society, which is primarily operated through programs interacting over the internet. The MSME sector and new businesses are primarily moving to the cloud to take advantage of the emerging virtual market prospects and to change their work culture to the online arena. As a result, workplace communication that previously took place behind closed doors and in locked storage rooms with data has transitioned to a more public setting, with files being sent through the public internet to public facing servers. As many of the servers for Public/Hybrid Cloud models are owned jointly by two or more parties/stakeholders, this creates a whole new set of security and compliance issues. As a result, data in transit, i.e. data moving in and out of the cloud, as well as data at rest, i.e. data stored in the cloud, must be encrypted so that no third party can access it without the owner's permission. Data from a client application, such as an Enterprise Communication Application, would be encrypted using updated algorithms and accessible securely through a set of Access Control capabilities with Least Privilege Access Policies in this suggested study model. The data is then packaged and sent over SSL Layers to a server-side application instance running in a public cloud (here)/private cloud, which decrypts the data and sorts it accordingly before saving it to object-based storages, NoSQL databases, and ledger databases with high availability and security at rest. The data at rest is further encrypted, and when requested, it can be packaged and given back to the client application with the essential encryption in transit conditions met. The transactions are carried out using role-based assigning systems and least access privilege access mode, thus obliterating the ideas of data eavesdropping, personal security risks, and so on.

Chapter 2 discusses the use of cloud technology which has grown in recent years. Cloud computing has become an essential component of modern life. Many businesses have been attracted to relay because of the on-demand service providing flexibility enabled by cloud technology. It is not necessary to purchase servers, databases, or other advanced technologies in order to start a new business. Simultaneously, data security in the cloud is extremely concerning and necessitates some attention. With the use of the user's cloud records, switches, and routers, cybercriminals can gain access to the user's systems in a variety of methods. Cloud computing is distributed computing, and it is impossible to imagine cloud computing without these techniques. The security procedures are still in their infancy. Identifying the cyber criminal's cybernetic proof is critical. Cloud service providers rarely give cloud security analysts access to cloud logs or virtual machine instances. For cyber criminals to abuse cloud computations at any time, they only need cybernetic evidence. To prevent cyber criminals from intruding, security procedures must be strengthened. Cloud forensics is one approach to carry out such tasks. There is a lot of research going on in this subject, but there are still a lot of problems to tackle. HPCBC is a high-performance cluster-based computing (HPCBC) technology that can be employed in IoT and AI applications instead of supercomputers. HPCBC uses a parallel processing system. Cloud forensics could be given a new direction with the support of high-performance cluster-based computing, according to this article. Simultaneous imaging and upload, as well as encryption, are available for the files. With the Remote desktop connection, the files should be processed in real-time stream processing. This survey article offers a variety of perspectives on cloud forensic methods and methodologies.

Chapter 3 includes that in the last few decades, cyber-attacks have become far more common. According to statistics, 12.4 million attacks were documented in 2009, and this number has since climbed to 812.67 million known occurrences in 2018. To be fair, these are merely the documented cases; there are many more. Small cyber attacks to massive Ransom ware attacks or a mix of several complex cyber attacks that include advanced exploitation techniques and persistence capacity for long-term infiltration campaigns. However, the deployment of malware was a common thread in all of the cyber attacks that have occurred thus far. To counter these attacks, we must first comprehend malware's basic structure, functionality, and impacts on the target. This paper gives an in-depth look at malware architectures by studying the malware using a technique known as malware analysis, as well as other related methods that vary based on the type of malware and a closer look at several types of malware, as well as certain well-known malware methods.

Chapter 4 discusses that fraud is one of the most common sources of substantial financial consequences in today's society, not just for businesses but also for individual customers. The extraction of user profiles based on previous transaction data and then deciding whether or not an incoming transaction is a fraud based on those profiles is an important approach of detecting fraud. The suggested block-chain technology enables certified users to securely store, review, and exchange digital data, facilitating the development of trust, integrity, and transparency in online commercial connections. Block-chain systematically examines the resilience of block-chain-based reputation systems, with a focus on the secure and reliable extraction and transfer of data to customers. Block-chain uses cryptographic hashes generated from summarized shopping blocks that are signed and sent to enable a safe and secure online buying experience without the need for third-party intervention.

In Chapter 5, it is shown that the demand for blockchain-based identity management systems is especially evident in the internet age; we've been dealing with identity management issues since the internet's inception. Privacy, security, and usability have all been cited as major concerns. User identities are organized using identity management systems (IDMSs), which also manage authentication, authorization, and data interchange over the internet. In addition to a lack of interoperability, single points of vulnerability, and privacy concerns, such as allowing bulk data collection and device tracking, traditional identity management systems suffer from a lack of interoperability, single points of vulnerability, and privacy concerns. Blockchain technology has the potential to alleviate these problems by allowing users to track who owns their own IDs and authentication credentials, as well as enabling novel information ownership and administration frameworks with built-in control and consensus methods. As a result, the number of blockchain-based identity management solutions, which can benefit both enterprises and clients, has been fast expanding. We'll classify these frameworks using scientific criteria based on differences in blockchain architecture, administration methods, and other important features. Context is provided by scientific classification, which includes the depiction of significant concepts, evolving principles, and use cases, as well as highlighting important security and privacy concerns.

In Chapter 6, the concept of feed forward networks is introduced which serve as the foundation for recurrent neural networks. Simple writing analysis is the best analogy for RNN, because the prediction of the next word is always dependent on prior knowledge of the sentence's contents. RNN is a form of artificial neural network that is used to recognize a sequence of data and then analyze the results in order to predict the outcome. The LSTM is a type of RNN that consists of a stack of layers with neurons in each layer. This article also goes into the issues that each technology has as well as possible remedies. Optimization algorithms alter the features of neural networks, such as weights and learning rates, to reduce losses. Optimization Algorithms in Neural Networks is one of the sections. A section dedicated to some of the most current in-depth studies on Steganography and neural network combinations. Finally, for the prior five years, we give an analysis of existing research on the current study (2017 to 2021).

In Chapter 7, it has been found that cyber physical systems (CPS) will be used in the majority of real-time scenarios in the future. The use of such technologies is unavoidable in order to make the world smarter. However, as the use of such technologies grows, so does the need for improved privacy. Users will not be easily used to such systems if the privacy component is compromised. Because Cyber Physical Systems use a variety of heterogeneous sensor data sources, incorporating a high level of privacy is becoming increasingly difficult for system designers. The applicability of the precise penalty function and its benefits in increasing the privacy level of cyber physical systems will be presented in this chapter. We'll compare this to existing privacy-preserving strategies in cyber-physical systems and discuss how our suggested privacy framework could be improved in the future.

In Chapter 8, the increasing demands for the preservation and transit of multi-media data have been a part of everyday life over the last many decades. Images and videos, as well as multimedia data, play an important role in creating an immersive experience. In today's technologically evolved society, data and information must be sent rapidly and securely; nevertheless, valuable data must be protected from unauthorized people. A deep neural network is used to develop a covert communication and textual data extraction strategy based on steganography and picture compression in such work. The original input textual image and cover image are both pre-processed using spatial steganography, and then the covert text-based pictures are separated and implanted into the least significant bit of the cover image picture element. Following that, stego-images are compressed to provide a higher-quality image while also saving storage space at the sender's end. After that, the stego-image will be transmitted to the receiver over a communication link. At the receiver's end, steganography and compression are then reversed. This work contains a plethora of issues, making it an intriguing subject to pursue. The most crucial component of this task is choosing the right steganography and image compression method. The proposed technology, which combines image steganography and compression, achieves higher peak signal-to-noise efficiency.

Chapter 9 shows the number of mobile network-connected devices is steadily increasing. The 5G network will theoretically provide a speed of 20 gigabits per second, allowing customers to access data at a rate of 100 megabits per second. Around the world, there are estimated to be 5 billion gadgets. With the advancement of wearable technology, a typical client can now carry up to two network-connected devices or engage in D2D communication. Clients are attracted to the 5G network because it advertises reduced inertness information correspondence, faster access and data transfer rates, and a more secure nature. As the number of supporters grows, concerns about information and computerized assurance will grow in order to keep up with the integrity of data security. Similarly, with any type of data security, there are always concerns about the safety of clients and their sensitive information. This chapter will discuss how to secure the diverse structures that are associated with networks, where these networks are vulnerable to compromise, well-known attack tactics, and how to avoid technical discrepancies.

Chapter 10 has explored the modern Information Technology environment necessitates increasing the value for money while ignoring the potency of the gathered components. The rising demand for storage, networking, and accounting has fueled the growth of massive, complex data centers, as well as the big server businesses that manage several current internet operations, as well as economic, trading, and corporate operations. A data centre can hold thousands of servers and consume the same amount of electricity as a small city. The massive amount of calculating power required to run such server systems controls a variety of conflicts, including energy consumption, greenhouse gas emissions, substitutes, and restarting affairs, among others. This is virtualization, which refers to a group of technologies that cover a wide range of applications and hobbies. This can be applied to the sectors of hardware and software, as well as innovations on the outskirts of virtualization's emergence. This study demonstrates how we proposed using virtualization technologies to gradually transform a traditional data centre structure into a green data centre. This study looks into the reasons for the price profits of supporting virtualization technology, which is recommended by practically every major company in the market. This is a technology that can drastically reduce capital costs in our environment while also almost committing to low operating costs for the next three years while pursuing the finance. We'll talk about value in terms of cost and space, with space equating to future cost.

The security of big data is being studied, as well as how to keep the performance of the data while it is being transmitted over the network. There have been various studies that have looked into the topic of big data. Furthermore, many of those studies claimed to provide data security but failed to maintain performance. Several encryption techniques, including RSA and AES, have been utilized in past studies. However, if these encryption technologies are used, the network system's performance suffers. To address these concerns, the proposed approach employs compression mechanisms to minimize the file size before performing encryption. Furthermore, data is spit to increase the reliability of transmission. Data has been transferred from multiple routes after the data was separated.

If any hackers choose to collect that data in an unauthentic method, they will not be able to obtain complete and meaningful data. By combining compression and splitting mechanisms with big data encryption, the suggested model has improved the security of big data in a network environment. Furthermore, using a user-defined port and various pathways during the split transmission of large data improves the dependability and security of big data over the network projects in Chapter 11.

Acknowledgments

We express our great pleasure, sincere thanks, and gratitude to the people who significantly helped, contributed and supported to the completion of this book. Our sincere thanks to Fr. Benny Thomas, Professor, Department of Computer Science and Engineering, CHRIST (Deemed to be University), Bengaluru, Karnataka India, and Dr. Arup Kumar Pal, Assistant Professor, Department of Computer Science and Engineering, Indian Institute of Technology (Indian School of Mines) Dhanbad, Jharkhand India for their continuous support, advice and cordial guidance from the beginning to the completion of this book.

We would also like to express our honest appreciation to our colleagues at the Haldia Institute of Technology Haldia, West Bengal, India, and CHRIST (Deemed to be University), Bengaluru, Karnataka India, for their guidance and support.

We also thank all the authors who have contributed some chapters to this book. This book would not have been possible without their contribution.

We are also very thankful to the reviewers for reviewing the book chapters. This book would not have been possible without their continuous support and commitment towards completing the chapters' review on time.

To all of the team members at Scrivener Publishing, who extended their kind cooperation, timely response, expert comments, and guidance, we are very thankful to them.

Finally, we sincerely express our special and heartfelt respect, gratitude, and gratefulness to our family members and parents for their endless support and blessings.

Sabyasachi Pramanik
Department of Computer Science and Engineering, Haldia Institute of Technology,
Haldia, West Bengal, India
Email: sabyalnt@gmail.com

Debabrata Samanta
Department of Computer Science, CHRIST (Deemed to be University) Bengaluru, Karnataka
Email: debabrata.samanta369@gmail.com

M. Vinay
Department of Computer Science, CHRIST (Deemed to be University), Bangalore, India
Email: vinay.m@christuniversity.in

Abhijit Guha
First American India Private Limited, Bangalore, India
Email: aguha@firstam.com

Securing Cloud-Based Enterprise Applications and Its Data

Subhradip Debnath*, Aniket Das and Budhaditya Sarkar

Department of Computer Science, Institute of Engineering and Management, Maulana Abul Kalam Azad University of Technology, Kolkata, West Bengal, India

Abstract

In today's world that is run mostly through applications interacting over the internet, data security both inside and outside the client devices is a very critical topic. MSME sector and the new enterprises coming up are mostly shifting to the cloud space for grabbing up the opportunities of the virtual market that are coming up and shifting their work culture to the online space. Thus, the enterprise communication that was mainly happening in offline methods, behind closed doors, and locked storage rooms with files has now shifted to a more public space, files being routed through the public internet to public facing servers. Resulting in a whole new domain of security and compliance problems as many of the servers for Public/Hybrid Cloud models fall under a joint ownership between two or more parties/stakeholders. Thus, securing the data in transit, i.e., coming in and out of the cloud, and the data in rest, i.e., the data lying inside the cloud, needs to be encrypted such that no third party can access it without the consent of its owner. In this proposed research model, it is proposed that data from a client application as in an enterprise communication application are encrypted using modified algorithms which would be accessible securely through a series of access control functionalities with least privilege access policies. The data is further packed up and are transported over the SSL layers to an server side application instance running in a public cloud (here)/private cloud which shall decrypt the information coming through and sorts the data accordingly and further saves them into the object-based storages, NoSQL, and Ledger databases with high availability and security at rest. The data at rest is further encrypted, can be packed up, and sent back to the client application when requested with necessary encryption in transit criteria fulfilled. The transactions are carried out using role-based assigning systems

---

*Corresponding author: research.subhradip@gmail.com

Sabyasachi Pramanik, Debabrata Samanta, M. Vinay and Abhijit Guha (eds.) Cyber Security and Network Security, (1–26) © 2022 Scrivener Publishing LLC

and least access privilege access mode, thus successfully stopping the concepts of threats to privacy, data eavesdropping, threat to personal security, etc.

Keywords: Enterprise, architecture, secure, application, data, cloud, encryption, threats

1.1   Introduction

Human life is driven by data. In this century, every business decision that is undertaken is based on derivations of data collected over the years. Data warehouses and databases are overflowing with ever growing data, but the main concern at this point of time is the security of both data in transit, i.e., being sent over the public internet and the security of the data at rest. Security of the data does not only mean about its confidentiality but also its availability and integrity.

Due to the rapidly growing virtual market, data is at its abundance as starting from the startup companies, companies from the MSME sector and even the traditional core large companies are shifting and changing their business model to adapt to cloud. Thus, security of the applications along with the data has become a necessity rather than a choice.

Due to the rapidly increasing demands, which are producing a large amount of data, the users are facing problems of securely storing that data in a searchable format. Studies have also suggested that security and privacy are among the major factors of influencing a consumer's trust [1, 2]. Some researchers have worked upon the concept of securing the data through blockchain. However, blockchain integration makes the computations required, and unnecessarily complex and large computations of the blockchain are quite unnecessary when thinking of saving data that are important but come in too frequently. This concept was not introduced to just storing data cryptographically but from the concept of "transfer of assets from peer to peer".

Thus, in our proposed model, our objective is to help the data from users, (here) an enterprise software transfer their data through the public network by the use of a web-based software, facilitating encrypted communications over the public channels and keeping unnecessary computations to its bare minimum. Data, be it object-based or text or JSON data structure, can be passed through the system and can be checked up for malware. If the data transmitted is seen to be coming in through valid credentials and passes the security checks, then it would be stored in the NoSQL databases. For object-based files, the files would be checked for security exploits, and after passing the checks, it would be checked if the files could be scaled down and they would be saved over in the object storage buckets. Logs would be generated for every action undertaken by the user after log in and those corresponding logs would be added on to immutable ledger databases for further audits and checks with timestamps, so that every user in the system is accountable for their actions.

The proposed system has a highly scalable and available architecture. The number of systems provisioned in the architecture can grow/shrink according to the load. The proposed system is developed keeping in mind that the data stored can be queried easily, so that it can serve as a better alternative to the proposed blockchain systems that are being proposed widely. The suggested architecture can also check for intrusion and can perform malware analysis, spam detection, etc.

1.2   Background and Related Works

Every device produces metadata based on the client's request. For securing cloud base applications, metadata exchange is also necessary to maintain nondisrupting service. Any hacker can easily take advantage of those metadata and use that for any malicious intention like malware injection and many others. In this case, a hacker needs to inject malicious code or service of the valid instance running in the cloud. If the hacker is successful, then the cloud will suffer from deadlocks and eavesdropping which forces real users to wait until the process is not completed. This type of attack is also known as metadata spoofing attack. In this way, anyone can get access to the cloud easily [3, 4].

Imagining that Raspberry Pi is connected to the internet using a wireless router and it sends data to the cloud. Here, if any hacker joins the network, then he places himself between two communicating parties and relaying messages for them. Here, the hacker is also getting full access to the data, and he can also monitor and change the contents of messages.

SQL injection is an attack that toxins dynamic SQL statements to comment out certain parts of the statement or append a condition that will ceaselessly be true. It takes advantage of the planning flaws in poorly designed net applications to require advantage of SQL statements to execute malicious SQL code. Thus, in our proposed approach, we have used a NoSQL database. In a NoSQL database, traditional SQL injection should not cause a risk to the system.

If only HTTPS is used and data is not encrypted, then it is in readable form before being sent to a private network, so it can be manipulated by any third person intriguing in the system. So, SSL Certificate (Secure Socket Layers) is used which ensures that it remains impossible for anyone else other than the receiver and sender to read the data by using encryption algorithms already integrated in it. However, HTTPS can be decoded using SSL man in the middle (MITM) through various ways. One of them is enabling the packet routing feature on hacker machines and running a DNS spoof so that the victim connects to hacker machine through HTTP/HTTPS port [5].

In the paper "Security Enhancement for Data Migration in the Cloud", J. R. N. Sighom *et al.* discussed regarding securing data in the cloud are one of the key roles. To maintain the privacy and security of data, researchers have combined several encryption algorithms like IDA (Information Dispersal Algorithm), SHA 512 (Secure Hash Algorithm), and AES 256 (Advanced Encryption Standard). The encrypted data is split into several parts. During the decoding process, the validation stages are observed first. IDA is used after the reconstruction of encrypted data, and it is reconverted into the initial data using AES 256. Consistent with the result, the common execution time is higher when the decoding time process is verification 1.453 [6].

Researchers have also tried to improve the security of data in the cloud by using the DES (Data Encryption Standard) and AES (Advanced Encryption Standard) algorithm together. Cloud computers well describe the set of resources or services that it offers on the internet, to meet the requirements of cloud providers [7].

Cloud computing systems have come a long way in implementing and executing applications in a sandboxed environment minimizing threat, and maximizing reliability, scalability, availability, and security. Although there has been much research to make the cloud platforms interoperable in between multiple organizations by organizing and reorganizing the cloud federation [8, 9], i.e., giving the companies the power to collaborate and share resources among each other. Multiple federation architecture is being proposed such as cloud brokering, aggregation, and cloud bursting and is worked upon to find out the most suitable among them [10]. However, there have been issues of portability and interoperability among them [11]. Primarily, the partially coupled federation is being followed where the company private servers and the services hosted on the public cloud are interoperable and there is an understanding and sharing of resources between the servers depending on the flow of traffic and load.

1.3   System Design and Architecture

1.3.1   Proposed System Design and Architecture

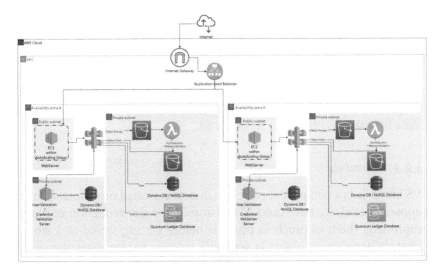

Figure 1.1 Proposed system design architecture.

1.3.2   Modules

1.3.2.1   Compute Instances

Amazon Elastic Compute Cloud, commonly known as EC2, is a computer service provisioning virtual servers on demand. The instances can be auto-scalable based on requirements, and it is highly flexible as one instance can be launched in a few minutes and configured to cater the needs. The web server applications are hosted on the servers. The servers are configured to be autoscalable and to scale out on the occasion of high traffic or load. On the occasion that the CPU or memory remains unutilized, then the auto-scaling further kicks in to scale-in the number of compute instances to save resources. Figure 1.1 shows proposed system design architecture.

1.3.2.2   API Gateway

Provisioned in the VPC, the API Gateway facilitates the use of REST API to congregate data requested from the web application and provides public endpoints for further future expansion of the client side architecture.

1.3.2.3   Storage Bucket (Amazon S3)

In our proposed architecture, we are using Amazon Simple Storage Service (Amazon S3) which provides secure, high-scalable, and durable object storage. Simply log in and seamlessly move and share data stored in S3 across any storage resources employing a unified, intuitive interface. Here, we are storing the data like large files and databases, which is being shared among themselves. In our proposed model, we have stored the static data or data in rest (i.e., object) in Amazon S3.

1.3.2.4   Lambda

AWS Lambda is a compute service which gets activated on demand. In our proposed model, we have used AWS Lambda for size reduction of files by compressing them as much as possible before getting stored in a storage bucket. Whenever an object is sent to a storage bucket from the server, lambda is called. It takes the object from the storage bucket and reduces the size by compressing them and stores them in another storage bucket, data being encrypted at rest.

1.3.2.5   Load Balancer

Load unbalancing is a serious problem that inhibits the performance and efficiency of compute resources. In our proposed model, the load balancer distributes the incoming traffic or load among the compute instances equally to maintain the balance of the server. Problems like server overload or under-load can be avoided using load balancer. Load balancer improves the real-time necessary constraint parameters like response time, execution time, and system stability [12].

1.3.2.6   Internet Gateway

In our proposed model, the Internet Gateway links the Virtual Private Cloud (VPC) with the public internet.

1.3.2.7 Security Groups

Security groups are instance level firewalls. Security groups can be configured to stop incoming and outgoing traffic in instances. In our proposed model, an advantage of using security groups is that it is a straight full service which means any rule applied to incoming rules will also be applied in outgoing rules.

1.3.2.8 Autoscaling

Autoscaling feature helps in cost saving and efficient use of resources without human intervention. In our proposed model, autoscaling determines performance metrics which acts as good indicators for conveying the load on a resource. Autoscaling performs operations on CPU utilization, bandwidth usage, and memory utilization. Here, the user need not overprovision a server to meet the needs during high usage. During peak demands, autoscaling automatically increases computing services and other necessary resources and decreases during low usage periods, thus saving cost and optimum utilization of services and resources [13].

1.3.2.9 QLDB

Amazon QLDB is a ledger database that provides an immutable, verifiable, transparent, and cryptographically transaction log centrally. It can be used to track and any application data change over time.

However, relational databases are not immutable and changes are hard to track and verify. Alternatively, blockchain frameworks can be used as a ledger but it adds complexity as an entire blockchain network needs to be set up and the nodes are required to validate each transaction before it can be added to the ledger.

With Amazon QLDB, effort of building your own ledger-like applications is eliminated. QLDB is immutable; it cannot be altered or deleted and can be easily verifiable if any unintended modifications are made. QLDB provides SQL-like API, a flexible document data model, and full support for transactions. With QLDB data can be replicated to other AWS services to support advanced analytical processing. QLDB is serverless so it is scalable according to my needs so I pay for what I use. In our proposed model, all the records of data and various other files are stored and maintained in QLDB.

1.3.2.10   NoSQL Database

In our proposed model, we have chosen NoSQL databases as it is perfect for our applications requiring flexibility, high-performance, scalability, and highly functional databases since it does not have any schema. The document type/JSON type files are stored in this database.

Sensitive data are secured using encryption algorithms mentioned in our architecture. The JSON files are being encrypted before getting stored inside the database.

1.3.2.11   Linux Instance and Networking

Instances widely provided by the public cloud provider services can be used or virtualized compute instances can be provisioned for hosting the application on private servers. In this project, we have used an AWS EC2 instance to set up the server side application on the instance for the client devices to communicate and transmit the messages. EC2 also provides additional security, and moreover, the compute capacity is easily resizable according to the demand.

Private servers can also be spun up if not going through with public cloud providers. The instances need to be spun up with updated hypervisors keeping scalability and durability in mind. Networking needs to be managed internally in that case and NAT gateways need to be set up to facilitate communication of the virtual instances through a public facing IP.

1.3.2.12   Virtual Network and Subnet Configuration

A specific virtual private network is required to be configured for the application spanning two or more availability zones for higher availability and application reliability. One public subnet and two private subnets need to be launched for each of the availability zone that we have accounted for. Private subnets would contain the user access and data, and the storage services and only the web application instances that are launched into the public subnet would be allowed to access. The application instances would be able to access the services provisioned into the private subnets through the private endpoints which are not exposed to the public internet. Thus, all the user/application data residing in the system cannot be accessed without prior authentication and authorization through the public endpoint.

1.4 Methodology

1.4.1 Firewall

In our proposed architecture, every incoming and outgoing data coming inside or going outside the cloud needs to be passed through the network firewall or VPC. Network firewall prevents several attacking problems like data exfiltration, insider attack, and many more. Here, we have created policies which are suitable for the organization. Every incoming and outgoing package can be blocked, filtered, and monitored. In addition, if any malicious activity is detected, then that can be blocked easily without affecting the entire system.

1.4.2 Malware Injection Prevention

The cloud or private server can receive data only from its client application. That data is always encrypted by the client application and never executes in the cloud without proper authentication, authorization, and validation of data. Inside the cloud, only specific actions can be done according to the privileges of the client which has been assigned by the organization. Apart from these, it can be prevented also from the VPC.

1.4.3 Man-in-the-Middle Prevention

Client application encrypts each and every data which it sends to the cloud. In addition, in the cloud after verifying, i.e., whether the client is trusted or not it will decrypt the data and perform the rest operations respectively. Since the data is encrypted by double layer encryption no middle man can tamper the data as a result MITM attack cannot be possible, i.e., no one can tamper the data in between the client and cloud.

1.4.4 Data at Transit and SSL

We have proposed to use TSL (Transport Layer Security), an updated and more secure version of SSL having advanced encryption algorithms integrated in it, giving extra security.

Nowadays, the encryption algorithms are all of single level encryption and hackers can easily hack the single level encryption so we propose to use multi-level encryption. First, we will encrypt the data using DES encryption technique on which we apply AES encryption technique giving a second level of encryption. Even by acquiring the data, decrypting such levels is a difficult task [14].

1.4.5 Data Encryption at Rest

To store big data files which have been uploaded by the client or organization in cloud for their use are stored, using several encryption algorithms like IDA (Information Dispersal Algorithm), SHA-512, and AES-256 (Advanced Encryption Standard) combinedly. This encrypted data is stored into Amazon S3 by splitting it into several parts. This encryption happens in server side, i.e., within the cloud. When any client or organization needing the data, it will undergo a decryption process, i.e., IDA is used to synchronize the encrypted data and it is reconverted into the initial data using AES-256 and SHA-512.

1.4.6 Centralized Ledger Database

After analysis of data, the JSON document is stored in QLDB. As the documents arrive, they will be stored in the journal one after another. If any document is changed, then a copy of it is maintained in a ledger called history. The rest remain in the current ledger. So, whatever data is in QLDB even if it gets deleted or updated is stored in the ledger and is easily viewable. For verifying data in QLDB, a SHA-256 secure hash file is generated from where the integrity of the data can be verified.

1.4.7 NoSQL Database

An encrypted JSON document will be stored in the hosted NoSQL database. The database would be encrypted at rest. While fetching data from the database, the files will be decrypted after checking the authorization details. After verifying the user to authorize or not, files can be updated from the database. In this way, data breaching can be avoided to a great extent.

1.4.8 Linux Instance and Server Side Installations

The server side application is developed using Python Django. Python version 3.x is recommended for development. Our application is developed using Python 3.8. The suggested required libraries and their versions are also provided in Table 1.1.

Table 1.1 Libraries and their versions.

Cryptography	Encryption (like AES)
Django-dynamodb-sessions	For NoSQL
Dynamodb-json	DynamoDB Json
Boto3	AWS SDK for Python (Boto3) to create, configure, and manage AWS services

The EC2 that was set up during testing was a T2 instance of the Micro specifications with 1.0 GiB RAM and 1vCPU. The application was set up in the Linux environment, and a startup script was put in place so that it would spin up the application whenever the instance starts. The application took in responses in a form of Rest API calls, and thus, the server provisioned is set up under a security group with network ingress egress allowed on Port 80.

For secure shell connectivity to the server for maintenance and optimizing and security purposes, the SSH port is kept open in the security group. This enables the administrator to connect to the server instances over the public internet securely. RSA keys are also advised to be used for encrypted secure login.

In a public cloud service, the servers and the security groups can be set up inside a virtual private cloud within public subnets facilitating public

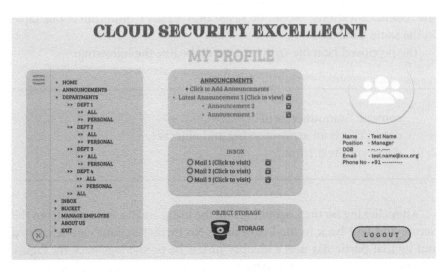

Figure 1.2 Home or my profile page from manager's point of view.

facing servers within a secure sandboxed environment so that the whole operation runs securely. Whole setup can also be done using integrated platforms (platform as a service) such as infrastructure as a code such as cloud formation services. Figure 1.2 shows home or my profile page from manager's point of view.

In our proposed model, the managerial role in the organization is the administrator of the system suggested. The name of the roles in our proposed model may vary and can be changed according to the enterprise specifications, but the logic behind the operations is suggested to be kept the same. The manager has the highest access privilege than the other users in the system. Here, he/she can control document transactions and user managements monitoring and tracking the access granted to the respected users. From the Profile page of the manager, he/she can create or delete (CRUD) any announcements, and small synopsis of unread or latest communications are also viewed in the home page.

The data of the announcement, or the communications that are being sent, are sent in the JSON format by the client machines which are encrypted using DES encryption first and then AES over it. After going through the public internet and reaching the server endpoint, the encrypted data packet is decrypted. Further, the data is analyzed for infections or malware. If the data is found to be free of such things, then the JSON data is analyzed. If the content key in it contains the value "announcement", then the data within is saved in the Announcement Table in the NoSQL database. Here, in our proposed model, we use DynamoDB because of its high scalability, serverless structure, and single-digit millisecond latency. Similarly, the "communications" would be saved over in the Communications table in the same database.

The proposed Json file structure would be like the following:

```
{
    content: "announcement",
    data: ['this is an array of string and objects'],
    data-type: 'text/html'
}
```

After clicking on the Logout button, the users are disconnected from the server and sent back to the Login page. No further actions can be carried out by that particular user's identity unless he or she logs back in. Figure 1.3 shows home or my dashboard page from employee point of view.

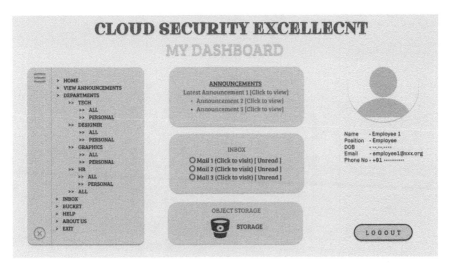

Figure 1.3 Home or my dashboard page from employee point of view.

Here, it shows the profile of the employee in the organization from where he/she can view the profile, get necessary updates (i.e., from Announcements, Inbox), and perform the job. From the Home or My Dashboard page, employees see the announcements, small synopsis of unread or latest mail. On clicking over the object storage, it will be redirected to storage or bucket page. From the navigation dashboard, employees can go to any page (only eligible pages) according to their choice. Apart from all these, users can also logout from the page by clicking on the Logout button at bottom right of the page. For the users to store object-based files, the users are authenticated and the client side of the software verifies the file and compresses it after encrypting. Here, we use double layer security, i.e., for the first layer we have used the DES encryption, over that a second layer of encryption, i.e., AES is applied over it. Further, encrypted compressed objects are sent over the public internet and are in a S3 bucket through the REST API that is put in place. After a new object is created over in the primary S3 Bucket, a serverless lambda function gets invoked and the encrypted compressed file is decompressed and decrypted accordingly. Further, after a series of actions verifying the authenticity of the file sent, the file is compressed and stored in another S3 Bucket from where it would be retrieved when required. A life cycle policy is put in place where the older objects which are not required frequently are transferred to an economical tier, and the other much older objects are transferred over to glacier object storages for archival purposes. Figure 1.4 shows inbox page from manager's point of view.

Figure 1.4 Inbox page from manager's point of view.

Here, it shows the inbox page of the manager in the organization from where he or she can send mail within the organization. Just by entering the client id of the employee, the mail will be received to the employee's inbox. It can contain any number of documents by attaching it with the storage bucket. Here, past mails or drafted mails can be edited, modified, and sent. If the manager wants to send the mail to the entire department, then it can also be done by tagging the entire department. All those details, i.e., data in transit and data in rest will be encrypted and safely stored in cloud such that no third party applications cannot take the data without the owners concerned [15]. Employees have the access to view the mails sent to them and reply to them. Figure 1.5 shows flowchart of inbox, and Figure 1.6 shows storage bucket from manager's point of view.

Here it shows the Storage Bucket page of the manager in the organization. Manager can upload any data in the storage bucket and can share it easily within the organization. Employees can do their work by making a copy of the data and can submit it when they finish. When a manager needs to search any files he or she just needs to search by the file name or client id in the search field. Apart from that, the manager can also sort the table according to his or her own preference. Managers have the permission to view, create and delete the files of all the employees. Employees can only access the files or documents only for those they have been eligible for.

To save the files of the Storage Bucket, we have chosen Amazon S3 for our model. It is highly scalable and any amount of objects can be stored in it.

INBOX

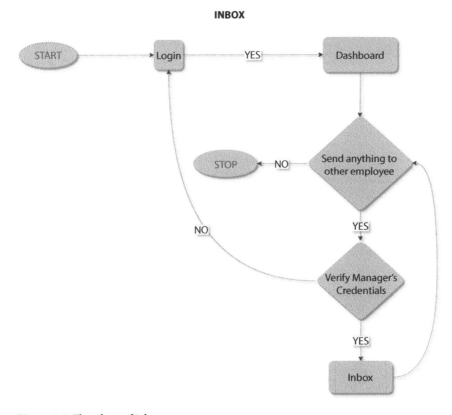

Figure 1.5 Flowchart of inbox.

Figure 1.6 Storage bucket from manager's point of view.

STORAGE BUCKET

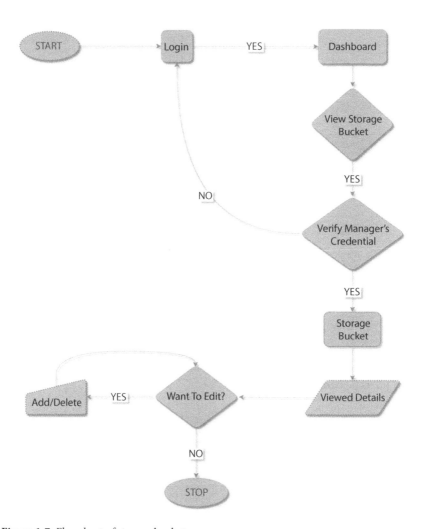

Figure 1.7 Flowchart of storage bucket.

A log will be maintained for storage and deletion of objects in QLDB safely. Figure 1.7 shows flowchart of storage bucket, and Figure 1.8 shows Manage Employees page from manager point of view.

Here, it shows the Manage Employees page of the manager in the organization. The managers can add new employees, update employees, and delete employees in the organization. Apart from that, he or she can also

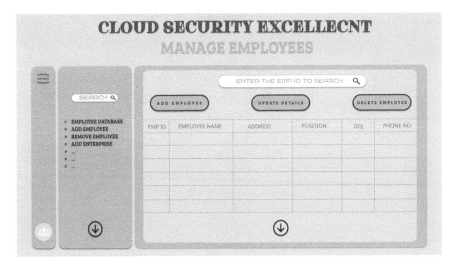

Figure 1.8 Manage employees page from manager point of view.

add and manage enterprises. Manager can search employee details just by entering the employee id of the employee in the search field. Manager has full authority over the employee, i.e., if he or she wishes to suspend any employee from accessing the application, then he or she can do so. Employees cannot access the Manage Employees page from their end as, at every step, manager's credentials will be checked before giving allowance inside the system.

In our proposed model, we have used NoSQL databases because they are highly scalable and large volumes of data can be stored without having any specific architecture. Editing on these databases is quite fast and easy. If development is made using modern agile methods, then relations database is not the right option as it slows you down, but in NoSQL databases, the level of preparation is not needed making work faster. Moreover, cloud-based storage requires data to be spread across multiple servers. A highly scalable database is required for such production and NoSQL databases perfectly fit in the case. Figure 1.9 shows flowchart of employee database, and Figure 1.10 shows announcement page from manager point of view.

Here, it shows the Announcement page of the manager in the organization. Here, the manager can view, edit, add, and delete announcements. The manager can send announcements to the entire department by entering the department id of them.

In our proposed model, we have selected NoSQL databases for storing the announcements. As it has no predefined schema, storing important

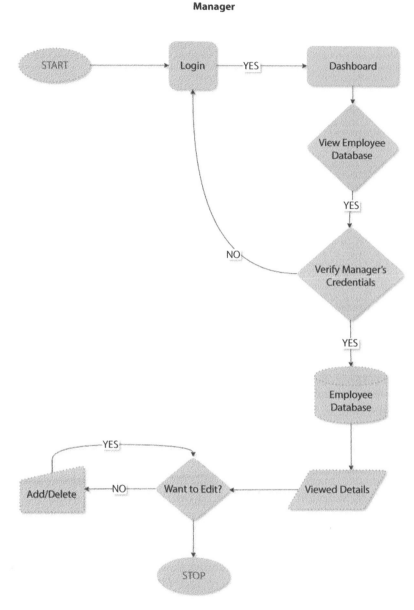

Figure 1.9 Flowchart of employee database.

announcements or deleting them later can be done with great ease. We have chosen multi-level encryption. We will use DES and AES encryption to encrypt the database before pushing it to QLDB. DES is a symmetric

Figure 1.10 Announcement page from manager point of view.

encryption algorithm converting data into block ciphers. It uses key sizes of 64 bits.

AES encryption is the most robust security protocol against hacking. It uses higher key sizes such as 128, 192, and 256 bits of encryption. It is one of the safest open source security solutions widely used commercially for encrypted data storage.

First, we will encrypt the data using DES and generate a key and further encrypt it using AES providing a second level of encryption.

The encrypted files are stored in QLDB (Quantum Ledger Database), a ledger database holding all records. These files can be decrypted again and viewed in QLDB if needed. We have chosen QLDB for our proposed model as it is a NoSQL database, with some additional features. Figure 1.11 shows flowchart of creating announcement, and Figure 1.12 shows group access control modifier by manager.

In our architecture, a highly strict policy for least access privilege model is followed to ensure that no user gets access to resources more than he is supposed to. The Group Access Control Modifier thus provides that opportunity for the immediate senior managers assigned to the users to access their control privileges. This ensures that no information flows in and out of the system that is not asked to be retrieved by an authenticated user with necessary access. The Group Access Control Modifier is the GUI of a backend architecture with a JSON file containing the detailed Access Policy for specific users. Whenever the Access Policies are changed over in the GUI, the contemporary JSON file updates itself accordingly.

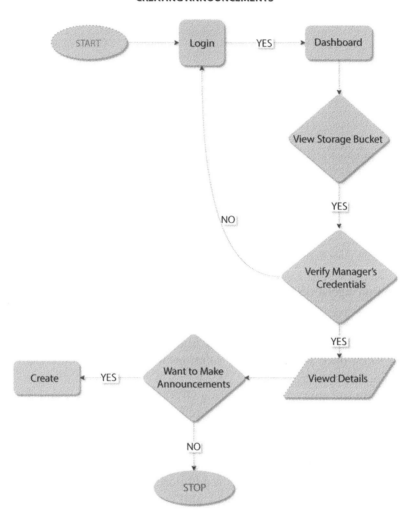

Figure 1.11 Flowchart of creating announcement.

Figure 1.12 Group access control modifier by manager.

1.5   Performance Analysis

1.5.1   Load Balancer

Load balancers are used to provide low latency to users especially at high usage periods and distribute the loads across multiple compute instances. Combining it with the autoscaling groups also enables our architecture to scale up and scale down as per requirements. In the absence of load balancers, higher traffic on instances would lead to higher packet loss and higher latency due to overloaded traffic, on a fixed number of compute instances. It would also lead to unbalanced load on web servers resulting in crashing of the servers. Due to the load-balanced architecture, a user may face a latency slightly above 1–5 ms, due to the load balancer operating at layer 7 and also since the instances are provisioned on demand automatically so it saves costs to a great extent.

1.5.2   Lambda (For Compression of Data)

In the above screenshots, it is shown using Lambda, a 3-MB .jpg file is compressed to 9.8 KB in a couple of seconds. In our proposed model, if a user accounts for the data transfer of 51.2 MB per day, then at an average, about 1,000 users are responsible for uploading about 50 GB of data per day. That number turns to 1,500 GB of object-based data saved by the end of a month. Figure 1.13 shows before compression of data (raw data), and Figure 1.14 shows after compression of data (compressed data). Due to the huge amount of data that needs to be handled, it is highly efficient to compress the data, keeping it intact to reduce costs on long term storages and cost incurred on egress traffic. By the method implemented in our proposed model, the 50 GB of data per day can be compressed into as less as 125 MB per day. It is almost a 500% decrease in the data size, saving costs to a great extent, making our proposed model much more economical.

Figure 1.13 Before compression of data (raw data).

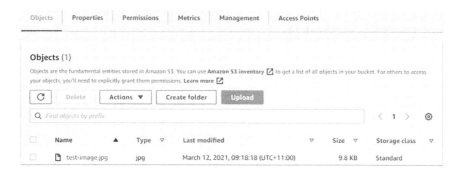

Figure 1.14 After compression of data (compressed data).

1.5.3   Availability Zone

The high latency is faced by the user if the user tries to access the application far away from an availability zone. However, having multiple availability zones, the users get the choice of using the closest zone from their location, as the compute instances can be cloned in multiple availability zones. In this way, the latency is 1–2 ms maximum, highly decreased.

1.5.4   Data in Transit (Encryption)

Encrypt and decrypt data blocks of varying sizes from 0.5 to 20 MB). Experiments performed on ECB and CBC modes. In ECB mode, DES algorithm takes 4 s for a 20-MB data block. In CBC mode, the time taken by the DES algorithm on a 20-MB data block is slightly more than ECB. Due to its key-chaining nature, more processing time is required. The average difference between CBC and EBC is 0.059896 s.

On both ECB and CBC modes, AES algorithm takes approximately 16 s for the same 20-MB block for encryption and decryption.

1.5.5   Data in Rest (Encryption)

AES encryption algorithm provides security and speed. It is the most efficient symmetric algorithm because AES-256 bit encryption can produce 2256 keys. To understand this thing, 232 is about 4.3 billion and it exponentially grows after that. We can assume this to be 250 keys per second (approximately one quadrillion keys/second a very plentiful assumption). One year is equal to 31,557,600 s (approximately). That means one billion supercomputers are required to check about 275 keys per year, while the age of the universe is 234 years only which is less than .01% of the entire key possible. Thus, it is practically not possible to figure out the AES-256 bit key. In addition, apart from that we are also using SHA-512 for extra protection of data. In real world, imagining a CPU like "Intel Xeon L5630" has four core, each core an process 610 MB/s of AES-256 bit data, i.e., around 2,440 MB/s which is enough for encryption and decryption data of 10 gigabit. The SHA-512 bit in "Intel Core 2" of 1.83 GHz process under Windows Vista in 32 bit node takes 99 MiB/s and 17.7 cycles per byte. Thus, the cloud does not get overwhelmed for encryption of huge data.

1.6   Future Research Direction

In our proposed model, data is encrypted as a result no one can tamper with our data; hence, we need to think about the metadata of the encrypted data which is being sent from client/user to server (cloud). Here, we can introduce some error detection schema like checksum. Checksum is a numerical value which is based on the bytes in encrypted data. The sender client will calculate the value of data and send the value with the data. The cloud server will use the same algorithm to check whether the numerical value is the same or not. If such a concept can be introduced in future, then we need not to depend on VPC. Apart from that, machine learning algorithms as well to verify the authenticity of the user can be used.

Blowfish is a symmetric encryption algorithm. During encryption and decryption, data blocks or cipher blocks are divided into fixed lengths. We can think of Blowfish for our future research because it provided remarkable results on ECB and CBC modes having the lowest latency among AES and DES with just around 3 s in both the modes, whereas AES had a whooping latency of around 16 s. One noticeable thing is that Blowfish has a 448 long key yet it outperformed other encryption algorithms [15].

We can think of reducing the Lambda Execution time by putting the dependency files in a separate library so deployment packages can be unpacked faster. Distribution of files according to deployment packages and function's code class files in a separate file reduces Lambda Execution time than keeping everything in a single large file with too many class files having function's code as Lambda has to execute the full large file then.

1.7   Conclusion

In our proposed model, we have suggested a system where data entry, data modification, and data management all are done through a client side application through which the data can be encrypted and sent over to the server side application. From the data encryption at transit to the data encryption at rest, everything is managed by the application itself. Here, in the suggested system design, we have implemented our concept in the form of an enterprise application to be used for communication between multiple levels of users. We have implemented a role-based access control/identity-based access control concept, depending on which different authorizations are allotted, which can be customized by higher levels of roles. Comparing with the existing systems, our system design is robust, scalable, and durable. The load is balanced between multiple availability zones, read-replicas are deployed, and autoscaling groups are deployed keeping the sudden increase of users in mind. Our system design proposes a much more secure way of transmission of classified data across networks, thus keeping the integrity of the data durable.

References

1. Khan, W.Z. *et al.*, "Data and Privacy: Getting Consumers to Trust Products Enabled by the Internet of Things," *IEEE Consum. Electron. Mag.*, 8, 2, 35–38, 2019.
2. Khan, W.Z. *et al.*, "Enabling Consumer Trust Upon Acceptance of IoT Technologies through Security and Privacy Model," in: *Advanced Multimedia and Ubiquitous Engineering*, pp. 111–17, Springer, Jazan University, Jizan, Saudi Arabia, 2016.
3. Tripathi, A. and Mishra, A., "Cloud Computing Security Considerations". *IEEE International Conference on Signal Processing, Communications and Computing (ICSPCC)*, 2011.
4. Rahaman, M.A., Schaad, A., Rits, M., Towards secure SOAP message exchange in a SOA, in: *SWS '06: Proceedings of the 3rd ACM workshop on Secure Web Services*, New York, NY, USA, ACM Press, pp. 77–84, 2006.
5. Chomsiri, T., HTTPS Hacking Protection. *21st International Conference on Advanced Information Networking and Applications Workshops (AINAW'07)*, Niagara Falls, ON, Canada, May 21-23, 2007, vol. 1, pp. 590–594, 2007, doi:10.1109/ainaw.2007.200.
6. Sighom, J.R.N., Zhang, P., You, L., "Security Enhancement for Data Migration in the Cloud". *Multidisciplinary Digital Publishing Institute (MDPI)*, 9, 23, 1–13, 2017.
7. Kumari, S., Princy, Reema, Kumari, S., "Security in Cloud Computing using AES & DES,". *Int. J. Recent Innov. Trends Comput. Commun.*, 5, 4, 194–200, 2017.
8. Rochwerger, B. *et al.*, "Reservoir—When One Cloud Is Not Enough," *Computer*, 44, 44–51, Mar. 2011.
9. Keahey, K. *et al.*, "Sky Computing," *IEEE Internet Comput.*, 13, 5, 43–51, 2009.
10. Ferrer, A.J. *et al.*, "OPTIMIS: A Holistic Approach to Cloud Service Provisioning," *Future Gener. Comput. Syst.*, 28, 1, 66–77, 2012.
11. Petcu, D., "Portability and Interoperability between Clouds: Challenges and Case Study," in: *Lecture Notes in Computer Science*, Institute e-Austria Timi, vol. 6994, pp. 62–74, Springer, Soara and West University of Timi, Soara, Romania, 2011.
12. Afzal, S. and Kavitha, G., Load balancing in cloud computing – A hierarchical taxonomical classification. *J. Cloud Comput.*, 8, 22, 2019. https://doi.org/10.1186/s13677-019-0146-7.
13. White, J., Dougherty, B., Schmidt, D.C., Model-driven auto-scaling of green cloud computing infrastructure. *Future Gener. Comput. Syst.*, 28, 2, 371–378, 2012.
14. Kumar, N.G., Polala, N., Kumari, D.A., New approach for securing cloud applications. *2018 2nd International Conference on Inventive Systems and*

Control (ICISC), Coimbatore, India, January 19-20, 2018, pp. 689–693, 2018, doi:10.1109/ICISC.2018.8398886.

15. Alabaichi, A., Ahmad, F., Mahmod, R., Security analysis of blowfish algorithm. *2013 Second International Conference on Informatics & Applications (ICIA)*, 2013, doi:10.1109/icoia.2013.6650222.

High-Performance Computing-Based Scalable "Cloud Forensics-as-a-Service" Readiness Framework Factors—A Review

Srinivasa Rao Gundu[1], Charanarur Panem[2*] and S. Satheesh[3]

[1]Keysoft Computer Education, Mehdipatnam, Hyderabad, India
[2]Karwar Government Engineering College, Karwar, Majali, India
[3]Malineni Lakshmaiah Women's Engineering College, Pulladigunta, Guntur, India

Abstract

In present days, usage of cloud technology has increased. Cloud technology has become an integral part of human life today. This on-demand service provision flexibility support of cloud technology has attracted many companies to relay. It does not need to purchase servers, databases, and their related sophisticated technologies for the establishment of any new company. Simultaneously, security of data in the cloud is much alarming and requires some attention. Cybercriminals have many ways to intrude into the user's systems with the help of the user's cloud logs, switches, and routers. Cloud is distributing computing and one can never think of cloud computing without these mechanisms. Still, the security mechanisms are in infancy. Identifying the cyber culprit's cybernetic evidence plays an important role. Cloud service providers generally do not provide the cloud logs and virtual machine instances to the cloud security analyst. Cybernetic evidence is enough for cyber culprits to abuse cloud computations at any moment. There is a need to strengthen the security mechanisms to avoid the intrusion of cyber culprits. Cloud forensics is a way to do such activities. Many types of research are done in this field, but many more challenges need to be solved. High-performance cluster-based computing (HPCBC) are alternative to supercomputers, and can be used widely in IoT and AI. HPCBC works on parallel processing mechanism. This paper suggests that with the help of HPCBC, cloud forensics can be given a new

Corresponding author: panem.charan@gmail.com
Srinivasa Rao Gundu: ORCID: 0000-0001-7872-5114
Charanarur Panem: ORCID: 0000-0002-7872-8902

Sabyasachi Pramanik, Debabrata Samanta, M. Vinay and Abhijit Guha (eds.) Cyber Security and Network Security, (27–46) © 2022 Scrivener Publishing LLC

direction. The files can be had simultaneous imaging and upload and encryption. The files should be processed in real-time stream processing with the remote desktop connection. This survey paper provides various insights into such cloud forensic procedures and techniques.

Keywords: High-performance computing, cloud crime, network forensics, digital evidence, cloud storage, cloud technology, technical dimension, evidence segregation

2.1   Introduction

Cloud computing's founder John Mc Karthy wished for computing to be treated as a utility, and he hoped for widespread public participation. With cloud computing, he has achieved his goal. The electronics-based revolution has begun in the late mid-1950AD. This electronics-based revolution has continued until the present. Without massive storage infrastructure, cloud technology could not be successful. One can access the cloud services using any of the devices and also their location is not at all a matter. Cloud technological advancement has improved computational capability by reducing the restrictions such as device-oriented computing and location-based computing. Cloud is a ubiquitous extensive information technology service delivery platform and a promising technology.

The cloud crime can be defined as "a criminal activity in a cloud environment where the cloud itself becomes an object, subject or tool for the crimes". There are many cloud crimes are reported until now. One such well-known cloud crime was "Zeus botnet controller." It was reported in 2009. Similar such incidents are reported in 2014 in iCloud hack and, in the same year, in Sony pictures. A year later, two more incidents occurred in Home Depot and Anthem.

Every technology carries a few benefits and limitations. Cloud is not an exception for this. Even though the cloud is affordable, scalable, and fault-tolerant technology, it has some technical issues too. User's data is stored on the World Wide Web platform which is prone to get hacked. Cloud environment also makes a path for attackers to create susceptible conditions. Regardless of the circumstances, the security and integrity of the data stored in the cloud must always be maintained, and users must be assured that their data is safe and secure. Some cloud forensics [1] technologies are currently available to locate information about the attackers and their associated data. The implementation of computer forensics principles and procedures in a cloud computing environment is known as cloud forensics. Network forensics is a subset of it. To confirm the cyber-criminal and punish them, one must gather digital proof [2].

The cloud forensics method is divided into four steps by the National Institute of Standards and Technology (NIST). Data collection, evaluation, analysis, and reporting are the steps involved. Furthermore, any cloud forensic model should be able to access any cloud evidence, the entire network should be accessible to the investigator, and all available server resources should be pooled through virtualization. The model should be run on a priority-based processing schedule. Cloud forensics is a paradigm for the community cloud that falls under the Software-as-a-Service (SaaS) and Infrastructure-as-a-Service (IaaS) service models [3]. Public cloud models should not be used for cloud forensics investigations because sensitive data is involved.

2.2   Aim of the Study

The aim of the study is to find a way to establish the following:

1. The cloud forensic tools need to be affordable and less cost
2. Forensics needs to be introduced as a service.

2.3   Motivation for the Study

There is a need to comprehend cloud computing and its associated problems, as well as new developments in cloud forensics. From a technological standpoint, these issues include dealing with a variety of data stored in numerous locations, leveraging cloud resources that create solid evidence, and protecting the evidence's integrity [4].

Furthermore, larger volumes of data on the cloud cannot be properly managed and processed without risking contamination or compromising the integrity of the evidence. Analyzing digital evidence is quite challenging. It necessitates the development of a new digital criminal system tracing mechanism. It manages a large volume of data across numerous servers and domains in a distributed environment [5].

Scalability refers to the ability to scale up or down IT resources in response to changing demand. Cloud forensics aims to find out the digital evidence and acquire such, authenticate them and report them. Google Drive and Drop-box are some of the cloud storage services which allow users to upload their data to the World Wide Web at any moment [6].

This creates a big challenge for cloud forensic investigators. Cyber culprits are presently using this as an advantage for uploading a large amount of data and sharing them to the other computer which leaves no traces at all. Normally, logs are low-level data, making it difficult for the average user to comprehend what they mean [7].

Cloud forensics uses the same investigative technique as traditional forensics, but with the added challenge of mixing several physical and logical locations. Location and time are two technological challenges.

In most cases, cloud forensic investigators will load a duplicate of the evidence onto a stand-alone workstation in the examiner's lab; nonetheless, the capacity to receive digital evidence from remote places is required [8]. The average upload speed in the United States is currently approximately 7 Mbps. Keeping this in mind, transmitting 1 TiB of data will take 12 days (300 hours). In this sense, the table below provides some approximations [9].

2.4 Literature Review

The researcher Raghavan (2013) [10] has categorized the total cloud forensics area in to five major parts. (i) Before the analysis, collected data is heterogeneous in nature with a large amount. This data will be in binary format. Therefore, it is much complex, and it needs a sophisticated minimizing technique. (ii) Apart of being the data is in heterogeneous in nature and also in large volume, such high volume of data does not have a proper technique to analyze. Some more complexities are added to this with different operating systems and different file formats. (iii) There is a need of consistency and correlation between the available tools. (iv) There is no proper automation for the analysis of largely stored volumes of information. (v) There are different time zones and different clock drift issues are there. There is a need to make a unified timeline. Today, more research studies are done but it is possible to categorize as per Raghavan's classification. Ukil (2011) [11] addressed a few security concerns relating to the Internet of Things (IoT), which are also linked to cloud forensics. The problems revolve with accessibility, authenticity, and non-repudiation. These are crucial for data usage that is legal. Encryption technology can be used to overcome such problems. At the same time, high-end computation necessitates a large amount of energy. According to Alex and Kishore (2014) [12], forensic investigators have an impact on a few topics. According to them, cloud service providers are used by the majority of cloud forensic investigators. In general, cloud service providers have the ability to alter evidence; as a result, the entire investigation process may take a different path. Forensic monitoring plane (FMP) is currently being installed outside of cloud premises in order to reduce reliance on cloud service providers. Aniello Castiglione (2013) [13] described new attacks that use a novel way to capture network data from online services such as web pages, conversations, documents, photos, and videos. TTP can be used to collect information on behalf of the investigator. To evaluate the approach in an experimental setting, they used LIENA, a proof-of-concept prototype. Using this method, network packets and interpretation data are automatically acquired from remote sources. A digital notary who acts as a third party is presented to certify both the acquired and the obtained. Juan-Carlos Bennett and Mamadou H. Diallo (2018) [14] presented a forensic pattern-based technique. To develop a semiformal architecture, this method employs object-oriented approach concepts. The cloud evidence collector and analyzer were built to collect, evaluate, and analyze evidence in order to acquire more and better network evidence in the quickest time possible. Simou (2018) [15] proposed a framework that offers a conceptual model in conjunction with a set of forensic restrictions for tracing cloud forensics-enabled applications. This approach also aids in the completion of the forensic process in a timely manner, allowing developers to design forensic-ready cloud systems.

Palash Santra (2017) [16] published a comparative study that demonstrates the importance of log analysis when compared to cloud forensics approaches. Because log data is the most crucial data for a successful cloud forensics procedure, the authors recommended Boolean and Euclidean cryptography approaches to safeguard log data. They also argue that it is possible to avoid harmful behavior in the cloud by implementing knowledge-based systems that use fuzzy logic and data mining.

Sugandh Bhatia and Jyoteesh Malhotra (2018) [17] have developed a reliable framework for ensuring security and privacy in cloud computing technologies so that businesses may use it. It disseminates all technological knowledge to the technicians that work in the organizations. Organizational preparedness may also be forecasted using this methodology. This type of appliance has the ability to control a whole enterprise.

Palash Santra (2019) [18] presented a thorough comparison of cloud forensic techniques in IaaS. The author of this research presented a parallel analysis based on several forensics methodologies offered for the Infrastructure as service architecture. To do this study in IaaS, all of the processes in the cloud forensics paradigm, such as evidence gathering, collecting, analysis, and presentation approaches, have been appropriated.

Ezz El-Din Hemdan and D. H. Manjaiah [19] have suggested a digital forensic accession for investigating cybercrime in a private cloud environment. They devised an experimental environment in which forensic processes might be implemented on a private cloud. Data capture and collection from virtual machines are the most important phases in the cloud forensic procedure. They pioneered the use of live forensics and dead forensics to analyze virtual computers in a private cloud setting.

Mazda Zainal, Ahmed Nour Moussa, Norafida Ithnin, and Ahmed Nour Moussa (2020) [20] suggested a conceptual bilateral cloud forensics–as-a-service paradigm to address the constraints of previous research in which the system is deployed and managed by the cloud service provider. In this paradigm, both the customer and the service provider can gather data, validate the forensic analysis process's equality, and use this information to resolve disputes that arise from independently acquired data. This model's success is contingent on two factors: The quality of the forensic evidence gathered by the consumer is also determined by the comparison, and the conflict resolution process can be used to reach mutually acceptable conclusions.

2.5   Research Methodology

The Research Methodology includes three dimensions:

1. Technical dimension: The information is needed to collect which is flexible and static and which can be proved. Such collected information should be processed with available criminal-related logical procedures in a distributed computing environment.
2. Organizational dimension: In a distributed computing environment, it is particularly considered. They are the cloud customer and the cloud service provider.
3. The applications hosted on the cloud: Therefore, one cloud service provider's services are hooked to other cloud service provider's services also. The dependence on numerous parties makes the investigation process very hard. Therefore, it becomes very hard.

2.6   Testing Environment Plan

The experimental plans for testing key parts of the cloud forensic tools operating mechanism are listed below. A few tests must be conducted throughout each phase of the technique to determine the viability of its execution. Some tests aim to establish benchmarks for the underlying components as well. The table below lists the systems that must be tested before cloud forensics may be implemented.

A HPC cluster with a high number of nodes should be present. A high-performance computing machine is required to host this cluster. Virtualization software is installed on the virtualization cluster nodes, allowing one node to operate as many nodes. The tests may then be carried out to see how effective they are. Then, each physical node will have additional virtual computers serving as nodes. This would enable the virtualization cluster to have a larger number of nodes, each with 25 GB of RAM.

Task processing must be set up from the start. These duties will be performed on the evidences, as well as potential imaging and encryption of the evidence for transmission over the Internet. This level's tests should all be done on a workstation.

High-performance computing allows data to be processed quickly and complicated computations to be performed quickly. Any computer with a 3-GHz CPU will suffice to do this high-performance computation. A computer like this can do over 3 billion operations per second. Similarly, a supercomputer has comparable capabilities. A supercomputer will have tens of thousands of nodes working together to complete tasks within a certain time frame. Parallel processing is a term used to describe this sort of computer activity. Today, high-performance computers can do miracles. It makes significant progress in a variety of fields, including science and technology. IoT, artificial intelligence, and 3D imaging are just a few examples of technologies that benefit from it.

Computation, networking, and data storage are all part of high-performance computing operating mechanism. A cluster is a collection of computers networked together for high-performance processing. All of the software and algorithms would be running at the same time. A high-performance computer cluster typically consists of thousands of processing machines. All of the servers are connected through a network. Each server will thus be referred to as a node. Such nodes in all clusters would operate at the same time, and the outputs would be in the form of high-performance computing as a result of this parallel working mechanism.

Today, workstation clusters are alternative to supercomputers. Generally, it had like these work station clusters for all high-performance computing needs. Parallel hardware or software designs can be divided into two categories. Distributed memory and shared memory are the two types of memory.

Distributed memory systems consist of a group of networked computing nodes that do not share memory but can communicate through a high-speed network. In shared memory systems, cooperative processes have access to a shared memory address space that may be accessed by all processors. Multiprocessing in shared-memory systems is achieved by the use of shared data structures or software emulation of message forwarding semantics. In distributed memory systems, parallelism is done by running many copies of the parallel program on distinct nodes and communicating with one another to coordinate computations. Application data, synchronization information, and other data that governs how the parallel program runs are frequently included in messages from a distributed memory parallel program.

The cyber analyst may upload, analyze, and analyze evidence obtained using the cloud forensics application. The cloud forensics analyst would have access to the client's computer, allowing them to connect to the cloud forensics program and upload digital evidence. The client will verify the cloud forensics analyst's identity before establishing a secure connection to the cloud forensic tool. The cloud forensics analyst will find work by picking the digital forensic tools that will be executed using the available secured connection. The cloud forensics analyst will next use the client to upload a disc image to the cloud forensic tool. While the picture is being uploaded, a few of the chosen forensic instruments will start; some programs do not require the whole disc image. Tools that require the whole image will be executed once the photo has finished uploading. The findings will be saved to the working directory because the tools will operate in a cluster. The cloud forensics analyst will authenticate and connect to a virtual machine remotely during the processing and analysis of the evidence. The virtual computer's connection will be safeguarded. Only the virtual computer with the cloud forensics expert's evidence will be accessible. As the tools finish on the cluster, the findings are displayed on the virtual computer. They need access to tools that are unable or unwilling to work on a cluster during this virtual machine. The cloud forensics analyst can use the output of these tools, as well as other tools on the virtual computer, to examine and analyze their case. Virtual computers cannot access evidence that belongs to another cloud forensics expert because they are segregated from one another. The cluster, and hence the analysis virtual machine, has access to the client's evidence in a knowledge store. Evidence is encrypted at the client, decrypted on the cluster, and re-encrypted before being transferred to the data storage. The information will be encrypted for cloud forensics professionals using the analysis virtual machine.

The cloud forensic tools will be made up of three parts. They are the customer, the investigators, and the processing parts as a consequence. After completing the initial job configuration, the customer will be able to contribute evidence to the tool. In order to study the evidence in the investigative part, the user is given a virtual machine to utilize. In the processing stage, the forensics tools will be executed on a cluster. With the aid of a virtualization cluster, many virtual computers will handle the strain for the tools. On the virtual machines, an agent will operate, receiving payloads and analyzing those using forensic tools. On a typical blade server, one or more virtual machines can be found.

2.7   Testing

The aim of this test is to figure out how many nodes each forensic cloud user has. Begin by allocating all nodes to all cases evenly, starting with a single case. Increase the number of instances by one until the processing speed becomes unacceptably slow. Keep track of how many nodes a particular case requires to be effective.

The processing performance would be improved if faster storage was employed. By up to 225%, the virtualization cluster outperformed both the workstation and the HPC cluster. Additional testing with a shared storage device is required. Despite the fact that the HPC cluster and workstation cluster performed similarly, it can be said that the HPC cluster is still more cost-effective and practical. Table 2.1 shows systems needs of cloud forensic tool implementation. To attain the 3,072 threads on the HPC cluster are utilized, 384 workstations would be required. It would require 96 virtualization nodes to match our HPC cluster's threads thread for thread.

Intel® Xeon® Processor X5660
12M Cache, 2.80 GHz, 6.40 GT/s Intel® QPI
CPU Specifications:
Cores: 6, Threads: 12, Processor Base Frequency: 2.80 GHz, Max Turbo Frequency: 3.20 GHz, Cache: 12 MB Intel® Smart Cache, Bus Speed: 6.4 GT/s
Memory Specifications:
Max Memory Size: 288 GB, Memory Types: DDR3 800/1066/1333, Max # of Memory Channels: 3
Max Memory Bandwidth: 32 GB/s, Physical Address Extensions: 40-bit

Table 2.1 Systems needs of cloud forensic tool implementation.

Name of component	RAM	CPU	Cores	Threads	Disk space
HPC cluster	25 GB	Intel Xeon	10	20	100 Mib/s
Virtualization	135 GB	Intel Xeon	10	20	1G B/s
Cluster Work station	8 GB	Intel core i7 processor	5	10	100 Mib/s

2.7.1   Scenario 1: Simultaneous Imaging and Upload and Encryption

Scenario 1 includes setting up the first processing activities that need be conducted on the evidence, as well as potential imaging and encryption of the evidence for Internet transmission.

The data processing should begin at the same time as the imaging procedure. To speed up processing, the client should allow for simultaneous data transmission and picture creation. The purpose of the test is to see how simultaneous imaging and network transmission of evidence affects

Table 2.2 Data transfer calculations.

Evidence size	Speed (measured with respected to 100 Mbits per second)	Speed (measured with respected to 10 Mbits per second)
100 GB	03:55:04	01:27:23
500 GB	22:43:21	00:09:30
1,000 GB	33:12:28	01:12:27
5,000 GB	155:22:15	01:22:41

Table 2.3 Evidences usage in testing processing.

	Disk image	Realistic image
Compressed Image	0.89 GB	4.3 GB
Un-compressed Image	2 GB	45 GB

Table 2.4 Outputs of one node/one cluster.

*	1st Parameter	2nd Parameter	3rd Parameter	4th Parameter	5th Parameter	6th Parameter
Factors related	High-Performance Computing	Virtualization	Workstation	High-Performance Computing	Virtualization	Workstation
Speed per 1 s	112.12	41.22	105.46	900.1	498.12	764.3
Speed in MIB/s	19.44	43.23	21.07	46.33	74.34	46.2
Speed in MIB	2 GB	2 GB	2 GB	4 GB	4 GB	4 GB
Threads	10 Nos	10 Nos	5 Nos	10 Nos	10 Nos	5 Nos
RAM	24 GB	24 GB	8 GB	24 GB	24 GB	8 GB

Table 2.5 Outputs of workstation clusters.

Factors related	Disk image				Realistic image			
	1st Node	2nd Node	3rd Node	4th Node	1st Node	2nd Node	3rd Node	4th Node
Seconds	32.1	41.3	23.4	4.9	500	200	197.3	45.3
Speed per 1 s	13.4	12.2	18.7	103.4	22.4	55.6	57.8	225
Speed in MIB/s	0.5 GB	0.5 GB	0.5 GB	0.5 GB	1 GB	1 GB	1 GB	1 GB

Table 2.6 Outputs of high-performance clusters.

Factors related	Disk image				Realistic image			
	1st Node	2nd Node	3rd Node	4th Node	1st Node	2nd Node	3rd Node	4th Node
Seconds	32.1	41.3	23.4	4.9	500	200	197.3	45.3
Speed per 1 s	13.4	12.2	18.7	103.4	22.4	55.6	57.8	225
Speed in MIB/s	0.5 GB	0.5 GB	0.5 GB	0.5 GB	1 GB	1 GB	1 GB	1 GB

Table 2.7 Outputs based on virtualization cluster.

Factors related	Disk image				Realistic image			
	1st Node	2nd Node	3rd Node	4th Node	1st Node	2nd Node	3rd Node	4th Node
Seconds	32.1	41.3	23.4	4.9	500	200	197.3	45.3
Speed per 1 s	13.4	12.2	18.7	103.4	22.4	55.6	57.8	225
Speed in MIB/s	0.5 GB	0.5 GB	0.5 GB	0.5 GB	1 GB	1 GB	1 GB	1 GB

performance. The client should be run twice: once to just upload the test data to the server and again to submit the test data while concurrently creating an image of it. This will be used to test if the client can perform both tasks at the same time while maintaining a 120 MB/s upload pace. Each node had 24 GB of RAM and 12 threads. Table 2.2 shows data transfer calculations, and Table 2.3 shows evidences usage in testing processing. Table 2.4 shows outputs of one node/one cluster. Table 2.5 shows outputs of workstation clusters and Table 2.6 shows outputs of high-performance clusters. Table 2.7 shows outputs based on virtualization cluster.

Encryption must be applied to the evidence being communicated between the client and server to maintain the data secrecy and integrity during transmission. The Advanced Encryption Standard (AES) has been acknowledged by the NIST as a well-known, trustworthy, symmetric key encryption technology. For data security during network transmission, this is deemed to be sufficient.

2.7.2   Scenario 2: Real-Time Stream Processing

Processing data as it becomes accessible to the server is required to streamline the analysis process. Processing digital evidence can be done in two ways. Bulk data analysis and a file-based method are the two options. Bulk data analysis treats data chunks as a whole, regardless of their structure.

To put it another way, it does not need file system structure knowledge to accomplish its job. These approaches are perfect for analyzing the stream of data that the forensic cloud client sends forth.

The data received must be chunked and delivered to each tool, with nodes assigned as appropriate. Many programs utilize file-based methods to handle data at the file level. The forensic cloud cluster is able to do file-level analysis by extracting files from a stream in real time.

It is feasible to reassemble files from a stream in real time and make them available to clients, as demonstrated by the latency-optimized target acquisition prototype discussed in. The nodes are the clients in this scenario. The files can then be handed to appropriate tools for file-centric processing after they have been made available.

2.7.3   Scenario 3: Remote Desktop Connection, Performance Test

The cloud forensic investigator connects to a distant virtual machine using VDI's built-in remote desktop protocol. There are two protocol alternatives for VMware Horizon View VDI: PCoIP and Microsoft's RDP.

More functionality, such as USB redirection and multi-monitor support, are available with PCoIP. The usefulness of the remote desktop protocol will be determined in this test. Connect to the available cloud forensic tools to find out.

2.8   Recommendations

After making the decisions, examine reports and use forensic tools to see if the virtual machine is still usable. The virtual machine should respond fast and with no visible lag. It is vital to set a baseline of how quickly a forensics workstation can handle digital evidence before deciding on the best processing choice for digital data in forensic cloud tools. The virtualization cluster and the HPC cluster must both use parallelization to test the speeds that each tool could attain. It may be possible to identify which distributed processing method is the most effective based on the speeds of each tool in various settings. In order to determine the most efficient and successful use of a forensic cloud system, a range of components of the work flow must be examined. These tests demonstrate how much capacity and processing power can be handled by a forensic cloud installation. The purpose of this test is to see if data can be uploaded to a forensic cloud. Using multiple data set sizes, each data set is uploaded and downloaded separately from different forensic cloud providers. Keep track of how long it takes for each file to upload. Calculate how long a single user would take to perform the task. This test is used to see if a forensic cloud environment can handle a high volume of uploads. At the same time, upload and retrieve a data collection of 500 GB or more from two forensic cloud sites. Keep track of how long it takes for each file to upload. Increase the number of upload sites by one and re-upload the files. Keep track of how long each file takes to upload. Continue to add one facility at a time until the upload time for any user becomes unacceptably long. The Nodes per Job Test is used to determine the most appropriate number of nodes for each work. Apply each tool offered to the user to a 1-TiB or bigger data set. Add for that tool to be used with each run of the tool. Continue until there are no more nodes available or until adding another node improves performance no more. Keep track of the number of nodes that each job requires.

2.9   Limitations of Present Study

To completely construct a functioning prototype of the forensic cloud, there is still a lot of work to be done. One of the goals of this article is to list the problems that cloud forensics encounters in order to initiate a community discussion. This will give us with valuable input that it can be utilized to improve the prototype it is being working on. It can be performed a full evaluation of digital forensics tools to identify whether tools can be parallelized suitably for usage in cloud forensics, as only a tiny portion of technologies were discussed at the conclusion of this study.

2.10   Conclusions

As the number of forensic needs increases, the advancement in this field is also needed. Different categories of millions and trillions of files need to be checked. It is not possible to check them manually, and it needs some atomized mechanism to scan all of them. An efficient tool would do the matter. The presently available tool takes a few hours of time, and it needs to be quick enough. With the help of high-performance computing, it could be achieved in this work with in very less time. Existing tools are being adapted to work in this context. Cloud forensics enhances the inquiry by offering a remote investigation environment that allows investigators to use licensed tools. This article has attempted to offer an architectural vision of cloud forensics in the future. The following are the benefits of this model: (i) By utilizing the capabilities of a high-performance computing platform and customizing current tools to function inside this environment, it reduces the total processing time of huge amounts of data. (ii) It provides smaller departments with the opportunity to utilize commercial software remotely if they do not have access to it. (iii) It allows for cooperation. Because the data is kept in the cloud, it is feasible for someone with proper authority from the case owner to have access to the case and perform additional analysis. (iv) The case on the cloud might potentially provide legal authorities access to the investigators' findings. It has provided a test strategy for assessing various implementation components. These tests may be used to assess the architecture's suitability for an inevitable cloud forensic plan deployment.

2.11   Scope for the Future Work

There is still a lot of work to be done in order to create a fully effective forensic cloud prototype. This includes figuring out which tools are made to function on discrete items like files and which are made to run in parallel. The deployment of cloud forensics as a platform-as-a-service was not examined in this study. Tool developers can use a cloud forensics environment to design and test parallelized digital forensics solutions if they have access to one. It will have an API that will make it simple for investigators to connect to forensic Cloud. You can construct a tool that uses parallel processing without writing parallel code using this API.

Acknowledgements

We wish to thank Late Mr. Panem Nadipi Chennaih for his continues support for the development of this research paper and it is dedicated to him.

References

1. Bennett, J.-C. and Mamadou, H.D., *A Forensic Pattern-Based Approach for Investigations in Cloud System Environments*, pp. 1–8, 2018, doi: 10.1109/CSNET.2018.8602908.

2. Simou, S., Kalloniatis, C., Gritzalis, S., Katos, V., A framework for designing cloud forensic-enabled services (CFeS). *Int. J. Comput. Appl.*, 178, 34, 0975 – 8887, July 20192018.

3. Santra, P., Roy, A., Majumder, K., A Comparative Analysis of Cloud Forensic Techniques in IaaS, in: *Advances in Computer and Computational Sciences. Advances in Intelligent Systems and Computing*, vol. 554, S. Bhatia, K. Mishra, S. Tiwari, V. Singh, (Eds.), Springer, Singapore, 2018.

4. Bhatia, S. and Malhotra, J., CSPCR: Cloud Security, Privacy and Compliance Readiness - A Trustworthy Framework. *Int. J. Electr. Comput. Eng.*, International Research on Permanent Authentic Records in Electronic Systems (InterPARES), 1–56, 8, 2018, doi: 10.11591/ijece.v8i5.pp3756–3766.

5. Santra, P., Roy, A., Majumder, K., A Comparative Analysis of Cloud Forensic Techniques in IaaS, in: *Advances in Computer and Computational Sciences. Advances in Intelligent Systems and Computing*, vol. 554, S. Bhatia, K. Mishra, S. Tiwari, V. Singh, (Eds.), Springer, Singapore, 2018.

6. Hemdan, E.E.-D. and Manjaiah, D.H., Digital Forensic Approach for Investigation of Cybercrimes in Private Cloud Environment, in: *Recent Findings in Intelligent Computing Techniques. Advances in Intelligent Systems and Computing*, vol. 707, P. Sa, S. Bakshi, I. Hatzilygeroudis, M. Sahoo, (Eds.), Springer, Singapore, 2019.

7. Moussa, A.N., Ithnin, N., Zainal, A., CFaaS: bilaterally agreed evidence collection. *J. Cloud Comput.*, Journal of Cloud Computing: Advances, Systems and Applications (2018), 7, 1, 1–19, 2018, 2018. https://doi.org/10.1186/s13677-017-0102-3.

8. Choo, K.R., Esposito, C., Castiglione, A., Evidence and Forensics in the Cloud: Challenges and Future Research Directions. *IEEE Cloud Comput.*, 4, 3, 14–19, 2017, 2017.

9. Ruan, K., Carthy, J., Kechadi, T., Crosbie, M., "CLOUD FORENSICS,", in: *Advances in Digital Forensics VII, IFIPAICT, IFIP International Federation for Information Processing 2011*, vol. 361, pp. 35–46, 2011.

10. Raghavan, S., Digital forensic research: Current state of the art. *CSI Trans. ICT*, Springer link, 1, 91–114, 2012, doi: 10.1007/s40012-012-0008-7.

11. Lillis, D., Becker, B., O'Sullivan, T., Scanlon, M., *Current Challenges and Future Research Areas for Digital Forensic Investigation*, 2016.

12. Alex, M. and Kishore, R., Forensics framework for cloud computing. *Comput. Electr. Eng.*, Elseviwer and available at: Science Direct, 60, 1–13, 2017, doi: 10.1016/j.compeleceng.2017.02.006.

13. Amato, F., Castiglione, A., Cozzolino, G., Narducci, F., A semantic-based methodology for digital forensics analysis. *J. Parallel Distrib. Comput.*, Revista de Direito, Estado e Telecomunicacoes (Sci Indexed Journal), 138, 121–138, 2020, doi: 10.1016/j.jpdc.2019.12.017.

14. Ferguson-Boucher, K. and Endicott-Popovsky, B., *Forensic Readiness and Information Governance in the Cloud*, International Research on Permanent Authentic Records in Electronic Systems (InterPARES), Canada, 2011.

15. Simou, S., Kalloniatis, C., Gritzalis, S., Mouratidis, H., A survey on cloud forensics challenges and solutions. *Secur. Commun. Netw.*, Security and Communication Networks Wiley Online Library, 9, 6285–6314, 2016, doi: 10.1002/sec.1688.

16. Santra, P., Roy, A., Midya, S., Majumder, K., Phadikar, S., Log-Based Cloud Forensic Techniques: A Comparative Study, ACM Digital Library, NewYork, USA, 2018, doi: 10.1007/978-981-10-4600-1_5.

17. Bhatia, S. and Malhotra, J., Towards Performing Classification in Cloud Forensics with Self Organizing Maps. *International Journal of Electrical and Computer Engineering(IJECE)*, 8, 5, 94, 2020.

18. Santra, P., Roy, A., Majumder, K., A Comparative Analysis of Cloud Forensic Techniques in IaaS, Springer Nature, Singapore, 2018, doi: 10. 1007/978-981-10-3773-3_20.

19. Hemdan, E.E.-D. and Manjaiah, D.H., *Exploring Digital Forensic Investigation Issues for Cyber Crimes in Cloud Computing Environment*, 2015.

20. Moussa, A.N., Ithnin, N., Zainal, A., CFaaS: bilaterally agreed evidence collection. *J. Cloud Comput.*, 7, 1, 2018, doi: 10.1186/s13677-017-0102-3.

3

Malware Identification, Analysis and Similarity

Subhradip Debnath[1]* and Soumyanil Biswas[2]

[1]*Department of Computer Science, Institute of Engineering and Management, Maulana Abul Kalam Azad University of Technology, Kolkata, West Bengal, India*
[2]*Department of Electronics and Communication, Institute of Engineering and Management, Institute of Engineering & Management, Kolkata, West Bengal, India*

Abstract

Cyberattacks have grown to a much greater extent in the decades. According to statistics in the year of 2009, 12.4 million attacks were recorded, and recently, in 2018, it has raised up to 812.67 million known cases. To be told, these are only the known cases, and there are many which are unrecorded. Ranging from small cyberattack to large ransomware attacks or to a combination of several sophisticated cyberattacks which consists of advanced exploitation techniques and persistence capability for a long-term intrusion campaigns. However, the common part among all the cyberattacks that have happened so far was the use of *malware*. To mitigate these attacks, we have to understand the basic structure of malware, working features, and its effects upon the target. This paper provides an in-depth overview on malware types, by analyzing the malware via a process called malware analysis, and other related processes depending on the type of malware. It is actually the process which is conducted just after digital forensics and incident response (DFIR). It is the process of detection of malware and malware infection in a particular host or network. After getting any sort of suspicious file or malware, malware analysis is done. Although this paper does not focus on *DFIR*, it does focus on malware and different well known mechanisms of malware.

Keywords: Reverse engineering, statically linked library, dynamically linked library, portable executable

Corresponding author: research.subhradip@gmail.com; https://subhradip.tk

Sabyasachi Pramanik, Debabrata Samanta, M. Vinay and Abhijit Guha (eds.) Cyber Security and Network Security, (47–70) © 2022 Scrivener Publishing LLC

3.1 Introduction

Let us start with a definition of malware. Malicious software, sometimes, known as malware, plays a significant role in the majority of computer intrusion and security events. Malware is defined as software that causes harm to a user, machine, or network. Malware encompasses viruses, Trojan horses, worms, rootkits, scareware, and spyware. While different types of malware perform different things, malware analysts (those who analyze malware) have a collection of tools, tactics, and approaches at their disposal when it comes to studying malware. Malware analysis is the process of dissecting harmful software to figure out how it works, how to recognize it, and how to defeat or remove it. Malware identification refers to the process of determining the type of malware that has been discovered.

3.1.1 Goals of Malware Analysis and Malware Identification

The goal of malware analysis is usually to figure out what went wrong and to make sure we have found all infected workstations and files. When investigating suspected malware, our goal is usually to figure out exactly what the suspect code can do, how to identify it on any network or device, and how to measure and limit the harm it might cause. Once the files that need to be examined have been determined, a malware analyst will create signatures to detect malware infections on our network. Malware analysis can be used to create host-based and network-based signatures for malware detection. Malicious/notorious code is detected on victim PCs using host-based signatures or indicators. These indications can detect files that the virus creates or modifies, as well as registry modifications. Malware indicators, unlike antivirus signatures, focus on what malware does to a system rather than the malware's features, making them more successful in detecting malware that changes form (polymorphic malware) or has been erased from the hard disc.

By monitoring network traffic, network-based signatures or indicators are utilized to detect malicious code. Without virus analysis, network signatures can be established, but there is a catch. Signatures developed through malware analysis are typically far more effective than traditional detection systems, with a greater detection rate and fewer false positives. After obtaining the signatures, the final goal will be to determine how the malware operates.

3.1.2   Common Malware Analysis Techniques

Majority of the time, while performing malware analysis, malware analysts only have the malware executable to perform the analysis, not the malware code, which will not be human-readable. So, by some magical tricks, the analyst will be able to ease work. They will be able to retrieve some pieces of information by those magical tricks. Those magical tricks and techniques are two most basic types of malware analysis techniques:

1. *Static analysis*: It is the process of getting information from the malware binary/executable without even executing/running it. The name is actually speaking for itself.
2. *Dynamic analysis*: Everything is the same as *static analysis* but the only difference is that it performs analysis on malware while it is actually in the running phase. Again, the name is actually speaking for itself.

In *dynamic analysis* before running the malware, the analysts have to create a safe (or isolated/quarantined) environment, so that running malware does not infect the OS environment. This is not required in static analysis, as static analysis does not involve running of any malware. Sometimes, dynamic analysis can be difficult, for the ones who do not have that much programming experience or knowledge. This is because most of the analysis done dynamically takes the use of a debugger or disassembler or decompiler or all the three. To know all those three tools, individuals must have solid understanding on *code debugging*, knowledge of low level language like *assembly language, operating system* (Windows and Linux) *registers*. It is also, sometimes, industrially recommended in a job offer that any individuals applying for code/malware analysis or reverse engineering roles should have a significant number of years of experience in the cyber security field [1]. This is because to ensure the individuals have much experience to deal with malware but this experience is not always necessary.

3.2   Background and Related Works

In the paper "Comparative study of two most popular packet sniffing tools-Tcpdump and Wireshark", P. Goyal *et al.* discussed using Wireshark and tcpdump [2]. All those important (hidden) things are captured by the author: the use of Wireshark and tcpdump in both offensive and defensive point and view and the comparison between their corresponding system requirements [3]. In a study "RegForensicTool: evidence collection and analysis of Windows registry", Bandu B. Meshram talked about providing a large amount of statistics, information and internals about registry keys and how they can be targeted by malware to perform persistence and other nefarious stuff. This paper also focuses on forensics and how to perform forensics when it comes to registry keys in the Windows Operating System. In this research paper, it emphasizes on reverse engineering much more than any other methodologies in malware analysis [4]. It is actually strongly agreed by authors, speakers, and other eminent security professionals as well handlers, dlls are much more than taken into account [5]. Real-world malware is analyzed with the tools and methodologies that are being discussed in this paper "Malware Analysis and Detection in Enterprise Systems" by T. Mokoena *et al.*

A malware analysis methodology named MARE is being discussed vividly. In the paper "Malware analysis reverse engineering (MARE) methodology & malware defense (MD) timeline", Nguyen, Cory Q. *et al.* claimed that MARE methodology is one of the most successful methods when it comes to malware analysis and reverse engineering [6]. The paper "Dynamic malware analysis in the modern era—A state of the art survey" by Or-Meir *et al.* is quite different [7]. This paper is focused toward the incident response and intrusion detection portion of cyber security. It covers anomaly detection, malware detection TTOs (Tactics, Techniques, Operations). Malware detection techniques based on training models are being seen nowadays. In the paper "Robust intelligent malware detection using deep learning", R. Vinayakumar *et al.* showed several forms of techniques using MLA (Machine Learning Algorithm) and DLA (Deep Learning Algorithm) to detect malware types, format, and threats [8]. A paper written by Souri, A. *et al.* "A state-of-the-art survey of malware detection approaches using data mining techniques" also focuses on data, when the topic comes to malware analysis [9]. This paper throws spotlight on detection of malware analysis based on data mining, behavior-based, and signature-based analysis [10]. The paper "A study on malware and malware detection techniques" by Tahir, Rabia majorly focused on malware obfuscation technique and their detection analysis and procedures of detections.

3.3   Proposed System Design Architecture

3.3.1   Tool Requirement, System Design, and Architecture

3.3.1.1   For Static Malware Analysis

Some tools will be needed for this type of analysis (not any particular safe environment). Some of the tools are online services and some of them are downloaded.

The *first tool* that any analyst uses before starting any malware analysis is using any open source malware scanner. In this paper, VirusTotal open source malware scanning service will only be discussed, as found online. VirusTotal allows users to *upload file*, *file hash* and *suspicious URLs*, to their database to check against all forms of antivirus scanner (presently 70 types). Their range of detection has a lot of scope, like metadata extraction, heuristic engines, and known-bad signatures [11].

The *second tool*, *any hashing tool*, is irrespective of using any *third party tool* or *command prompt/terminal*. *Hashing* or *cryptographic hashing* is a type of one way algorithm which converts the input key/string into a fixed length output key/string, respectively, based on the type of hashing algorithm used upon the input object. This is basically a common method to identify any malware uniquely. The malware is run through a hashing algorithm which in turn produces a unique hash that identifies that malware which acts like a fingerprint of the hash. Figures 3.1 and 3.2 show Linux code.

Let us perform Message-Digest Algorithm 5 (MD5) hashing:

```
root@reveng ~# md5sum file.txt
efa717f3019d1916f60e6919171d0864   file.txt
```

Figure 3.1 Linux.

The content of the file is as follows:

```
root@reveng  # cat file.txt
Hey You !! , Ya you who is looking at this paper.
You can do anything you want !!
```

Figure 3.2 Linux.

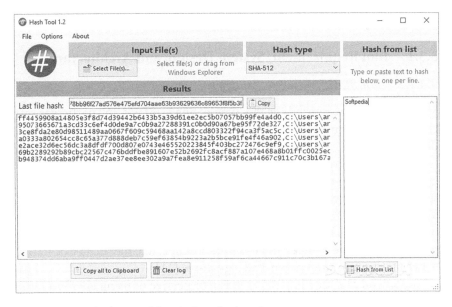

Figure 3.3 GUI hashing tool for windows: hash tool.

In the above explanation, hashing is done in the Linux platform; likewise, you can also perform the same in Windows platform as well. You can also use GUI softwares like this. Figure 3.3 shows GUI hashing tool for Windows: Hash Tool.

In many books and online platforms, the use of MD5 hash function and the Secure Hash Algorithm 1 (SHA-1) are still prevalent, to detect malware types. However, the thing is that MD5 and SHA-1 are prone to breakage of integrity. Both of them were found to be prone to hash collisions. Goal of the *third tool* is finding *debug symbols/PDB(program database) symbols/ strings*. By searching through these *symbols* is the easiest way to get hints about the functionality/working of a program. For example, if the malware is programmed to connect to a remote ip address, then there is a possibility to see the *remote ip address* or *URL* stored as a string in the program. Figure 3.4 shows Linux terminal.

However, in this example, the external ip address is not revealed, only the *bind ip address* is. However, the idea is the same. Now, a question can strike people's mind: "How *string utility* (the tool that we used above in image to extract strings from executable file) works?" Basically, *strings utility* performs searches in two stages as follows.First, when it searches for strings in an executable, it searches for ASCII or Unicode or both strings. It ignores the text and formatting present in the executable file. Second,

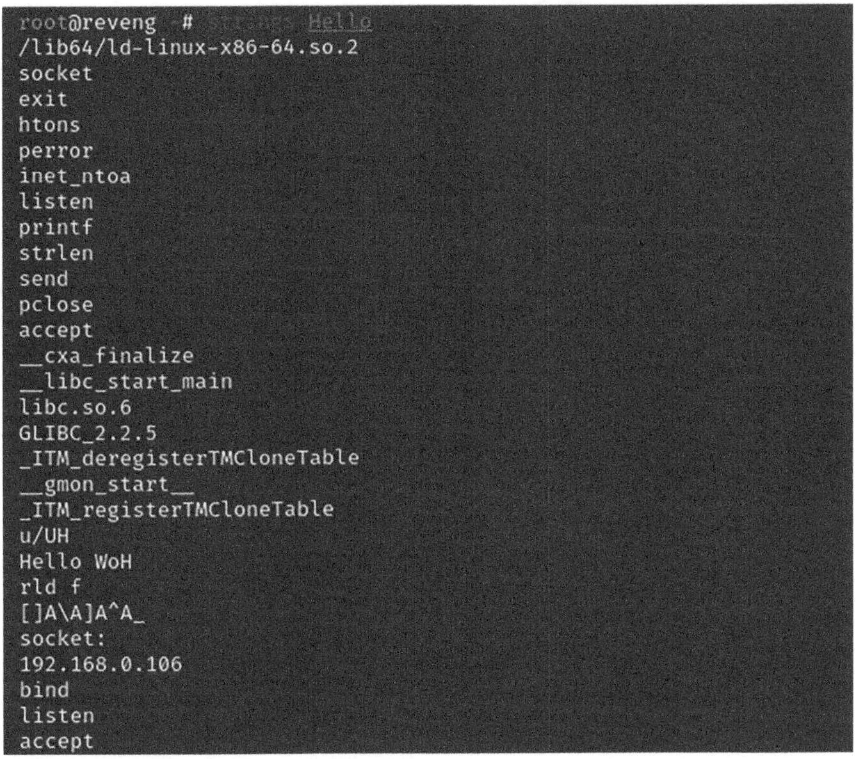

```
root@reveng  #  strings  Hello
/lib64/ld-linux-x86-64.so.2
socket
exit
htons
perror
inet_ntoa
listen
printf
strlen
send
pclose
accept
__cxa_finalize
__libc_start_main
libc.so.6
GLIBC_2.2.5
_ITM_deregisterTMCloneTable
__gmon_start__
_ITM_registerTMCloneTable
u/UH
Hello WoH
rld f
[]A\A]A^A_
socket:
192.168.0.106
bind
listen
accept
```

Figure 3.4 Linux terminal.

it narrows down searches by picking those ASCII and Unicode strings, which have three or more characters, ending with a NULL terminator string (0x00). Over time, maldevs (malware developers) are becoming clever and cunning. While writing malware they implement a special type of mechanism called *packing/obfuscation*. This specific technique makes the strings present in the malware—*obfuscated* (encrypted or hidden or replaced by normal program strings in such a way strings utility fails to identify it). Another subset of *obfuscation* is *packing*. The goal of using it is also the same but it has a different strategy. It compresses the malware so that most of the strings do not get detected by conventional static analysis. So, to detect this packer, analysts need another type of tool. So, the *fourth tool* is the *packer identifier* tool named *PE-bear*. From a high-level, *PE executable* is basically a *file format* found in x86 and x86_64 versions of Windows Operating System. *PE format* actually holds all valuable information related to the file within a data structure. Figure 3.5 shows PE-bear.

GUI software to analyze *PE*:

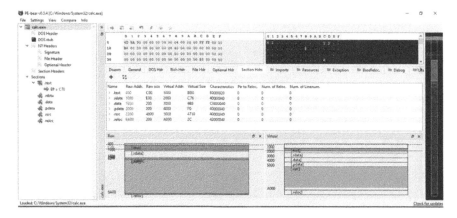

Figure 3.5 PE-bear.

In the above image, *PE-bear* is used to open the *calc.exe* file. For those users who are more cmd/terminal fanatic, they can use a tool called *dumpbin.exe*. Figure 3.6 shows snipped image of the result produced by dumpbin (Windows).

Apart from strings, there are several factors to consider while undertaking any type of malware research. There are also additional topics we should discuss, such as Linked Libraries and Functions. More than strings,

```
C:\Program Files (x86)\Microsoft Visual Studio\2019\Community>dumpbin /headers c:\Windows\System32\calc.exe
Microsoft (R) COFF/PE Dumper Version 14.29.30037.0
Copyright (C) Microsoft Corporation.  All rights reserved.


Dump of file c:\Windows\System32\calc.exe

PE signature found

File Type: EXECUTABLE IMAGE

FILE HEADER VALUES
            8664 machine (x64)
               6 number of sections
        340C410 time date stamp
               0 file pointer to symbol table
               0 number of symbols
              F0 size of optional header
              22 characteristics
                   Executable
                   Application can handle large (>2GB) addresses

OPTIONAL HEADER VALUES
             20B magic # (PE32+)
           14.20 linker version
             C00 size of code
            6200 size of initialized data
               0 size of uninitialized data
            1870 entry point (0000000140001870)
            1000 base of code
       140000000 image base (0000000140000000 to 0000000140000AFFF)
            1000 section alignment
             200 file alignment
           10.00 operating system version
           10.00 image version
```

Figure 3.6 Snipped image of the result produced by dumpbin (Windows).

they are the most important considerations when it comes to malware analysis. All of the libraries and functions utilized in malware are linked to the malware via import functions. Imports are code libraries, such as sys (in Python), that provide functionality related to any Operating System, that are used by one programme but are actually present in another programme. By linking, these libraries are linked to the main executable. Programmers employ link imports in their applications so that they do not have to re-use the same functionality across many projects. Statically, at runtime, or dynamically, these Code libraries can be connected. The reason these libraries are considered the most crucial is that they can truly define the malware's functionality and power. In the Linux world, statically linked binaries are the most frequent type of binary. When a library is statically linked to an executable, all of the library's code and functions are copied into the executable, resulting in an extremely large executable. Because nothing in the PE file header indicates that the file contains any linked code, analysts find it difficult to distinguish between statically linked code and the executable's own code when studying code. Static linking is diametrically opposed to dynamic linking. The library or library functions are not copied into the file. It retrieves those sections from the library as needed, rather than maintaining a copy, resulting in a file that is a fraction of the size of a statically linked file.

Runtime linked code is used by *maldev* when they want to obfuscate or pack any malware.

In *Windows*, using *Dynamic linking library (DLL)* is more prevalent than using *statically or runtime linking*. *PE file header* of the malware stores the library name that would be loaded whenever the particular

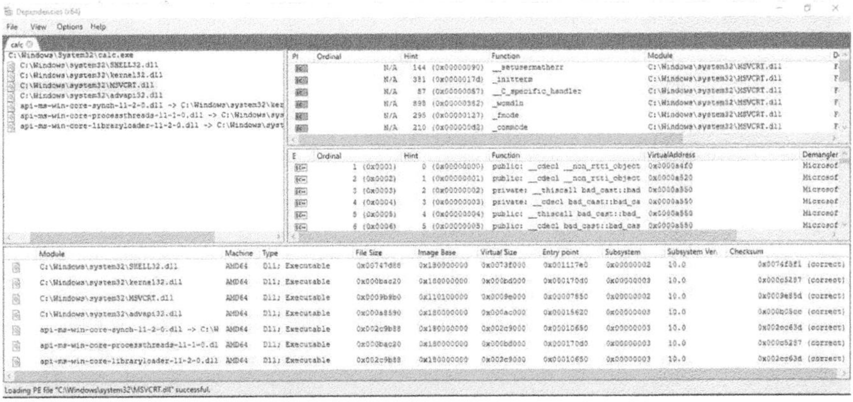

Figure 3.7 Dependencies (Windows only).

malware calls them. In the below picture, an open source GUI tool is used named *Dependencies*. This is basically the modified version of erstwhile *Dependency Walker*. Figure 3.7 shows Dependencies (Windows only).

This tool can be used to view imported dlls and imports linked to an executable when an executable runs. A running DLL linked to an executable can tell a malware analyst a lot about its functionality.

3.3.1.2   For Dynamic Malware Analysis

When malware analysis performs dynamic analysis, they must run them in an isolated environment, as new/unknown malware can do anything. It is always better to have precaution. So, to develop an isolated (air-gapped) environment, virtual machines can be used. There are many vendors present in the market like, vmware (recommended), virtualbox, Microsoft Hyper-V, to name a few. More or less all of them thrive on the same concept of running virtual machines. Anyone can use this open source project (made with powershell) for making a virtual machine environment

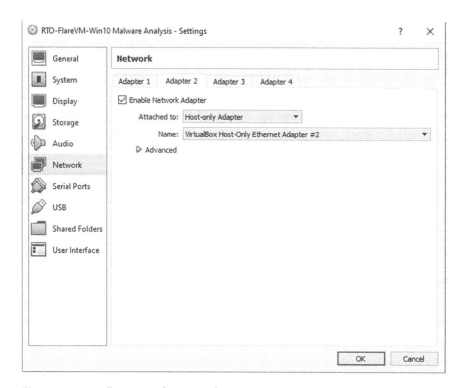

Figure 3.8 Virtualbox network port configuration.

specially dedicated to malware analysts. Users just to set up a machine (Win), then after opening it, they simply have to run this script (but before that, it is highly recommended to read the documentation present in the project repository). The most important things to keep in mind while configuring a virtual machine dedicated to malware analysis are basically two things.

First, let us look at the network configuration: changing network to Host-only adapter: This functionality, which, malware is contained within a virtual computer. The configuration of Virtualbox's network ports is shown in Figure 3.8.

Second, installing "Guest addition disk image". From the Virtualbox menu, select Devices > Insert Guest additions to begin the installation. This will improve the user experience by making the mouse and keyboard more responsive. Figure 3.9 shows Guest addition.

However, there is *one catch*. Many malware (advanced) catch this process running in the background, and then, it obfuscates its original nature or it creates another fake identity to hide its malicious intent. As malware authors know that these files are only used by OS when the OS is running on a virtual machine, that is, there is a high chance of the malware being analyzed or reverse engineered. So, to protect the malware from being exposed they do this thing. So, enabling this is only useful when the malware analyst becomes completely sure that the malware does not scan the host for this file type. Figure 3.10 shows VBoxService.exe file.

There are some techniques of malware analysis related to configuration of the isolated machine on which malware is being dissected. Suppose the analyst opens the virtual machine in order to analyze a malware. So, he/

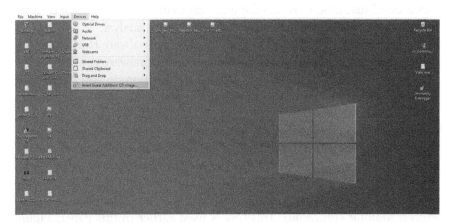

Figure 3.9 Guest addition.

Figure 3.10   VBoxService.exe file.

she starts analyzing the malware in a dynamic phase. So, the malware does its work, and it infects those things which it was designed to. If, for some reason, the analyst again wants to analyze the same malware, then he/she again has to set up a fresh VM, which is not possible again and again. So, by taking a snapshot, we can jump right back to the 1st previous fresh (base image) install state of the machine.

When malware analysis does not provide any success while performing string or static analysis, due to packing or obfuscation, it is time to jump to the domain of dynamic analysis. From surface level, *dynamic analysis* yields more results or increases the chances of success when compared to *static analysis* as when malware is obfuscated, in dynamic analysis, that particular malware is executed, that means, when it is executed, it performs de-obfuscation to reveal the function to utilize that particular function, thereby revealing the function to the malware analyst.

Another thing to be kept in mind is that when malware runs in an isolated environment, just like *VBoxServices.exe*, the malware can also detect whether the host machine has an internet connection or not. If the malware finds internet connection is missing, then it also acts as a trigger alert for the malware to keep its secret. That is the reason why malware analysts use *fakenet*. Fakenet is basically a simulation of a network so that malware can interact with the network and hence will not get notified that the host operating system is running under a virtual machine, thereby showing its inner motives to the analyst within a safer environment. *Monitoring process* is also an essential step in Malware Analysis. They do that using *Process Monitor (Procmon).* This tool is used earlier in this paper. Figure 3.11 shows Process Monitor (Windows only).

Figure 3.11 Process Monitor (Windows only).

We can also perform filtering by *opening Filter > Filter* to open the Filter menu.

Malware analysts can view processes in detailed form using an advanced task manager tool, process explorer. Figure 3.12 shows Process Explorer (Windows).

When it comes to dynamic analysis, checking registry keys is a very important task just like checking dynamic imports and functions. In many research papers, when it comes to checking registry in malware analysis, *regshot* is preferred the most. In this paper, another with advanced functionality is *accessenum.exe.* It also does the same thing. Figure 3.13 shows AccessEnum (Windows).

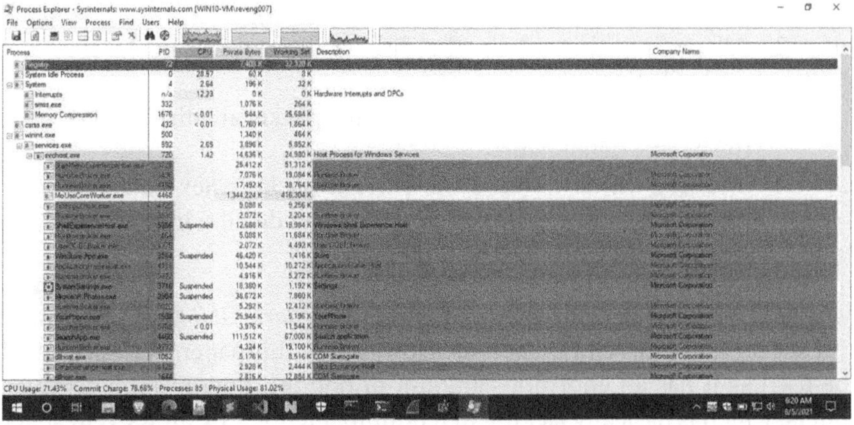

Figure 3.12 Process explorer (Windows).

Figure 3.13 AccessEnum (Windows).

It is important because malware can set up persistence, open a file/run a process, or thread after every reboot, etc.

Another thing which is very important is *packet capturing*. The most famous tool for this is present out there used by most of the blue teamers, Wireshark. This tool, on the other hand, can be used for both good and evil. It can be used to investigate networks and network utilization, troubleshoot application problems, and observe protocols in action. Like Mr. Robot, it can sniff passwords/credentials, reverse engineer network protocols, steal confidential data, and listen in on internet chatter at nearby coffee shops.

The Wireshark display is divided into four sections:

1. The filter box is used to narrow down the number of packets presented.
2. All packets that satisfy the display filter are listed in the packet listing.
3. The contents of the presently selected packet are displayed in the packet detail pane.
4. The hex window shows the current packet's hex contents. The hex window is linked to the packet detail window, and any selected fields will be highlighted.

Again, there is a controversy of using *wireshark GUI* tool or another packet capture tool (CLI), *tcpdump*. However, in this paper, Wireshark will be used as it has an enormous amount of options, buttons, and complex filters, which is basically lacking in tcpdump. Figure 3.14 shows Wireshark display structure (Windows/Linux).

Figure 3.14 Wireshark display structure (Windows/Linux).

Some important wireshark queries are as follows:

- ip.addr == x.x.x.x && ip.addr == x.x.x.x
- (or ip.src == xxxx && ip.dst == xxxx - for a destination)
- tcp.seq == x
- !(arp or icmp or dns)
- browser.comment == "An embedded \" double-quote"
- http.content_type[0:4] == "text"
- tcp.port in {80 443 8080}
- http.request.method in {"HEAD" "GET"}
- (ipx.src.net == 0xbad && ipx.src.node == 0.0.0.0.0.1) || ip

So, this is all for any malware analyst to set up before running a dynamic malware analysis. When it comes to malware analysis, running *dll* is much more challenging in comparison to *exe*.

Last, the main tool is the debugger. Any tool can be used, namely, WinDbg, *Ollydbg*, *IDA* (*free/pro*), *Ghidra*, and *binary ninja*. This tool can be used to analyze malware by the process called reverse engineering (RE), a more focused process in malware analysis. Although it is not necessary that RE is only needed while performing malware analysis, it can also be used to reverse or break or get the initial value from which or for which the malware or software or driver is or was made. Basically, backtracking is the process of production to get the initial value [11]. This is known to be the hardest section when it comes to malware analysis. It is the portion where, basically, the knowledge of the individuals, who are performing the RE, depends irrespective of which tools/methodologies they use.

Knowledge of Windows or Linux internals (depends on the file type of malware—PE or ELF exe), Assembly language, knowledge of disassembler and debugger, knowledge of C/C++ based on Operating System internals, and courage of getting up after getting failed as there is no great malware analyst or Reverse Engineer out there who can perform reverse engineering or malware analysis on the first try. RE is that field in cyber security which needs much more number of tries before getting success.

These are all the tools and techniques that are used successfully to perform a malware analysis dynamically.

3.4   Methodology

Currently, there is no structured method for analyzing malware. However, a malware analysis methodology is important so that this process steps do not get mingled, as well as aiming to get more fresh jobseekers to get into the malware analysis industry, who do not have a high amount of experience. The aim of the malware analysis methodology is to keep the malware

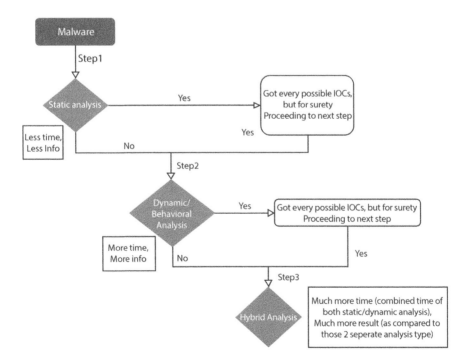

Figure 3.15 Flowchart.

analysis process structured, so that, in the near future, this process can be automated. After that, the safeguarding software can ensure the organization's network. The malware analysis methodology examines the malware's consequences on the system. However, the time, tools, and abilities of the malware analyst required for malware analysis methodologies are different. Figure 3.15 shows flowchart.

In this paper, the above steps will be discussed as to why this particular strategy will yield the most number of IOCs as well as kill switches side by side within a considerable amount of time.

At first, malware analysts should jump for static analysis. As the vulnerability caused by the software may be obtained by string analysis only. There is a possibility that the malware author did not obfuscate the software. So, doing dynamic analysis ahead of doing static analysis would be a foolish job, as it will not only yield no result but also would be a waste of time. Another thing, doing dynamic analysis before getting any of the strings in form of IOCs from static/code analysis, may lead to difficulty of finding out the exact path to find the final *Kill Switch*. The main thing is we should not jump straight into dynamic analysis soon after getting malware unless any information is already known. After doing static analysis and getting those strings/PDB strings, malware analysts either can establish the mindset of the malware or malware author or also can get the kill switch. Getting a *kill switch* with static analysis is not that much of a possibility as per the open source malware analysis reports available on the internet. Assuming if analyst got the kill *switch*, then he or she can terminate the malware analysis process. However, this paper would not recommend that. Always being one step ahead of the malware will be the best thing when it comes to malware analysis.

By *static malware analysis*, analysts can extract the basic strings. Analysts can use those tools that are mentioned in the tools section under static analysis. With that they can get to know the information from which C2 Server (Command and Control server), that is, from which IP (internet protocol address), the connection is being established. This address is most often hardcoded in the binary. By this method, analysts can also know how malware performs persistence. There is a possibility that the Strings *utility* will yield out "CreateProcessA", which can show that malware binary is creating another process. This can give the analyst an idea that the malware is trying to open a process in the operating system. The process can be known in the dynamic analysis phase. All these which are being got in this process are all hints which will be useful in the next (big) step/process. After extracting strings, analysts can try to find out whether malware is packed/obfuscated or not. He/she can use the PEiD tool to know which

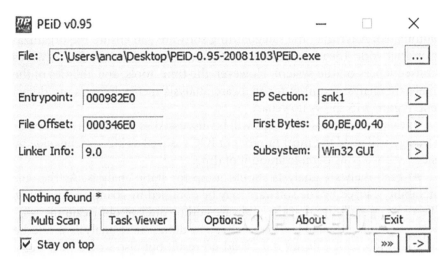

Figure 3.16 PEiD tool (Windows only).

open source packer type is used with the malware, if any. Figure 3.16 shows PEiD tool (Windows only).

In above image, "Nothing found *" was shown, that means, either the malware is not packed/obfuscated or the malware is obfuscated with some

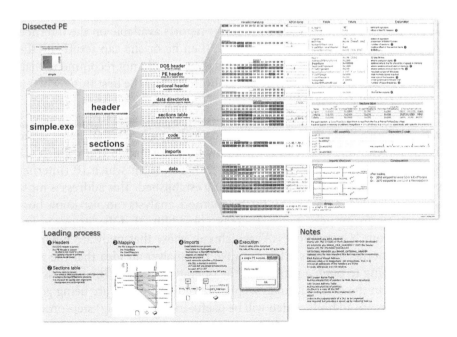

Figure 3.17 Portable executable dissected.

other software, which does not match any of the packing hashes present in the PEiD hash database. Then, malware analysts have some work to do in the dynamic analysis phase of this methodology. In addition, if the malware is found to be a PE binary, then the analyst has more work to do in comparison to Linux binary (ELF executable). He/she has to know the core portions of it. Figure 3.17 shows Portable Executable dissected.

This image basically shows the core structure of PE. Only knowing DOS headers, imports, data, and section tables are important. Only these will be required immensely. After, they can perform the analysis deeply. After getting every possible thing from malware in malware analysis, it is now time for malware analysts to go to phase2/step2 of this methodology, that is, *dynamic analysis*. Now, the malware analyst will put the malware into a debugger/disassembler and run it, to find out results in the form IOCs, during runtime. Most suggested debugger/disassembler, Ghidra. It is also mentioned earlier. Figure 3.18 shows Ghidra (Windows and Linux).

With this tool, every software can be debugged. Whether the software is kernel based or user mode based, everything can be done. As the topic moved to the kernel, a specific thing should be told about it. Functions do not work the same in the kernel as in the user mode. In other words, functions in the kernel work a bit differently than the user functions do. Writing to files from kernel space has the advantage of being harder to detect by local antivirus. This is not the most secure approach to write to a

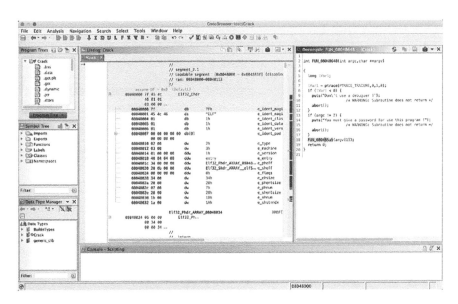

Figure 3.18 Ghidra (Windows and Linux).

file, but it can fool malware experts looking for important system calls in the user space to "CreateFile" or "WriteFile" routines. The standard Win32 functions are not as easy to use in kernel mode as they are in user mode, which makes it difficult for maldevs, although similar functions are frequently utilized in malware built in kernel mode. Because the CreateFile and WriteFile functions are not available in kernel mode, the NtCreateFile and NtWriteFile functions are utilized in their place. By debugging the kernel, a malware analyst can dynamically analyze the code that will be run as a result of the DeviceIoControl call. The analyst must first determine where the driver is located in the kernel. If the malware analyst attaches industrially recognized debuggers to the malware binary, then he or she will be notified as soon as the kernel module is loaded. It is usually more convenient to begin examining the malware function with IDA and then switch to WinDbg if more analysis is required. It is important to remember that the Windows kernel employs a UNICODE STRING structure, which is considerably different from the user-space wide character strings. Figure 3.19 shows WinDbg (Windows only).

The driver object can be difficult to locate at times, but there are tools available to assist. Analysts can identify the device object from the user-space application and then utilize the device object to locate the driver object.

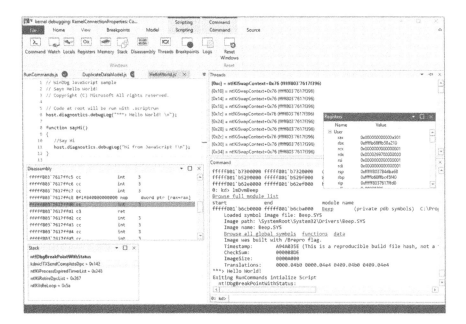

Figure 3.19 WinDbg (Windows only).

Then, using the name of the device supplied by the CreateFile system call from user-space code, users can use the "!devobj" command to acquire information about device objects. Static analysis is considerably easier to understand than dynamic analysis. Now, after completing dynamic analysis, if malware analyst thinks, more things to be searched, then he/she can hop to Hybrid analysis. Hybrid analysis analyzes the signature of any malware code. Then, it matches it with the other behavioral parameters; in this way, *malware similarities* are found. It is for the improvement/ development of the malware analysis methodology. Hybrid analysis mitigates the limitations of static or dynamic malware analysis methodology. There are relative studies and existing malware analysis methodology present for malware analysis. *Machine learning* (ML) and *deep learning* overcome the disadvantages of the malware analysis methodology faced by malware analysts. Nowadays, malware analysts are using advanced malware analysis techniques. Comodo Forensic Analysis is a forensic analysis tool that has the ability to recognize malware. It enables organizations to inspect their frameworks for malware. Thereby, it can push organizations to improve their security barriers.

3.5   Performance Analysis

All tools mentioned here in this paper are all highly sensitive and accurate, unless they are not backdated. These tools are highly reliable when topic comes on analyzing performance of the analysis. Those three steps will forever be useful, even after M.L. gets into the picture related to malware analysis and reverse engineering. Malware analysis is a crucial domain, when it comes to fighting against APTs and cybercrime, this paper can provide some help to fight against the malware in a structural way.

3.6   Future Research Direction

In future, ML will be highly used in malware detection, although there is a very less chance of using ML to perform malware analysis. Analysts can take help, but on the whole process, ML cannot be used as of the techniques present out there in the industry as of now. Although traditional approaches are classified into static, dynamic, and hybrid approaches, hybrid approaches are far more powerful when it comes to analyzing malware. It can provide a detailed description of the features in a traditional

ML workflow. It introduces new research directions such as data science, deep learning, and multimodal approaches.

3.7   Conclusion

We offered efficient malware analysis approaches in our proposed model. The purpose is to have a more in-depth understanding of the actions that an unknown malware sample can carry out. Furthermore, the tools presented here are essential for analyzing malware in kernel mode in Windows. WinDbg is triggered when a kernel driver is used for malicious purposes, and it subsequently generates an alarm. Our approach works by observing how a software responds to unusual input. Everything will be excellent if all of the actions outlined here are taken diligently and in the correct order.

References

1. Bhojani, N., *"Malware Analysis."*, pp. 1–5, 2014, doi: 10.13140/2.1.4750.6889.
2. Goyal, P. and Goyal, A., "Comparative study of two most popular packet sniffing tools-Tcpdump and Wireshark,". *2017 9th International Conference on Computational Intelligence and Communication Networks (CICN)*, pp. 77–81, 2017, doi: 10.1109/CICN.2017.8319360.
3. Patil, D.N. and Meshram, B.B., "RegForensicTool: evidence collection and analysis of Windows registry.". *IJCSDF*, 5, 2, 94–105, 2016. doi: 10.17781/P002064.
4. Cappers, B.C.M., Meessen, P.N., Etalle, S., van Wijk, J.J., "Eventpad: Rapid Malware Analysis and Reverse Engineering using Visual Analytics,". *2018 IEEE Symposium on Visualization for Cyber Security (VizSec)*, pp. 1–8, 2018, doi: 10.1109/VIZSEC.2018.8709230.
5. Mokoena, T. and Zuva, T., "Malware Analysis and Detection in Enterprise Systems,". *2017 IEEE Int. Symposium Parallel Distributed Process. Appl. 2017 IEEE Int. Conf. Ubiquitous Computing Commun. (ISPA/IUCC)*, 1, 1304–1310, 2017. doi: 10.1109/ISPA/IUCC.2017.00199.
6. Nguyen, C.Q. and Goldman, J.E., "Malware analysis reverse engineering (MARE) methodology & malware defense (MD) timeline.". *2010 Information Security Curriculum Development Conference*, pp. 8–14, 2010, doi: 10.1145/1940941.1940944.
7. Or-Meir, O. *et al.*, "Dynamic malware analysis in the modern era—A state of the art survey.". *ACM Comput. Surv. (CSUR)*, 52, 5, 1–48, 2019. doi: 10.1145/3329786.

8. Vinayakumar, R., Alazab, M., Soman, K.P., Poornachandran, P., Venkatraman, S., "Robust Intelligent Malware Detection Using Deep Learning,". *IEEE Access*, 7, 46717–46738, 2019. doi: 10.1109/ACCESS.2019.2906934.

9. Souri, A. and Hosseini, R., A state-of-the-art survey of malware detection approaches using data mining techniques. *Hum. Centric Comput. Inf. Sci.*, 8, 3, 1–22, 2018. doi: 10.1186/s13673-018-0125-x.

10. Tahir, R., "A study on malware and malware detection techniques.". *Int. J. Educ. Manage. Eng.*, 8, 2, 20–30, 2018. doi: 10.5815/ijeme.2018.02.03.

11. Chikofsky, E.J. and Cross, J.H., "Reverse engineering and design recovery: a taxonomy,". *IEEE Software*, 7, 1, 13–17, Jan. 1990. doi: 10.1109/52.43044.

4

Robust Fraud Detection Mechanism

Balajee Maram[1]*, Veerraju Gampala[2], Satish Muppidi[1] and T. Daniya[3]

*[1]Department of CSE, GMR Institute of Technology, Rajam, Srikakulam,
Andhra Pradesh, India*
*[2]Department of Computer Science and Engineering, KoneruLakshmaiah Education
Foundation, Vaddeswaram, Guntur, Andhra Pradesh, India*
*[3]Department of IT, GMR Institute of Technology, Rajam, Srikakulam,
Andhra Pradesh, India*

Abstract

In today's world, fraud is one of the leading sources of significant financial consequences, not just for businesses but also for personal customers. The extraction of
user profiles based on their past transaction data, and then determining whether
or not an incoming transaction is a fraud based on their profiles, is an essential
method of detecting fraud. The proposed blockchain method allows certified users
to store, examine, and exchange digital data in a secure atmosphere, which aids in
the development of trust, integrity, and visibility in online business relationships.
Blockchain systematically analyzes the robustness of blockchain-based reputation
systems, which focuses on the extraction and transmission to customers in a safe
and trustworthy manner. Blockchain employs cryptographic hashes, which are
produced from summarized shopping blocks that are signed and transmitted that
provides a safe and secured online shopping for an highly efficient manner without any interference of third parties.

Keywords: Blockchain, robust, cryptographic hashes, key frames, summarized
shopping blocks, online purchasing

*Corresponding author: Balajee.m@gmrit.edu.in

Sabyasachi Pramanik, Debabrata Samanta, M. Vinay and Abhijit Guha (eds.) Cyber Security and Network
Security, (71–94) © 2022 Scrivener Publishing LLC

4.1   Introduction

Blockchain technology provides a fresh approach to developing reliable distributed networks. Originally created as a network service for identifying double spending in bit coin systems, blockchain is now applied in a wide range of business applications that require scattered users to trust each other. A blockchain, at its most basic level, is a distributed record technology network that is implemented by numerous users, each of whom stores a local record of transactions. Accuracy in the ledger is accomplished through consensus methods involving all parties [1]. Business regulations are typically written as intelligent transactions that demand blockchain availability in real-world scenarios. In the healthcare field, an intelligent agreement can be built to enrol clients who are likely to purchase the company's policies, as well as to allow them to file claims and obtain reimbursements. If the requests or behaviors do not follow the terms of the agreements, then the intelligent-based distributed ledger will automatically prevent any unauthorized transactions [2].

To record, authenticate, and manage transactions, it creates and operates a highly virtualized public blockchain on the framework known as Ethereum. This technique establishes a mechanism for calculating the transaction's computing cost, frequency, and intensity. Furthermore, blockchain systems like Ethereum, which employ decentralized applications to perform complicated trades, need every deal's data or the information that processes on it to be exposed and each miners to simulate running each agreement [3]. This will result in the disclosure of user data. For instance, a user can create a shared ledger to send a particular quantity of ETH to some other user at a specific moment. If an opponent knows background knowledge about one of the involved individuals, then it may be able to reveal and link that individual to true identity. Ethereum was picked due to its widespread adoption by both consumers and companies in the industry. The insights gained from the contributions are based on a review of 30 activities that took place and were registered on the virtual Ethereum blockchain [4]. According to the existing studies in this area, the existence and integration of blockchain could have a significant impact on operations in sectors such as manufacturing, transportation, provenance, purchasing, finance, administration, supply chains, and the agro-based business. Blockchain technology also provides a fertile ground for scientific study. However, most of this field's knowledge is still largely theoretical, with minimal or no tangible findings or real-world applications [5].

They claim that a majority of researchers have highlighted their concerns over confidentiality, safety, and pricing [6].

One of the most significant considerations for blockchain is efficiency. To establish a new record of transactions on the blockchain, a highly stringent authentication procedure is required, which results in a substantial delay in validation time and wastage of computational resources. A transaction now takes around 10 min to be verified. Several more nodes are also working to process and validate transactions. Fraud prevention errors when a customer purchases goods or services using his/her credit card or an online payment site and then requests a reimbursement with the product or service intact. When a consumer disputes a transaction, the bank or online payment platform will provide a refund while the customer retains ownership of the item, because consumers frequently make statements that appear convincing and trustworthy.

These problems severely restrict the breadth of blockchain applications. Present blockchain approaches, for example, are typically unsuitable for the networks because IoT technology can have limited computing capabilities or must operate on extremely minimal power. It is one noteworthy example of blockchain application in the economic sector. Blockchain uses the robustness-based reputation systems, which focuses on the extraction and transmission to customers in a safe and trustworthy manner. Online transaction confidentiality regulations and the security protocols for online transactions are generally classified in to the ledger's reliability across entities. Due to the differences in architectural style and business operations among banking firms, as well as the use of hand-operated procedures, unification, removing, and insolvency procedures among lenders not only produce higher trading fees from clients and the depth business by interacting of lenders, but they are also subject to mistakes and inconsistency [7].

The blockchain technology is made up of six core aspects.

i. The primary characteristic of blockchain was that it does not require a centralized site to register, process, or update information; instead, data may be recorded, stored, and upgraded in a distributed network.

ii. The blockchain device's file is accessible for every site, and it is also apparent when updating the information, hence why blockchain can be accepted.

iii. The software that is freely Individuals may use blockchain technology to develop any program they need, and also, most blockchain systems are accessible to anyone. Records can be checked openly, and individuals might use block-chain methods to develop any service they desire.

iv.   Due to the general shared foundation, each site on the blockchain network may securely transmit or monitor information; the concept is to entrust a single individual with the overall network, and nobody can interfere.

v.   All recordings will be retained indefinitely and cannot be altered until over than 51% of the nodes are taken forward at the same time.

vi.   Because blockchain technology addressed the endpoint trustworthiness issue, information movement and some-times even transactions may be done anonymously.

People in the internet world frequently conduct business with people they have never met in fact. In the online, reputation systems have been widely utilized as a useful approach for individuals to assess the integrity of a potential vendor. Present reputational systems, on the other hand, are prone to rating of fraud, detecting fraudulent rates is not easier since they might act intelligently to disguise users. They investigate possible strengths and limits of blockchain-based reputational systems in the context of two attack theme: ballot stuffing and badmouthing. They discovered that blockchain systems are efficient at avoiding bad mouthing and whitewash-ing assaults and restricted in identifying electoral fraud under Turing, con-tinuous attempts, and camouflaged intrusions [8].

Fraudsters frequently use the mentioned apologies to file a partial refund:

(i)   The purchase was not authorized by the cardholder.
(ii)   The products were not delivered within a prescribed period.
(iii) The products received by customers did not suit the characterization or the products received were probably damaged.
(iv)   The consumer decided to surrender the item and yet no refund was analyzed.
(v)   The consumer cancelled the arrangement.

Researchers' recommendations for preventing chargeback fraud are presented as follows:

(i) Verify addresses and preserve as much evidence as possible to substantiate the transaction;

(ii) Implement rigorous authorization and authentication. Allow customers to check their orders after entering all of their payment card details. Customers may also make final confirmation by email or phone;

(iii) Clearly and correctly describe products or services; and

(iv) Provide it to scammers to avoid long-term company harm.

Users submit false information because of privacy concerns, as described in the context of information systems, and it suggests that buyers and sellers interact using private and public keys with the use of blockchain technology. Customers might be given tokens by vendors in exchange for providing review. Customers, on the other hand, can unlined the rating. As a result, consumers do not have to fear reprisal and may offer useful opinions [9].

Digital fraud has long been studied by academics. Users act differently to introduce untruthful facts because the constructed mechanisms in expert machines differ. As a result, many forms of data fraud have been identified and summarized. For each fraudulent situation, several supervised or unsupervised learning algorithms for detecting fraud had been developed. Past research has substantially improves the accuracy of digital fraud detection; nonetheless, only a few models are capable of detecting all fraudulent data perfectly. Furthermore, the false input is properly recognized, we might be unable to accept the truth and make the appropriate judgement. Moreover, digital fraud might be motivated by a variety of factors, including issues about individual privacy or the desire to make unjustified gains. Such activities are not entirely eliminated by existing detection systems [10].

To summarize, blockchain technology is still in its development, and more study is needed to improve its security and efficiency. Researcher encountered several potential as well as obstacles in implementing blockchain in diverse commercial areas, as evidenced mostly by these special issue that examine current ideas. As an evolving field, blockchain has been recognized as a new way to address the requirements of people, technology, and organizations. As part of modern society, blockchain development is intended to solve concerns of trustworthiness, sharing, and confidentiality. Therefore, while chargeback fraudsters pose a major danger to online merchants' economic security, efficient technical tools to counteract it are missing, particularly in the area of chargeback fraud data exchange [11]. For a transaction, integrity has become a critical element that blockchain can supply. These characteristics are based on network security, which allows users to put their trust in the system when conducting commercial transactions. The technique will significantly minimize the number of regular individuals who commit fraud in online shopping environment and the fraudulent criminal activity will be discouraged as well.

4.2   Related Work

This section defines different efforts that have been presented for fraud detection and to secure the online transactions that are comparable during online shopping. It also discusses several projects that have made use of blockchain technology.

4.2.1   Blockchain Technology for Online Business

Blockchain has the potential to play a significant role in online business areas that it might be a viable option for a pay-as-you-go auto security policy. More precisely, all data from the online users are monitored to record the data in a blockchain database, which ensures that the data is tamper-proof and traceable, resulting in a faster and better customer experience, lower operational costs, and the prevention of fraud. Furthermore, by utilizing smart contracts, blockchain may be utilized in various other fields also to keep track of protection against blockchain for business application. The details are given in Figure 4.1.

To begin, it investigates the bit coin protocol under reduced conditions, ignoring details like as evidence and service reliability. To adhere to the network, they just utilize a tree-like model and assign each node a category that indicates whether it is an authentic transaction or an offensive block. They establish a limit value to reflect attacker-controlled computer resources, which determines the likelihood that perhaps the current item becomes an aggressive block. It uses several techniques to join the current site, which symbolizes the extraction and transmitting procedure in blockchain, depending on the transaction type [12]. This algorithm obtains all state of simulation process about blockchain.

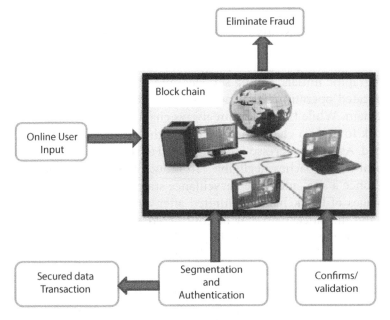

Figure 4.1 Block diagram of block-chain secured online shopping.

Algorithm 4.1

Input: R is the offensive strength.
Output: The whole status of the blockchain T
1: Create a blockchain having a truthful site as the first site P
2: Establish a distinct block based on the fire threat of the system;
3: repeat
4: predicated on the assaulting R's ability, make a new site;
5: if the new site is truthful, make a new.
6: process with the new site
7: else
8: select the site safer from the false site.
9: end if
10: if the site arises in condition T then
11: proceed with new site in T
12: end if
13: if the new site obtains secured site then
14: Start the blockchain with a truthful site
15: end if

16: until T reaches

17: process the entire sites as trustful site in blockchain T.

This model is represented by Algorithm 4.1, which excludes evidence, cryptographic initials, timing services, and other factors. Because these complicated operations have no impact on the overall structure of the blockchain. While the algorithm always enables a significantly lengthier network to undo a chain, there is always the potential of any site being reverted. As time progresses, the likelihood of such an occurrence diminish until it approaches negligible. To reduce the intricacy of our challenge, once a site enters the surveillance state, it may be turned offline. The stages of blockchain are limited after clipping off the surveillance state, and the blockchain may be considered a cyclic activity. Obtain the majority of the states, comprising truthful and attacker states, using a simulation method, and assess the likelihood of each truthful state been assaulted [13]. Consider the assaulting state to be the goal and examine the likelihood of any truthful state becoming an assaulting state. The sorts of assaults have yet to be completely defined, making detection extremely challenging. However, the attacking chance of each condition may be calculated. This technique will issue alerts to everyone if the likelihood is greater than a number provided that can also take certain defensive actions in the case of an attack.

Various mediators handle equities, securities, income certificates, store vouchers, and other items when using online transactions for trading and financial services. This not only raises trading costs but also raises the threat of certifications being purposefully falsified or forged. As a result, the system should ensure process security and confidentiality events from being interfered therewith. Clients of the online world networks should really be able to view transaction information during any time and from any place. The term "reliability" applies to both network and process affordability. Sometimes, in the event of a network assault, the software should function effectively at the design stage. The information of deals may be retrieved by authenticated persons without even being inaccessible, inaccurate, or altered at the process level. One of the most difficult aspects of exchanging virtual cash in a distributed platform is preventing and double or paying a crypto currency twice. In a centralized system, a trustworthy centralized payment gateway verifies whether or not a virtual currency has indeed been quintuple. To avoid dual, we require effective security protocols and remedies for interactions executed in a decentralized and distributed context [14]. For most economic online purchases, consumers prefer to get the least amount of data about their activities and accounts disclosed in an internet trading platform. The preceding is the bare minimum of information:

(i)   Each and every unauthorized consumer can obtain visitors' transaction records;

(ii)   The network manager or internet person involved cannot expose any customer's data to someone without his or her authorization; and

(iii)   Only those users' data should be permanently stored repeatedly and securely, even in the case of abnormal mistakes or cybercriminal.

In many semi-circumstances, such secrecy is beneficial. The difficulties of exchanging user information efficiently and securely between different lenders may lead to a significant expense of recurrent authentication process. It also exposes consumers' identities to the danger of exposure by some providers [15]. In certain circumstances, either both partners to the agreement may be hesitant to reveal their true identities to another. Individuals should demand that actions connected to personally cannot be correlated, which is separate from personal confidentiality (not exposing one's true identity). Because now all of a recipient's interactions are connected, it is simple to extrapolate additional data regarding the account balance and the kind and regularity of transactions. Interested or hostile individuals can predict (reasonably deduce) the actual user credentials with strong certainty using factual analysis about interactions and profiles combined with some existing understanding about the individual.

4.2.2   Validation and Authentication

A cryptographic method is used to validate the authenticity of a bit of data in an authenticator. It is also a technique for ensuring that data has not been interfered improperly. A digitally signed method is composed of three main parts. The first part is the symmetric key computation, which generates key pair: the first is used includes and considered confidential and is termed "the encryption keys"; another is released publicly and is utilized to authenticate whether reply has the confirmation agreed to sign with the appropriate credentials and is named the public key. The authentication algorithm is the next integral part. It creates a certificate on the incoming sequence that is backed up by the encryption key provided. The validation algorithm is the other integral part. It accepts three parameters: validity, a document, and a session key, and it verifies the confirmation of the text using the shared key before returning a numerical expression. Both qualities should be included in into something and safe authentication scheme [16]. The basic requirement is that genuine signs be verified. Identities are inherently secure, which is the next criterion. It implies that an opponent who knows your key pair will almost certainly be unable to fake identities on certain communications.

The hash pointer is one of the most important components for constructing the blockchain utilizing hash tethered memory. A hash pointer is a cryptographic hash of content that points to the database's storage site. As a result, a hash pointer can be used to see if the content has been altered therewith. Hash pointers are used to relate partitions collectively in such a distributed ledger. Blockchain level of safety shows the location in which the content of the preceding block is kept, with the hash pointer directing to the preceding block. The hash value is one of the most important components for constructing the blockchain utilizing hash tethered memory. A hash value is a cryptographic hash of content that points to the database's storage site. As a result, a hash value can be used to see if the content has been altered therewith. Hash value is used to relate partitions collectively in such a distributed ledger. Blockchain level of safety shows the location in which the content of the preceding block is kept, with the hash value directing to the preceding block. Furthermore, customers may publically verify the hash of the saved information to determine that it has never been altered with lastly; the opponent's alteration will be exposed, because storing this single core hash reference of the blockchain network essentially makes the overall network tamper-resistant. Customers can go assigned to a particular node in the list and validate it from the origin.

The benefit of using an unique identifier is that it proficiently validates the truthfulness of a comment by utilizing public key encryption, in which the text author authorizes it with her encryption key prior to actually submitting it out, and the beneficiary can now use the recipient's key pair to verify the document's authenticity. Across most software cases, the pair of keys may be obtained from a trustworthy third person. A cryptographically infrastructure is used to maintain shared key by constructing a signed contract among individuals' identifiers (such as identity, email, and pin) and their cryptographic [17]. An authentication and authorization registers and keys are used to achieve this linkage. On the basis of the binding's security level, the verification procedure is effectively transformed into proposer proof of identity. As a result, in these circumstances, the key pair might be considered identification. Without a centralized system to establish a client in a network, blockchain embraces decentralized authentication mechanism. Participants made their own key pairings. Customers have complete control about how many shared key they create, refers to these identifiers (cryptographically hash) as identities. These identities are really real identities created by individuals since there is no centralized administration of secret key.

4.2.3   Types of Online Shopping Fraud

On the internet, fraudsters use a variety of methods to commit fraud; a research was performed on how information is stolen in online shopping. The following are some of the many methods used to steal the information.

4.2.3.1   Software Fraudulent of Online Shopping

Credit card numbers and expiration dates are obtained using software. Because it employs the statistical method that credit card businesses or issuers use to produce credit card numbers for their credit card customers or users, some of these developed applications are capable of creating legitimate credit card details like credit card firms or issuers. Credit card information is hacked and stored in a database, which is then displayed to online credit thieves via software. In certain situations, black-hat hackers utilize this approach to sell their stolen credit card details to other online credit card thieves with limited computer knowledge [18].

Black hat hackers with highly qualified software or computer knowledge infect a computer system by installing and instantaneously attempting to run sniffers or keylogging software programs that log all virtual keyboard input information and activities on a file with the personal gain intention of retrieving personal credit card details data, etc. Spam mail is employed by fraudsters to infect customers' computers by inviting them to download for free apps or software. When those emails are read and downloaded, key logger sniffers are immediately downloaded, placed, and run on the customers' computers. Whereas the sniffer is running on the user's browser, it records all of the user's typing inputs across a network [19]. As a result, with this viral programme, any user might unwittingly reveal their personal genuine information. This application is often distributed or supplied to other fraudsters who lacked computer expertise or abilities.

The introduction of the EMV standard (originally Euro pay, MasterCard, and Visa) significantly enhanced the degree of security for concrete block shops. The EMV chip in cards, on the other hand, does not provide safety for online transactions, making it easier for thieves to use stolen cards.

When consumers argue their dealings with a company, they might emerge fraudsters and receive both the funds and the products.

Technically swiped credit card details refer to online purchases and sales made with a payment method that has been stolen. Cyber payment fraudsters with no technical computing skills purchase hacked financial information on these platforms to use for fraudulent online currency for various products and services on the internet.

A black-hat hacker creates software, which is then installed and used to monitor online activity on the user's browser. They copy the digital or financial websites that the customer usually visits and direct the user to use it with the intent of recovering private or confidential data by following and monitoring the user's website actions on the online. The second example is phoney merchant sites, which are websites that supply consumers with low-cost items in exchange for credit card transactions. When personal information such as credit card is used to pay a bill on a fraudulent website, the customer's credit card is stolen [20].

4.2.4   Segmentation/Authentication

Client segmentation is the technique of dividing consumers into groups based on common behaviors or other characteristics. The groupings should be homogenous within itself and diverse in relation to one another. The main goal of this approach is to find a high-value client base or customers with the greatest potential for development or profit [21].

Effective segmentation findings are used to create tailored marketing campaigns as well as effective business strategy and tactics. One of the most important decisions a company must make is whether or not to segment its consumers and how to go about doing so. This would be determined by the business' ideology as well as the products or services it provides. The sort of segmentation criteria used will have a significant impact on how the company works and proposes its strategy.

Zero segments: This refers to how the firm treats all of its clients in the same way. In other sense, there is really no distinct strategic plan, and a singular intensive distribution effort is used to reach out to the whole target consumers. Single segment: This refers to a firm's focus on a specific subgroup or segment of clients within a narrowly focused customer base. Second or even more segments: This indicates that the firm is focusing on multiple groups within its own client base, with separate marketing techniques developed for them [22].

Hundreds and thousands of segments: This implies that the firm treats each consumer as an individual and offers a new deal for them. Following the identification of the firm's client base and the number of segments on which it intends to target, the business must choose the criteria on which it will segment its users and this information are stored in the blockchain database. Factors to consider when segmenting an online business to consumer marketing firm include the following: age, gender, education, nationality, economy, profession, and passion.

Systems have become important. Regularity and recurrence financial includes the length of time since the last purchase, the regularity with which the client trades, and the overall amount worth of the contract. A social factor includes the purchase history, brand consciousness, and life experiences. Factors to consider when segmenting an online business to consumer marketing firm include opinions, attitude, lifestyle, self-interests, inspiration, and priorities, which are all psychographic: location, postcode, environmental circumstances, metropolitan area distinction, and economic growth [23].

The procedures below can be used to discover segments in a client base on a wide scale that has to be stored in the blockchain database. Examine the current client base: analyzing regional dispersion, familiar with online shopping, and search engine site statistics, among other things.

Establish a thorough grasp of every client: understanding and predicting consumer behavior by linking each client to a collection of choices: the goods, activities, and information they are involved in. When commencing customer segmentation, a company must have a planned approach and goal in mind. The techniques outlined below can be used to identify client segments on a large scale [24].

Analyze your present clientele: Among many other factors, analyzing geographical dispersion, familiarity with internet purchasing, and web search site analytics. Obtain a deep understanding of each client: knowing and forecasting market trends by associating each customer with a set of options, such as the items, services, and data they purchase.

4.2.4.1   Secure Transaction Though Segmentation Algorithm

In blockchain, processors are used to build an elevated hash algorithm, and the key fragment calculation information hash is retrieved from memory. Following the calculation of the hash value, the outcome is enclosed and sent to the storage device to finish the blockchain's storage [25].

The block holds all transaction details, such as transaction generation time, transaction record reference number, transaction hash value, blockchain's expenditure location and quantity of expenses, and other sorts of transactions. During the transaction, a Merkle value will be created.

The transaction's hash node value ensures that all destinations can indeed be frequently exchanged and falsified. To increase data integrity even further, a proactive adjustable hash has been introduced to the blockchain, which is made up of several types of hash algorithms that may be employed individually or in sequence [26].

The hash algorithm evaluation step will be introduced even before deal is created, and then, the suitable hash function will be picked from the hash list. The unit node competes to discover the hash value using the chosen hash algorithm. The block will be pushed to some other node in the blockchain for confirmation after the hash value has been discovered.

During the interaction, the detector material on the location collects data. The detector transmits digital to the unit networks and requests that it be saved by the process. The blockchain network will upgrade the transaction if individual nodes effectively finish transaction processing. The practice area layer data is then returned to the management plane by the blockchain network [21]. After that, block extraction will begin. The blockchain network gets the incident node when block mining is completed and distributes the block and validate request to certain other sites. For validation, other sites employing the hash method validated the data block [27].

At regular intervals, the concept picks a new cryptographic hash and the two partners probably and modify for a different hash algorithm to make things safer. Many encryption methods use the hash function as a key component. The use of hash functions for various operations is an essential aspect of blockchain technology. Hashing is a way of computing a substantially distinct output for practically any amount of input by implementing a hash function to it. It enables users to receive user input and hash data separately and get identical outputs, demonstrating that the information has not modified. As a result, for blockchain and its implementations that include confidential trades and private information, secrecy and anonymity represent a significant problem, and it is devoted to a discussion of several key areas of research which may aid in improving online security and transactional secrecy on blockchain.

Take SHA256 as an example of how a hash algorithm can be optimized and implemented on proactive changeable computers. The algorithm's flow resolves the algorithm's computing performance. The following is the exact implementation formula:

$$P = \frac{b \times g_{max} \times M}{c} \tag{4.1}$$

P refers for throughput, b for block size, g for maximal clock rate, M for network series, and c for computation time in Equation (4.1). Speed and flow are related to the number of network series. We may employ prediction and CSA methods to decrease critical route delays, as well as full-pipeline SHA1 and SHA256 algorithms, to increase the algorithm's performance.

The following enhancement of SHA256 can be expanded to SHA1. The hash method SHA256 generates a 256-bit hash code for communications having duration of not over than 264 bits, which is referred to as a plaintext block. The authentication is a 32-byte range that may be expressed as a 64-character alphanumeric text.

The SHA256 algorithm divides communication flow into five phases:

Add great many 0 bits to the input data until 448 bits. Then, add 64-bit length to the input data until 512 bits.

(i)   Group the 512-bit spliced data into 16 groups: M0–M15.

(ii) Set the starting values of a, b, c, d, e, f, g, and h to h0–h7 and the vectors k0–k63 and h0–h7.

(iii) Repeat from 0 to 63 and afterwards modify the parameter t.

(iv) Let $h0 = h0 + a63$, $h1 = h1 + b63$, $h2 = h2 + c63$, $h3 = h3 + d63$, $h4 = h4 + e63$ (4.2)

(v) $h5 = h5 + f63$, $h6 = h6 + g63$, $h7 = h7 + h63$. output h0–h7.   (4.3)

From the processing of the SHA256 algorithm, it can be seen that the key is to update the values of "a" and "e", which requires multiple addition operations and 64 cycles of iteration. Therefore, the optimization of these two operands will play an important role in reducing the time consumption of the algorithm.

4.2.4.2 Critical Path Segmentation Optimization

The difficulty to state the link among different facts or two observable entities of the system with strong certainty is referred to as fragments. Confidentiality refers to the condition of being unidentifiable and unidentified. Even though the blockchain guarantees online anonymity by providing pseudo-identity as reinforcement for a recipient's privacy, it lacks to provide individuals with the security of event fragments [28]. Inherently, a recipient's entire anonymous can only be maintained by providing both online anonymity and untraceability if the user constantly interacts with the platform using pseudo-identity. Every data is confirmed on the record with the identities of the transmitter and recipient and, therefore, accessible simply by those who use the related credentials of the transmitter and recipient; this does not ensure full confidentiality for blockchain networks. By doing a basic scientific calculations of the locations used in transactions, anybody may link a customer's purchase to subsequent financial transactions of users accounts. Analyzing information about the user, for example, can immediately show the amount and total sum of money deposited into that person's account. Instead, several identities can be linked to submit trades from a particular network. More significantly, if a recipient's address is linked to real-world identity, then it may lose anonymity and hence confidentiality for all processes linked with that account. Furthermore, due to its open aspect of the blockchain network, anybody can seek to execute a de-anonymization attempt invisibly and without the intended users ever recognizing that is being targeted or that her actual identities have now been exposed. Therefore, the blockchain implementation achieves pseudonymity but not unlink ability and thus not full anonymity defined by pseudonymity with unlink ability and argues that the blockchain system should be enhanced by other cryptographic techniques [29].

The characteristic that blockchain can guarantee privacy for all information or particular private information placed on it is referred to as information security. Even though the blockchain was created as a compared to other major record for the virtual currency network, its potential applications are far wider. Blockchain may be used to manage smart contracts, intellectual works, and the digitalization of corporate and organizational records, for instance. The secrecy of log entries, including as payment contents and locations, is, unsurprisingly, a desired safety precaution shared by all blockchain technologies. Currently, systems do not implement the security feature. Even if the pseudonym is being used as the transmission and reception of a payment rather than the true person, the transactional text and locations are available to the public. This is essential for fostering requirements exchange rather than the full blockchain being publically available [30].

The time-consuming use of SHA256 activity is mainly in the iteration phase of Step 4, and the most time-consuming part is the calculation of "a" and "e" values. Therefore, using a sensitive method of separation and integration with the same features of resource utilization can reduce the use of time. ht, kt, and wt in a critical way do not require additional sensible functions or do not depend on other current cycle operators. Therefore, the critical path of the algorithm is divided into the following formulas:

$$s_t = h_t + k_t + w_t, \tag{4.4}$$

$$a_{t+1} = \Sigma(e) + ch(e_t, f_t, g_t) + s_t + \Sigma a + maj(a_t, b_t, c_t) \tag{4.5}$$

$$e_{t+1} = \Sigma e + ch(e_t, f_t, g_t) + s_t + d_t \tag{4.6}$$

As a result, A and E variables will be revised and reduced from 6tADD and 5t ADD to 4t ADD and 3t ADD, respectively, in which t ADD represents the moment used by addition.

The fundamental functionality of the method is separated into three categories based on the features of the SHA256 method and the efficiency of crucial activities: W unit, divided S subsystem, and upgrade module a–h. By maximizing usage of resources, partitioning technique minimizes process time. As a result, each component will require 64 processing units, totalling 192 processing units. The input is also sent into w0 at same instant. The information is analyzed in sequence by the third network servers, etc. The production of the first data is not concluded through till 66th clock pulse, when all 192 entities are functioning [31]. When a significant quantity of data needs to be calculated, one kind of information is calculated in a clock period, reducing the time spent in the method by 64 steps. As a result, the method's overall performance and cost usage have substantially improved.

4.2.5 Role of Blockchain Technology for Supply Chain and Logistics

This paper examines whether this lack is because of an extra expense of innovation and distinguishes other potential causes. Likewise, the paper presents blockchain technology, clarifies the starting points of Bitcoin and blockchain's center design and framework, and investigates shrewd agreements. Far reaching and orderly writing examination recognizes the ideas of the utilization of blockchain technology in readiness corresponding to monetary advantages. Also, an assortment was made regarding the matter of applicable text. Another finding is that blockchain technology is vital for high worth resources. Simultaneously, the interest for straightforwardness and consistency of the information should be undeniably more significant than the security of delicate information. Notwithstanding the substantial use instances of blockchains, a model administration framework inside luxury supply chain will be presented, which shows the advantages of blockchain technology at each phase of each interaction [32].

This work intends to recognize the monetary advantages of utilizing BCT in coordinations through orderly survey of writing. Notwithstanding the two instances of substantial use, a model remediation measure has been presented, which shows the advantages of BCT at each progression of each interaction. In such manner, another comprehension of the extra worth of BCT can be seen. Organizations that do not have ability in BCT can utilize this paper to help them in their decision of innovation. Likewise, this paper gives authoritative data on recognizing ebb and flow employments of innovation, assessing their advantages, and along these lines featuring potential exploration openings. A publication is found to feature openings and can rouse organizations. The principle benefits of BC are that, not normal for customary appropriated data, no assertion or halfway record space is required, on the grounds that network members control one another. Thusly, BC makes agreement on the present status of the organization without requiring individual SC accomplices to trust one another. It likewise guarantees the honesty and consistency of the data put away in it. BCT is viewed as another innovation with numerous shortcomings and boundaries to reception. A key component is the low-level construction, which, related to the straightforward presentation, sets new well-being norms. Contrasted with the normal focal information, BCT is very perplexing, and a significant degree of safety is managed by high equipment and energy costs [33].

As a feature of business and the executives contemplates, research exercises have zeroed in on blockchain innovation (BCT) in resource the board and acquisition (LSCM) beginning in 2016, which contains information from 613 articles from contextual analyses research. It is in this way an effectively open passage point for scholastics and professionals regarding the matter of BCT at LSCM. Acknowledge compose network investigation and compound examination. In view of compound examination, this article isolates existing writing into five distinctive exploration gatherings, including speculation, thinking and assessing blockchain applications, and building BCT in supply chains.

Economic situations are changing and requesting, prompting a difficult cutthroat climate. Adjusting to this unique climate, synthetic acquirement has depended vigorously on collaboration, combination, adaptability, and validity among partners. To further develop the stream control of acquisition, extraordinary present day applications should be made. Blockchain innovation has secured itself as an important piece of the present serious climate. Organizations need to put resources into blockchain innovation to react rapidly to changing economic situations and requests in the present powerful business climate. In such manner, this explores the impact of the utilization of blockchain innovation on obtainment perceivability, acquisition adaptability, and dependence on providers. Second, factor examination and review investigation were performed with information got from 84 organizations.

Because of the examination, not set in stone that the utilization of blockchain innovation expands straightforwardness, adaptability, and dependence on supply chains. In view of these outcomes, it is recommended that organizations ought to put resources into blockchain innovation to make their deals more straightforward, adaptable and secure. Also, the blockchain assumes a significant part in building the trust of acquisition partners. At long last, the investigation incorporates further thought of the constructive outcomes and qualities of the blockchain in joint effort and reconciliation. Blockchain innovation is presumably perhaps the most broadly utilized ideas today. Since digitalization has gotten typical (even important), we have started to digitalize our resources. We consider this digitalization the change of realities into nothing and (information) that can be put away, sent, and investigated in a PC climate. We have started to investigate approaches to secure all advanced resources that we can utilize carefully (changed over to information) with this innovation.

Accordingly, blockchain innovation was first evolved to guarantee the security of advanced resources (e.g., digital currency). For this situation, the impact of the utilization of blockchain innovation on the adaptability of inventory network, straightforwardness, and trust has been examined. Blockchain innovation accompanies doubt since it is extremely new and obscure to organizations. Subsequently, organizations might see their interest in these advances as high danger. In this investigation, we have attempted to recognize a portion of the advantages that the innovation being referred to can offer organizations. For this reason, we have chosen to be straightforward, adaptable, and dependable, which are key components of supply chains, for example, research variety. Because of our examination, we have tracked down that the utilization of blockchain innovation altogether influences perceivability, adaptability, and dependence on supply chains.

Suitable writing underscores that organizations can build consumer loyalty and, thus, client dependability, by giving more conveyance measures. What is more, a reasonable perspective on the offer of merchandise can work fair and square of co-activity in the acquirement cycle by expanding trust between organizations. Also, adaptability in obtainment can be a significant instrument for organizations to accomplish supportable upper hand. As per research discoveries, blockchain is a significant and important innovation as far as three advancing stages. We accept this exploration will assist organizations with decreasing their questions about blockchain innovation. In the writing survey, led toward the start of this, we did not discover blockchain innovation testing with regards to the elements referenced previously. In such manner, we accept that the exploration model set up in our examination is the first, and we trust that this will be a significant commitment to existing writing. We likewise accept that the returns of this financing will help all assembling organizations. We can say the accompanying regarding the limits and further exploration: as far as possible is the example size a lot. In this manner, we were unable to build the example size further. At the point when these advancements become more broad later on, studies ought to be directed with bigger examples.

The blockchain technology can be applied to the transportation and logistics industry to get efficiency. Nowadays, manufacturing companies are suffering a lot in finding the vehicles to transport their goods even trucks are available in the world. Figure 4.2 shows the traditional supply chain mechanism.

The issues which were in traditional supply chain sector will be resolved with blockchain technology, because the blockchain technology can validate the data and acts like tamper proof in logistics industry with the mechanism, as shown in Figure 4.3.

The above diagram explains the need of blockchain technology functionality in supply chain which shares all the entities in the value chain. Reasons for blockchain implementation in the supply chain and logistics:

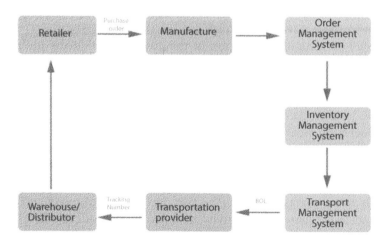

Figure 4.2 Traditional supply chain mechanism.

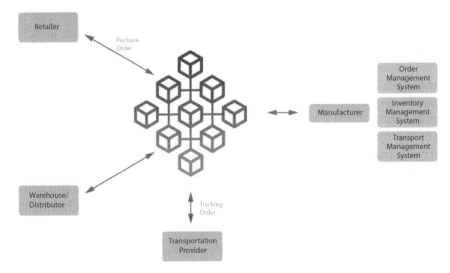

Figure 4.3 Supply chain using blockchain technology.

- Growth in transparency because it helps to reduce the redundancy in supply chain industry
- It helps to trace the updated information in the life cycle of supply chain.
- The payments are error-free and track all the transactions in central level. Here, smart contracts reduces the errors and delay time.
- It allows the enterprises to find out the fraud and who is the culprits.
- It enhances the delivery process and greater flexibility for tracking of goods.
- It improves the security since third party not able to modify the information that is stored in the chain.
- Once smart contracts are signed, then the ledger is used to track the goods and get the details who have those goods currently.

4.3 Conclusion

One of the most enticing frameworks of blockchain is its protection mechanism, which is focused on a global record and decentralized agreement. This may not indicate that blockchain technology is highly resistant to all types of thuggery and phishing; rather, it reviews the types of fraudulent and destructive actions that blockchain technology can inhibit, as well as the attacks to which blockchain technology has remained vulnerable, and proposes preventative measures for destructive actions. Consumers must own and manage the data they create in a reality where numerous parties gain ever-increasing capabilities to acquire and analyze personal information. With a concrete demonstration, our solution demonstrates whether blockchain technology could provide business users with the best privacy and information rights. The data can be securely saved from the fraudulent and made reliable in the present by using the algorithms in the proposed system to the blockchain. This allows the online shopping users to confirm the correctness of data in retrospect, without having to share it with anybody on a regular basis or putting their faith in a third-party provider.

References

1. Abdallah, A., Maarof, M.A., Zainal, A., Fraud detection system: A survey. *J. Netw. Comput. Appl.*, *68*, 90–113, 2016.
2. Al Khalil, F., Butler, T., O'Brien, L., Ceci, M., Trust in smart contracts is a process, as well, in: *International Conference on Financial Cryptography and Data Security*, Springer, Cham, pp. 510–519, 2017.
3. Atzori, M., Block-chain-based architectures for the internet of things: a survey, 2016.
4. Atzori, M., Block-chain-based architectures for the internet of things: A survey. SSRN, 2017, Available: https://ssrn.com/abstract=2846810, 2017.
5. Bandaranayake, B., Fraud and Corruption Control at Education System Level: A Case Study of the Victorian Department of Education and Early Childhood Development in Australia. *J. Cases Educ. Leadersh.*, *17*, 4, 34–53, 2014.
6. Berneis, M., Bartsch, D., Winkler, H., Applications of Blockchain Technology in Logistics and Supply Chain Management—Insights from a Systematic Literature Review. *Logistics*, *5*, 43, 2021, https://doi.org/10.3390/logistics5030043.
7. Müßigmann, B., von der Gracht, H., Hartmann, E., Blockchain Technology in Logistics and Supply Chain Management—A Bibliometric Literature Review From 2016 to January 2020. *IEEE Trans. Eng. Manage.*, *67*, 4, 988–1007, Nov. 2020, doi: 10.1109/TEM.2020.2980733.
8. Cai, Y. and Zhu, D., Fraud detections for online businesses: a perspective from block-chain technology. *Financial Innov.*, *2*, 1, 1–10, 2016.

9. Casado-Vara, R., Prieto, J., Corchado, J.M., How block-chain could improve fraud detection in power distribution grid, in: *The 13th International Conference on Soft Computing Models in Industrial and Environmental Applications*, pp. 67–76, Springer, Cham, 2018.

10. Chanson, M., Bogner, A., Wortmann, F., Fleisch, E., Block-chain as a privacy enabler: An odometer fraud prevention system, in: *Proceedings of the 2017 ACM International Joint Conference on Pervasive and Ubiquitous Computing and Proceedings of the 2017 ACM International Symposium on Wearable Computers*, pp. 13–16, 2017.

11. Chukwu, P.O., *Fraud in The Nigerian Banking Systems, Problems and Prospects: A Case Study Of First Bank Of Nigeria Plc, and Oceanic Bank Plc, Abakaliki Branch Offices*, University of Nigeria, Nsukka, Institutional Repository, 2011.

12. Christidis, K. and Devetsikiotis, M., Block-chains and smart contracts for the internet of things. *IEEE Access*, 4, 2292–2303, 2016.

13. Dhiran, A., Kumar, D., Arora, A., Video Fraud Detection using Block-chain, in: *2020 Second International Conference on Inventive Research in Computing Applications (ICIRCA)*, RVS College of Engineering and Technology Coimbatore, International Conference, Coimbatore, pp. 102–107, IEEE, 2020.

14. Dolgui, A., Ivanov, D., Potryasaev, S., Sokolov, B., Ivanova, M., Werner, F., Block-chain-oriented dynamic modelling of smart contract design and execution in the supply chain. *Int. J. Prod. Res.*, 58, 7, 2184–2199, 2020.

15. Efanov, D. and Roschin, P., The all-pervasiveness of the block-chain technology. *Proc. Comput. Sci.*, *123*, 116–121, 2018.

16. Francisco, K. and Swanson, D., The supply chain has no clothes: Technology adoption of block-chain for supply chain transparency. *Logistics*, *2*, 1, 2, 2018.

17. Gates, T. and Jacob, K., Payments fraud: perception versus reality—a conference summary. *Econ. Perspect.*, *33*, 1, 7–15, 2009.

18. Hastig, G.M. and Sodhi, M.S., Block-chain for Supply Chain Traceability: Business Requirements and Critical Success Factors. *Prod. Oper. Manage.*, 29, 4, 935–954, 2019, doi: 10.1111/poms.13147.

19. https://www.exlservice.com/blockchain-in-transport-and-logistics

20. Ilker, K.A.R.A. and Aydos, M., Cyber Fraud: Detection and Analysis of the Crypto-Ransomware, in: *2020 11th IEEE Annual Ubiquitous Computing, Electronics & Mobile Communication Conference (UEMCON)*, pp. 0764–0769, IEEE, 2020.

21. Irissappane, A.A., Jiang, S., Zhang, J., Towards a comprehensive testbed to evaluate the robustness of reputation systems against unfair rating attack, in: *UMAP Workshops*, vol. 12, 2012.

22. Liu, D. and Lee, J.H., CFLedger: Preventing chargeback fraud with block-chain. *ICT Express*, 2021.

23. Meidute-Kavaliauskiene, I., Yıldız, B., Çiğdem, Ş., Činčikaitė, R., An Integrated Impact of Blockchain on Supply Chain Applications. *Logistics*, 5, 33, 2021, https://doi.org/10.3390/logistics5020033.

24. Ostapowicz, M. and Żbikowski, K., Detecting fraudulent accounts on block-chain: a supervised approach, in: *International Conference on Web Information Systems Engineering*, Springer, Cham, pp. 18–31, 2020.

25. Schaub, A., Bazin, R., Hasan, O., Brunie, L., A trustless privacy-preserving reputation system, in: *IFIP International Conference on ICT Systems Security and Privacy Protection*, May, pp. 398–411, Springer, Cham, 2016.

26. Soska, K. and Christin, N., Measuring the longitudinal evolution of the online anonymous marketplace ecosystem, in: *24th {USENIX} security symposium ({USENIX} security 15)*, pp. 33–48, 2015.

27. Tan, B.S. and Low, K.Y., Block-chain as the database engine in the accounting system. *Aust. Account. Rev.*, 29, 2, 312–318, 2019.

28. Tapscott, D. and Tapscott, A., The impact of the block-chain goes beyond financial services. *Harv. Bus. Rev.*, 10, 7, 1–5, 2016. https://hbr.org/2016/05/the-impact-of-the-blockchain-goes-beyond-financial-services

29. Vandervort, D., Challenges and opportunities associated with a bitcoin-based transaction rating system, in: *International Conference on Financial Cryptography and Data Security*, pp. 33–42, Springer, Berlin, Heidelberg, 2014.

30. Vukolić, M., Rethinking permissioned block-chains, in: *Proceedings of the ACM Workshop on Block-chain, Cryptocurrencies and Contracts*, pp. 3–7, 2017.

31. Wang, Y. and Kogan, A., Designing privacy-preserving block-chain based accounting information systems. *Available at SSRN 2978281*, 2017.

32. Wei, W., Li, J., Cao, L., Ou, Y., Chen, J., Effective detection of sophisticated online banking fraud on extremely imbalanced data. *World Wide Web*, 16, 4, 449–475, 2013.

33. Wood, G., Ethereum: A secure decentralised generalised transaction ledger. *Ethereum project yellow paper*, vol. 151(2014), pp. 1–32, 2014.

5

Blockchain-Based Identity Management Systems

Ramani Selvanambi[1], Bhavya Taneja[1], Priyal Agrawal[1], Henil Jayesh Thakor[1] and Marimuthu Karuppiah[2*]

[1]School of Computer Science and Engineering, Vellore Institute of Technology, Vellore, India
[2]Department of Computer Science and Engineering, SRM Institute of Science and Technology, Delhi-NCR Campus, Ghaziabad, India

Abstract

The demand for blockchain-based identity management systems (IDMSs) is especially evident in the internet age; we have been dealing with identity management issues since the internet's inception. Privacy, security, and usability have all been cited as major concerns. User identities are organized using IDMSs, which also manage authentication, authorization, and data interchange over the internet. Conventional IDMSs are also plagued by a lack of interoperability, single points of vulnerability, and privacy concerns, such as allowing bulk collection of data and device monitoring. Blockchain technology has the prospect to palliate these issues by allowing users to monitor the ownership of their own identifiers and authentication credentials, empowering novel information proprietorship and administration frameworks with built-in control and consensus mechanisms. Thus, blockchain-based IDMSs, which have the ability to profit organizations and clients both, have started increasing rapidly. We will sort these frameworks into a scientific categorization dependent on contrasts in blockchain structures, administration models, and other notable highlights. Context is accommodated by scientific categorization by the representation of relevant concepts, emerging principles, and usage cases, while illustrating essential protection and privacy issues.

Keywords: Identity management system, blockchain, blockchain-based identity management, self-sovereign, authentication, authorization, data sharing

*Corresponding author: marimuthume@gmail.com

Sabyasachi Pramanik, Debabrata Samanta, M. Vinay and Abhijit Guha (eds.) Cyber Security and Network Security, (95–128) © 2022 Scrivener Publishing LLC

5.1 Introduction

Identity has a problem. If an individual's identity is dependent on paper, such as identity card or driving license kept somewhere, then it is vulnerable to theft, loss, and fraud. By enabling greater compatibility among departments and various other agencies, a digital identity eliminates bureaucracy and speeds up processes within organizations. However, if the digital identity is being kept on a centralized remote server, then it can be a hacking target. Millions of personal records, such as government photo id proof and bank account details, have been compromised, stolen, or leaked from businesses since 2017. The majority of today's identity management systems (IDMSs) are ineffective and obsolete. Digitization makes it possible for identities to be accessed and verified anywhere. However, being digital is insufficient. Private and safe identities are also needed. To summarize, existing internet IDMSs has evolved from the Leibniz's law–based identity management model used in separated environments to distributed, combined, and customer-focused IDMSs such as OpenID, which have been embraced by numerous online professional organizations such as Facebook and Google. In most federated domains, the IDMS of several large online service providers serves as the universal identity provider [18]. The interconnected identity solution, in reality, establishes a specific relationship between online service providers. As a result, we could only use one account to log in to other online services, like Facebook or Google. Users can manage their identity more easily thanks to the interconnected user-centric IDMS with partnerships. However, customers must have full confidence on these service providers, who sit in the middle and can see all of the interactions between each customer and the online applications used by them.

As a result, in this digital era of internet, removing unneeded third person organizations and providing a reliable identity provider in trustless networks is crucial. Thanks to its potential to replace intermediaries in transactions, blockchain technology, which was born out of Bitcoin, has gained a lot of attention over the last decade. The blockchain wave of thinking, which began with Ethereum in 2014, has spread to a wide range of fields, including monetary and financial services, governance, copyright, and even the Internet of Things (IoT). As cyber security threats become more prevalent in IoT, blockchain technology is gaining traction as a viable option for developing IoT security solutions in decentralized, trustless environments. Users and devices would be able to monitor their own identities without relying on third party organizations because of blockchains.

Traditional identity networks are fractured, vulnerable, and exclusive in today's world. By offering a centralized, interoperable, and tamper-proof platform, blockchain enables more stable management and storage of digital identities, with key benefits for businesses, consumers, and other application management systems [20]. While there are fairly flawed mechanisms for creating personal identification in the real world, such as identity documents, passports, and even birth certificates, there is no comparable mechanism for securing online authentication of personal identities or the identities of virtual entities. Hence, while governments could give types of actual recognizable proof, on the web, digital entities do not perceive public limits and computerized personality validation shows up from the start to appear to be a recalcitrant issue without a regulating worldwide entity. Blockchain innovation may offer an approach to tackle this issue by conveying a safe arrangement without the requirement for a trusted, local authority. It tends to be utilized for making an identity on the blockchain, simplifying it to oversee for people, enabling them with more noteworthy authority about that has access to their personal data and how they use it. By consolidating the distributed blockchain standard with identity authentication, a digital identity is generated that will play the role of computerized watermark that can be relegated to each online exchange [20].

This arrangement can also assist the company in checking the identities of each exchange continuously, thus, wiping out the pace of misrepresentation and misuse. Customers will actually want to sign in and confirm instalments without entering any of the customary username and personal information.

Blockchain technology offers the following benefits:

- **Decentralized Public Key Infrastructure**

  Decentralized public key infrastructure (DPKI) is the center of decentralized identity. Blockchain strengthens DPKI by creating a safe and trusted platform for disseminating the identity holders' hilter kilter search and encryption keys. The DPKI allows everyone to build or protect cryptographic keys on the blockchain in a safer, sequentially specified manner. These keys are used to allow others to verify computerized marks or scramble data for a specific character holder. Before DPKI, everyone had to buy or acquire advanced authentications from customary endorsement specialists (CA). There is no longer a need for a single CA as a result of blockchain innovation. As a result, DPKI can be a powerful tool in some situations, especially when it comes to obvious qualifications (VC). Many people nowadays use the expression "evident qualifications" (VCs) to refer to the computerized certifications that go along with cryptographic verifications.

- **Decentralized Storage**
Characters stored in blockchains are, by definition, more stable than those stored on incorporated staff. It is possible to decentralize current consolidated information storing systems while preserving faith and data respectability by combining the cryptographically protected Ethereum blockchain with distributed information storing systems like OrvitDB or InterPlanetary File System (IPFS). Decentralized capability systems that are designed reduce a substance's potential to gain unauthorized data access in order to exploit or alter a person's secret details [3]. One of the most critical facets of protecting data on the platform is autonomous power. Accreditations are usually kept directly on the client's computer (e.g., smart device and computer) or securely maintained by private character stores in a distributed framework.

    Character center points, such as uPort'sTrust Graph or 3Box, are examples of private personality shops [19]. Personalities are regarded as self-sovereign because they are highly affected entirely by the customer [5]. As a result, the customer has full leverage of access to relevant data and does not have to worry about access getting refused. Data under the client's management renders it more interoperable, allowing the customer to use information across several levels, for different reasons, and to prevent the customers from being protected in one point.

- **Manageability and Control**
In brought together personality model, the substance lending the character is for the most reasons responsible for the security of the character data. In a distributed personality structure, security converts into the responsibility of the customers, who might prefer to execute their own safety efforts or re-appropriate the assignment to some assistance such as a computerized bank vault or a secret key chief like application. Furthermore, blockchain-fueled, distributed character arrangements power developers to assail specialized data stores that are exorbitant and unproductive for the most parts.

5.2   Preliminaries

5.2.1   Identity Management Systems

Identity management is an organizational strategy for ensuring that individuals have sufficient access to technology services (ID management). This entails recognizing, authenticating, and authorizing a single person or a group of users for access to systems, applications, or networks [1]. This is accomplished by associating existing identities with user privileges and constraints set forth by the organization's regulations. Identity management includes both authenticating people and determining whether they have access to specific systems. Systems for identity management and access management go hand in hand. The purpose of identity management is authentication, while the goal of access management is authorization [26–35]. The main goal of identity management is to ensure that only authorized users have access to the software, services, or IT environments to which they have been granted access. Account provisioning and onboarding for new users, such as employees, partners, customers, and other stakeholders, are covered.

5.2.1.1   Identity Factors

An identity factor is one of several types of identity signs that are used by the IDMSs to authenticate a person's identity. There are four types of identity factors used by the modern IMS.

- **Knowledge Factor:** This includes something that the user knows like passwords and pin.
- **Possession Factor:** This includes something that the user possesses, like the keys, cards, and tokens.
- **Inheritance Factor:** This factor is used by many modern IMS. It includes something unique that the user inherits like biometric, face id, and iris scan.
- **Mobility Factor:** This includes the location of the users which can be determined by the user's IP address, mobile location, etc.

5.2.1.2   Architecture of Identity Management Systems

An IDMS includes the following components:

- **User**
  Users are the system's key enablers, taking advantage of the service provider and identity provider's different services. Not every user has the same degree of access in system.

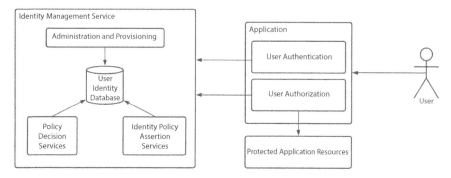

Figure 5.1 Identity management system architecture.

- **Service Provider**
  Service provider provides the services requested by the users upon successful authentication and authorization.
- **Identity Management Service Provider**
  The identity management service provider, which is at the heart of the architecture, is responsible for delivering identity services to users (such as registration, authentication, and management). User authentication is also provided by this module of the architecture.

Consider Figure 5.1, where the user tries to access the protected application resources. The user first provides an identity factor to the application system. The application requests for user authentication and authorization to the identity management service provider by sending user's identity factor. The IMS provider then authenticates the user by verifying in the database and then authorizes by checking the organizational policies [2]. Once the user identity is verified and response is sent back to application service provider, the application then provides access to the protected application resources based on user's authorities.

5.2.1.3   Types of Identity Management Systems

There are three types of IDMSs.

- **Independent IDM**
  The vast majority of online identities are stored in a single location. A single company owns and maintains the user

credentials. However, the independent identity registry concept has flaws. The identity provider has [21] control over the users' identity records, which can be revoked or misused.

- **Federated IDM**
  Authorization and authentication abilities can be provided throughout organizational and system limitations through federated IDMSs. It necessitates contractual arrangements on data ownership and agreements that a provider's identity is recognized by other providers. The identity provider manages user accounts individually, so there is no need for business directory integration. As a result, the vulnerability risk is minimized because credentials are not repeated, rather presented on request [18]. This technique is harder to execute and necessitates appropriate understanding and trust between online administrations.

- **Self-Sovereign IDM**
  Stakeholders must be able to manage their own online identities, according to the principle of self-sovereign identity [11]. Without depending on a centralized database of identity data, individuals and companies may record their own identity data on computers owned by them and provide their identity to those in need to verify it [4, 8, 25]. It gives users full power, protection, and portability of their data because it is independent of any single silo. Self-sovereign identity, according to the Sovrin Foundation, is "an Internet for identity where no one owns it, anyone can use it, and everyone can develop it".

5.2.1.4 Importance of Identity Management Systems

Identity protection is a vital component of an organizational security policy because it impacts both the organization's security and efficiency. Users are also given more access rights than they need to perform their jobs in certain organizations. In order to obtain access to an organization's data and network, attackers will use compromised user credentials [10, 23]. Organizations can protect their corporate assets from a variety of risks, such as phishing, ransomware, hacking, and other malware attacks, by implementing identity management. Identity protection programs provide an additional layer of security by making sure that user access protocols and rules are applied universally across an organization.

5.2.2   Blockchain

DLT (Distributed Ledger Technology), also known as "Blockchain Technology", is a decentralized open ledger with verified and approved information stored in it. A blockchain is a decentralized network comprised of millions of digital devices known as nodes.

5.2.2.1   Blockchain Architecture

Blockchain has a distributed architecture in which each node functions as a network administrator and joins the network voluntarily [21]. A blockchain is nearly impossible to hack due to the lack of centralized information in its architecture.

The blockchain architecture stores information in the form of blocks. Along with data, timestamp and a hash of the previous block are also maintained and stored in a block as shown in Figure 5.2.

5.2.2.2   Components of Blockchain Architecture

The major components of blockchain architecture include the following:

- **Node:** A node refers to a connected computer device in blockchain architecture.

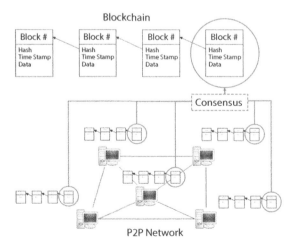

Figure 5.2 Blockchain architecture.

- **Transaction:** A transaction is a data record that is validated by blockchain nodes and acts as an almost immutable proof of authenticity.
- **Block:** As mentioned, it is the building block of the blockchain technology where each block acts as a sealed compartment containing data, native hash and hash of the previous block.
- **Chain:** It refers to the structured sequence of blocks in the blockchain.
- **Miners:** Miners are the nodes in the architecture, involved in verifying of a new block before appending it to the chain.
- **Consensus:** Consensus refers to the protocol for executing blockchain operations.

5.2.2.3 Merkle Tree

A blockchain is made up of different blocks that are connected to one another. A hash tree, also known as the Merkle tree, is used to efficiently and securely encrypt blockchain data. It enables the peer-to-peer blockchain network to quickly verify and transfer vast volumes of data from one node to the next node. A hash is connected with any activity on the blockchain network. These hashes are kept on the block in a tree-like structure rather than in chronological order, with each hash having a parent-child tree-like relationship. Because a block comprises many transactions, all of the block's transaction hashes are hashed as well, resulting in a hash of the entire block, Merkle root as shown in Figure 5.3.

5.2.2.4 Consensus Algorithm

A consensus algorithm is a process that allows all peers in a blockchain network to agree on the state of the distributed ledger. Consensus algorithms are used to maintain blockchain network stability and build trust between unknown peers in a distributed computing system. In reality, the consensus protocol guarantees that any new block added to the Blockchain is the only version of the truth that all nodes agree on. Many basic aims of the blockchain consensus algorithm include establishing an agreement, cooperation, co-operation, equal rights for all nodes, and each node's necessary

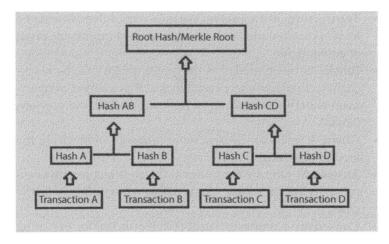

Figure 5.3 Merkle tree [Source: Cointral.com].

participation in the consensus process. As a result, a consensus algorithm seeks to discover a common ground on which the entire network can stand.

Various types of consensus algorithms and their working are as follows:

- **Proof of Work**
  This consensus algorithm is used to select the miner for the next block creation. For Bitcoin, the Proof of Work (PoW) consensus algorithm is utilized. This algorithm's main purpose is to swiftly find a solution to a complex mathematical problem. The first node to answer this mathematical problem, which requires a lot of computational power, gets to mine the next block.

- **Practical Byzantine Fault Tolerance**
  Practical Byzantine Fault Tolerance (PBFT) is just one of the numerous consensus mechanisms which are used with permissioned blockchain tech, here another new block is created if more than 66.66% of all verifying peers respond in just the same way. Although Hyperledger Fabric does not provide PBFT out of the box, it does allow users to incorporate this consensus mechanism in a modular fashion.

- **Proof of Stake**
  This is the most widely used alternative to PoW. The consensus on Ethereum has shifted from PoW to Proof of Stake (PoS). Validators invest in the system's coins by locking up some of their coins as stake in this form of consensus process,

rather than investing in expensive gear to solve a challenging mathematical problem. All of the validators would then validate the blocks. If validators believe a block may be linked to the chain, then they can validate it by wagering on it. Validators earn payouts proportional to their stakes based on the quantity of true blocks tied to the blockchain, and their stake adjusts appropriately. Finally, a validator is picked to construct a new block based on their economic stake in the network. As a result, PoS enables validators to come to a consensus through a reward system.

- **Proof of Importance**
  Proof of Importance (PoI) was a new consensus algorithm developed to overcome the problems with PoS and PoW algorithm. The concept driving this algorithm is that the nodes are just as important as their activities of the network. The active nodes in the network are then compensated. Each address is assigned a trust score, and as organization activity increases, the almost certain node will be remunerated for its loyalty and effort.

5.2.2.5   Types of Blockchain Architecture

- **Public blockchain architecture**
  The public blockchain architecture uses the PoW consensus algorithm and its relevant procedures. Transparent yet anonymous or pseudonymous transactions are possible with this blockchain architecture.
- **Private blockchain architecture**
  Private blockchain architecture restricts access of data to a small number of participants (organizations or individuals). Such architectures are created by companies having intention of raising net profits or performance. The participants' shared interests, as well as Byzantine fault tolerance (BFT) consensus algorithms and PoS, ensures private blockchain's reliability.
- **Consortium blockchain architecture**
  Anybody could connect to and access the blockchain in this type of blockchain architecture, but a user can only append details or attach a node with approval of other members. Organizations create blockchains like this to raise trust among its clients, users, and entire society. The existence of

Table 5.1 Comparison of various blockchain architectures.

Properties	Private blockchain	Public blockchain	Consortium blockchain
Access	One organization	Anyone	Multiple selected nodes
Participants	Known Identities	Anonymous	Known Identities
Consensus Process	Permissioned	Permissionless	Permissioned
Centralized	Yes	No	Partial
Efficiency	Very High	Low	High
Security	1. Pre-approved participants 2. Voting/multi-party consensus	1. Consensus Algorithm 2. Proof of Work/ Proof of Stake	1. Pre-approved participants 2. Voting/multi-party consensus.
Immutability	Possible to tamper	Tampering is almost impossible	Possible to tamper

confidence between participants, as well as the use of the same PoS and BFT consensus algorithms, contributes to reliability of the architecture.

Table 5.1 compares the three blockchain architectures.

5.2.3   Challenges

In spite of many promising norms and methods proposed in the internet time, basic difficulties of building compelling [20] IDMS for IoT stay strange, for example, performance, trust, privacy, and access controls.

- **Controlling Access**
  The objective of setting up personality frameworks in the IoT is to empower correspondences and appropriately manage the interaction of approval to gadgets and assets. Notwithstanding, with the appearance of IoT time, because of the rapid proliferation of jobs and methods, many

traditional access management models such as Role-based Access Control (RAC) and Access Control Lists (ACLs) models, which were intended for concentrated frameworks, have become outdated [14]. Moreover, an ever-increasing number of components and boundaries like time, area ought to likewise be thought about in planning access control arrangements. Yet, Attribute-based Access Control model targets taking care of this issue, the presence of concentrated character suppliers in Attribute-based Access Control model actually need to look up to the adaptability problem.

A common issue with current arrangements come from incorporated managerial gatherings (that is, directors or personality suppliers) that become crucial for allotting access rights, jobs, and credits, and, thusly, these arrangements are not appropriate for adaptable distributed IoT frameworks. The Capability-based Access Control (CAC) model gives a ton of considerations by prudence of its adaptability. In any case, it has a similar reason by which clients who solicit administrations need to depend on the confirmation of outsiders like character suppliers or testament specialists. This is clearly inadmissible in the trustless IoT environments, where each subject, for example, a human could build clients without the help of other halfway gatherings. As a result, the CAC paradigm only fits under limited circumstances.

Blockchain innovation is additionally used to configure access control frameworks for the IoT. Blockchain-based admittance controls dispose of the requirement for concentrated authorities to set admittance control strategies in obliged IoT gadgets. They depend on blockchain exchange information models to execute access control tasks to allow or deny access demands in IoT conditions. One more advantage is the inspecting of access control strategies, which can report unchanging exchanges in the blockchain.

- **Privacy**
  The security safeguarding alludes to the assurance of clients' sensitive data like character data, area, portability follows, and propensities from some other gatherings. From client's viewpoint, the protection saving incorporates two perspectives:

✓ Personality data security from character suppliers
✓ Delicate application information insurance from administration suppliers

To save the critical application details, various works in scholarly papers and the IT industry have been suggested, where instead of character data put away in personality suppliers. By and large, character suppliers and specialist organizations are limited together and they require some close to home data to verify clients. For example, clients may shield their area data from map specialist co-ops by debilitating the area administration; in any case, they overlook the spillage of their own personality data by character suppliers presented to security weaknesses [15]. Yet these proposed arrangements take care of the protection issue somewhat, their personality data is as yet presented to character suppliers.

Before blockchains, security saving is inadequate attributable to the presence of incorporated character suppliers. Administration accessors and administration proprietors need to allow full trust to their character suppliers. All in all, brought together character suppliers consistently hold data about assistance accessors and administration proprietors and could follow all exchanges between them. The blockchain innovation brings together all client characters dissipated among personality suppliers heavily influenced by clients. The plan of character arrangements is subsequently subject to a change in outlook by which clients choose to whom their delicate individual data could be uncovered (from client's point of view) rather than believing character suppliers to deal with their own information. Additionally, the presentation of zero-information confirmations in blockchains brings the specific revelation of delicate individual data into the real world.

- **Trust**
  Inside a similar security space, clients and specialist co-ops trust and depend on a similar character supplier, concede chime that their own data would not be undermined or misused by the personality supplier or outsiders. As a rule, character suppliers are dependent upon weaknesses which uncover individual data stores to be taken by de-freed

assailants (i.e., Equifax information break). The understood trust in personality suppliers gets problematic, making the unified character model outdated considering as to security saving and maintainability in the IoT period targeting interfacing everything [14]. In spite of the fact that organizations (i.e., Google or Facebook) look to offer general character suppliers for all digital clients and specialist co-ops, the increment number of online specialist organizations and personality suppliers makes computerized characters disengaged and divided over the Internet. In addition, the expense of correspondence and common validations increments quickly between various security spaces. Diverse personality suppliers additionally need to haggle to set up trust connections to united characters across security spaces.

Without a doubt, the blockchain-based personality of the board frameworks kills the need for needless data transparency to outsiders and has numerous beneficial properties such as immutability, non-partisanship, and protected time stamping that can be utilized to create faithful relationships. Lu *et al.* proposed a novel method for creating trust notoriety using personalized Ethereum tokens. However, these dispersed or conveyed approaches face various difficulties in establishing a stable structure or feedback mechanism for developing confidence relationships among all subjects and expert cooperatives. The systems can be self-governing modular applications that are updated in a distributed manner.

5.3   Blockchain-Based Identity Management System

5.3.1   Need for Blockchain-Based Identity Management Systems

To understand how blockchain technology could be employed as an IDMS, it is necessary to first understand how the present system's flaws have emerged. The internet is designed as a peer-to-peer, open network of links that allows any user to contact and engage with any other user without the need for a third party. As the internet became more privatized, third-party intermediaries formed, and they became an increasingly important aspect of the internet's structure.

Everything was taken over by a tiny set of firms, from giving website protection certificates to monitoring internet access to curating user online identities. These firms were able to accumulate vast amounts of personal information from anybody who used the internet, which was then stored on servers, thanks to this centralized control [9].

These servers can (and have) been penetrated and hacked by hackers resulting in stealing or manipulation of the critical identity data of users, and the accumulation of personal and critical data in the control of a limited number of organizations can further raise the possibility of potential data breaches in future. Hence, the need to store crucial identity data in a decentralized environment was raised.

The blockchain by configuration is decentralized; consequently, it gives a unified way to deal with identity management. In most of the best-in-class frameworks, clients store their personality in their individual decentralized wallets in this way killing the issues of centralization. This decentralization likewise gives a huge level of versatility and client control to such personalities. A blockchain identity additionally naturally gives a reasonable detachment between the jobs of authentication specialists and authorization specialists, subsequently debasing the likelihood of conspiracy of these specialists against a subject [13]. By and large authentication and authorization specialists might be totally decoupled, subsequently eliminating the motivation to abuse subject information. Finally, trust scales very well in the blockchain climate when contrasted with conventional focal worker arrangements. This is basically in light of the fact that, new contestants into the blockchain identity just need to believe the agreement calculation when contrasted with confiding in a worker or even a gathering of workers.

5.3.2   Approaches for Blockchain-Based Identity Management Systems

As previously stated, blockchain technology could provide a possible solution to the issue by allowing users to store data on a blockchain instead of on vulnerable servers. As data is stored on a blockchain, it is encrypted and cannot be modified or removed, making major data breaches extremely difficult for the intruders. While it may seem that data storage on a blockchain is a straightforward, high-level solution, there are a number of theoretical approaches to putting it into practice. One approach is to do away with the intermediaries by allowing people to store their identities and data directly on a blockchain, which they can carry with them anywhere they go online. If users' digital identities were cryptographically stored directly on a blockchain within an internet browser, then they would theoretically not have to provide sensitive data to any third party anymore.

Allowing users to encrypt their personal identity information into a blockchain that can be accessed by third party organizations is another choice. This method does not completely remove the requirements of intermediaries; instead, it removes the requirements for intermediary organizations to store confidential personal data on their servers directly.

5.3.3 Blockchain-Based Identity Management System Implementations

The invention of blockchain-based identity management and verification has been pioneered by a few firms. Several deployment strategies for designing digital identity schemes are mentioned below, organized by the types of blockchain used as the underlying technologies.

- **Blockchain with a closed network (private or consortium)**
  A permissioned network is created when digital identity is incorporated into a private or consortium blockchain [22]. This limits who is eligible to join in the network, and only for specific transactions and the parties involved in a deal will be aware of it and will have access to it and other parties will not.

  o **Waypoint**
    Waypoint is an Ethereum virtual machine–based decentralized multi-factor authentication scheme. This approach uses a Web API to execute identity authentication on the blockchain. It enables applications to protect various modules within a product by specifying multiple features, and it has both a mobile and desktop version. It has the capability of storing user activity and performing analyses for real-time behavior-based authenticating.

  o **UPort**
    It is a web-based program that makes use of consensus used Ethereum to create this. Smart contracts, smartphone app, and developer repositories are its three key components [6, 12]. A smartphone app stores the user's key. The center of the identity is Ethereum smart

contracts, which provide the logic that allows users to reclaim their identities if the user's phone is misplaced [25]. Lastly, it is possible for third-party developers to create apps using the developer libraries [19].

○ **Blockstack**
Decentralized services for naming (DNS), identification, storage, and authentication are provided by Blockstack. Developers can build serverless apps using JavaScript libraries without the need to be concerned with the actual infrastructure. Blockstack might possibly take the place of the traditional client-server architecture, where the information is controlled by the users, apps run on the client machine and the open Blockstack network executes functionalities on server side.

○ **Microsoft Decentralized Identity Foundation (DIF)**
Microsoft has built up an establishment for building an open-source decentralized character biological system for individuals, associations, applications, and gadgets. It utilizes four columns in another environment: decentralized personalities, blockchain character, zero trust information stores, and being generally discoverable [20].

○ **Cambridge Blockchain LLC**
This stage was created to permit monetary organizations to meet the strictest new information security rules, wipe out repetitive character consistence checks, and, furthermore, improve the client experience. By joining blockchain innovation with an off-chain individual information administration, they made an autonomous wellspring of truth through the organization impacts of exchanges among people and trusted parties.

○ **Netki**
Netki gives open-source and open-standard based advanced personality arrangements that permit monetary assistance organizations to achieve their consistence necessities on both private and public blockchains. Netki Wallet Name Service (WNS) makes an interpretation of simple to-recollect names such as "wallet.myname.me" into bitcoin (and certain other cryptographic currency) wallet addresses.

- ○ **KYC-Chain**

  This is a novel stage worked with the accommodation and security of DLT, permitting clients to deal with their computerized personality safely, while organizations and monetary organizations can oversee client information in a dependable and simple way.

- ○ **HYPR**

  HYPR gives decentralized biometric verification to get clients across versatile, work area, and IoT frameworks. It upgrades the client experience by permitting clients to browse voice, face, contact, and eye acknowledgment. By utilizing biometric verification, information penetrate misrepresentation can be kept away from [16].

- ○ **Guardtime's BLT**

  This is a blockchain standard for advanced character, a verification and mark convention planned to substitute RSA as the norm for computerized marks. In differentiation to the RSA's dependence on quantum-weak unbalanced key cryptography, BLT depends on Guardtime's quantum-secure Keyless Signature Infrastructure (KSI) innovation, which utilizes just hash-work cryptography.

- ○ **Evernym**

  Evernym is building up a modern character stage based on Sovrin, a private-area, global non-benefit that was set up to administer the world's first SSI organization. These devices and items are planned by the very group that made Sovrin to essentially facilitate the arrangement and combination of SSI foundation in various ventures.

- • **Open Blockchain (Public)**

  A public blockchain network is totally open and anybody can join and take an interest in the organization. The advanced character in open blockchain ordinarily has a boosting instrument to urge more members to join the organization.

  - ○ **Sovrin**

    Sovrin is a self-sovereign identity trust system that is decentralized and global. It is also the first global public service devoted solely to self-determination and verifiable statements. Self-sovereignty seeks to give any user or any organization a portable identity. The holder of a self-sovereign identity may show verifiable credentials in a private manner. Sex, age, educational history, and job details are examples of these credentials. The Sovrin protocol is developed completely on open standards and the Hyperledger-Indy Project, which is open source. By default, all Sovrin identifiers and public keys are pseudonymous.

o **ShoCard**

This simple-to-utilize advanced character based on a public blockchain information layer implies that organizations do not claim the client information. A client's personality is encoded, hashed, and afterward kept in touch with the blockchain, where it very well may be called up when required. Clients, basically, give banks impermanent admittance to the private side of this blockchain record to check character. Whenever that is finished, the bank makes its own record which can be counselled later on to discover that a certain individual is who they guarantee to be.

o **MyData**

MyData is a personal data management project commissioned by the Finnish government. The idea of usability, human-centric power, accessibility, and transparency drives this Nordic self-sovereign IDM. It can be used to protect the flow of information between the healthcare, government, and finance sectors. User controlled Oauth 2.0, OpenID single sign-on, and access, which control admittance to Web APIs, are at the core of MyData verification. Since any transition to mess with the blockchain is immediately identified, blockchain is utilized to convey control of criminal operations to the total organization of partners. This examination, which was led as a team with Sovrin, plans to improve advanced basic freedoms while likewise giving new freedoms to organizations to make imaginative individual information administrations. Also, it aims to counter the EU General Data Protection Regulation (GDPR), which has been effective since May 2018 and sets new guidelines for monitoring and handling personal data [17].

o **UniquID**

This gives character the board, incorporated with unique mark and other biometrics, on close to home gadgets. Fit to be sent in custom equipment, workers, PCs, cell phones, or any other portable devices. UniquID Wallet additionally runs on battery and low-fueled gadgets, giving honesty and interoperability at the edge of one's framework.

o **Bitnation**

This is an administration 2.0 stage fueled by blockchain innovation. Its objective is to offer the very types of assistance that administrations give, yet in a decentralized and deliberate way, unbound by topography. Bitnation has formulated distinguishing proof arrangements, for example, blockchain international IDs and marriage declarations.

o **Civic**

Metro's personality check and security instruments enable the two organizations and people to control and ensure their characters through the blockchain. They permit clients to enlist and approve their own personality data and lock their personalities to forestall wholesale fraud and deceitful action on their credit reports.

o **Bloom**

Bloom is a credit score and identity protection blockchain project devised on Ethereum and IPFS [25]. It is a robust protocol that allows holders of traditional and digital currencies to serve as loans to people who do not have a bank account or a credit score. In Bloom, users have created a BloomID id contract, which should be verified and attested by peer nodes such as friends, relative's, or the organization's device(s) [12].

o **Existence ID**

This permits clients to make an advanced personality container to store their records, to some degree like Dropbox, yet with a lot more elevated level of safety. Every client account is totally self-verified and zero-information on the client's close to home account. The protected network, a protected open data management program, encrypts and uploads identity documents saved to a digital identification capsule. The BloomIQ framework then records and monitors financial obligations, resulting in a BloomScore as credit worthiness metric for the client. Through defining a globally scalable and comprehensive credit profile, the bloom protocol eliminates the need for

Table 5.2 Overview of various blockchain-based identity management system.

Solution	Description	Network	Blockchain	Propose type	Auth	ID mgmt.
Waypoint	It is a distributed multiple identity factor based authentication system	Private	Ethereum	Company	Included	Not included
MyData	A Nordic initiative collaborated with Sovrin to build self-sovereign identity management system	Public Permissioned	Hyperledger Indy	Government	Included	Included
Sovrin	It is a distributed IDMS for self-sovereign identity based authentication	Public Permissioned	Hyperledger Indy	Non-profit organization	Not included	Included

(Continued)

Table 5.2 Overview of various blockchain-based identity management system. (*Continued*)

Solution	Description	Network	Blockchain	Propose type	Auth	ID mgmt.
ShoCard	It is an IDMS for protecting user's privacy	Public	Ethereum	Start-up	Not included	Included
Jolocom	It is a blockchain-based IDMS app for customers to possess their personal digital identity	Private	Ethereum	Start-up	Not included	Included
BlockStack	It is distributed services for storage, identity authentication and DNS.	Private	Ethereum	Start-up	Included	Included
Bloom	It is a blockchain project for identity management and credit scoring	Permissioned	Hyperledger	Open source	Not included	Included

(*Continued*)

Table 5.2 Overview of various blockchain-based identity management system. (*Continued*)

Solution	Description	Network	Blockchain	Propose type	Auth	ID mgmt.
Uport	It is a blockchain project for identity management	Private	Ethereum	Company	Not included	Included
CertCoin	A distributed identity authentication system based on NameCoin	Permissioned	Hyperledger	Open source	Included	Not included
BlockAuth	It is a blockchain-based identity registrar	Permission-less	Ethereum	Start-up	Not included	Included
UniquID	It is used for authentication and authorization process management of connected things	Permission-less	Ethereum	Open source	Not Included	Include
I/O Digital	Blockchain-based IDMS	Private	Ethereum	Start-up	Not included	Included

(*Continued*)

Table 5.2 Overview of various blockchain-based identity management system. (*Continued*)

Solution	Description	Network	Blockchain	Propose type	Auth	ID mgmt.
Cambridge Blockchain	Blockchain-based IDMS	Permission-less	Ethereum	Start-up	Not included	Included
Authenteq	It blockchain-based IDMS that uses facial recognition algorithm.	Permission-less	Ethereum	Company	Not included	Included
Kyc.Legal	It is a blockchain-based authentication and authorization system used to prevent fraud.	Permission-less	Ethereum	Company	Not Included	Included

conventional banking networks and anonymous, proprietary credit ratings.

○ **Open Identity Exchange (OIX)**
This is a non-benefit, innovation sceptic, community cross-area participation associated with the objective of speeding up the selection of advanced personality administrations in view of open principles. They distribute white papers to convey worth to the character environment as an entirety.

○ **Cryptid**
Cryptid is the up-and-coming age of distinguishing proof. Ebb and flow recognizable proof techniques, for example, state-gave driver's licenses are uncertain and effortlessly messed with. Cryptid dispenses with the chance of fake recognizable proof by adding factors of recognizable proof and encryption that are upheld by a conveyed, worldwide organization. The entirety of the information is encoded with the given secret word, after which it is for all time moved to the blockchain. The client is then given an interesting recognizable proof number that focuses on the data on the blockchain and can be put away on nearly anything from attractive strips to QR codes.

Table 5.2 summarizes various blockchain-based identity management and authentication implementations.

5.3.4   Impact of Using Blockchain-Based Identity Management on Business and Users

The following features of blockchain-based IDMs can be useful for its users and businesses:

- **User-optimized**
  The blockchain environment is profoundly practical and time-proficient. Also, the expense brought about in checking personalities gets brought down both for business and clients.
- **Transparent**
  Everybody associated with the organization can follow the exchanges recorded on the blockchain. Undeniable legitimacy exists for each made exchange.

- **Obscure**
  It guarantees the protection of the exchanges for the gatherings associated with the blockchain.
- **Decentralized**
  Rather than putting away the information on a solitary brought together worker, decentralization empowers the dispersion of data on each hub in the organization, lessening the odds of a solitary place of disappointment.
- **Universal Identity**
  Clients can request that the association confirm its character across the boundary too.

5.3.5   Various Use Cases of Blockchain Identity Management

Blockchain-based IDMSs have many use cases in various fields. A few of them includes the following:

- **Applying for a loan**
  Envision you need to apply for a credit or open another financial balance. Customarily, you need to present numerous character records for finishing the whole manual confirmation measure, requiring a long time to handle the advance or credit. Yet, a blockchain-based character could secure the interaction by sharing relevant data rapidly. Since a client might not need to keep up various IDs, the expense and endeavours could likewise be decreased.
- **Immigration**
  Aside from conveying identification, an explorer additionally needs to bring a particular arrangement of records for leeway and security checks at the air terminal. From booking a pass to passing security checks, getting onto a flight, and moving to another country, an individual can introduce a general blockchain-based character all through the whole interaction. An individual with a decentralized character would not need to go through confounded security checks and different methodology. Thus, blockchain character on the board can make the cycle more smoothed out for the two explorers and specialists.
- **Legal procedures**
  While going through any legitimate cycle, a client may need to submit distinctive character evidences like proof of age, proof of occupation, and address proof. With the assistance

of blockchain characters the executives, individuals probably would not need to convey various records any place they go. Lawful substances, also as government bodies, can confirm a person from a solitary blockchain-based character. Subsequently, a complete individual verification is not any more required.

- **E-commerce checkout**
  At whatever point people put in a request on the web, they are approached to fill in explicit data like name, email, telephone number, and address, and they need to rehash this cycle each time at whatever point they join at an online business webpage, making the entire interaction tedious and bulky. Thus, joining at various online business locales with a novel recognizable proof number can save clients time and exertion.

- **Previous employment verification**
  As of now, there is no fixed normalization to do a record verification of the representatives. It is fundamental for checking workers' data written in resumes, past letters, or reference letters in the worldwide business area. Approval of the data written in representative's resumes can be mentioned straightforwardly through the blockchain biological system with a client's consent.

5.4 Discussion

Despite the fact that identity security has been thoroughly researched and implemented, there are still a range of drawbacks and challenges. Although blockchain could successfully address few of these problems, still many concerns and implications have to be addressed.

5.4.1 Challenges Related to Identity

There is a chance that personal information stored on the user's end might be exposed to danger and abuse [20]. The following are some examples:

- **Identity factors leakage**
  Data can be leaked or valuable details about the participant can accessed if the identity factors were successfully compromised. As a consequence, the information that has been released may be utilized to promote such malicious actions.

- **Change in Identity**
  The person's identity shifts. In fact, the person's identity is not set and could be altered any time. Traditional, centralized identity providers may easily revoke or renew identity status, such as during promotions or the suspension of a river licence. However, because of the resilience of blockchain and the SSI, any alteration of person's identity data in a blockchain-based identity framework necessitates him/her [7]. As a result, changing one's identity can be difficult.

5.4.2 Cost Implications

With the above-discussed blockchain-based solutions for IDMSs, there are also economic implications.

- **Infrastructure**
  Since SSI is still so new, existing IDMSs and their supporting infrastructure can struggle to support it. As a result, infrastructure improvements would have financial consequences. User passwords, for example, will need to be substituted with certificates, and the service provider's authentication process will need to be strengthened. Certainly, equipment and process upgrades are just a portion of the total cost. Staff preparation and equipment repairs are two other expenses to consider. Infrastructure enhancements can be phased in to various stages to reduce costs.
- **Key Management**
  Losing the private key in a bitcoin-based system means losing the associated asset (e.g., Bitcoins). In such cases, it is not possible to reset the forgotten password, unlike a password-based system. As a result, integrating such a reset feature or outsourcing key management to a third-party is a viable option. Private key delegation management, on the other hand, runs counter to the SSI principle. There is also substantial maintenance cost associated with supporting SSI.

5.5 Conclusion

As demonstrated by all of the large-scale online account theft, credentials like username and passwords are extremely vulnerable and easy to guess.

For identity protection and authentication, current web services depend solely on online providers. There should be a better method of identity management that specifically permits admittance to explicit data and eliminates the requirement for each online specialist organization to store client's credentials. This chapter discusses an ideal solution for the above problem using blockchain-based IDMS in detail. It deliberates in-depth information about the traditional IDMSs architecture, identity factors, types of IDMs, and its importance in the current digital world, followed by basics of Blockchains, its components, various types of blockchain architectures, and challenges in IDMs especially in state-of-the-art technologies like IoT.

The chapter also briefs about blockchain-based IDMs, its requirement for solving the problems with centralized IDMs, various approaches followed for creating blockchain-based IDMs, various existing blockchain-based IDM solutions, their impact on individual users and organizations, and also the use cases of such systems in multiple sectors. Finally, challenges related to blockchain-based IDMs such as challenges related to Identity leakage, change of identity and development and maintenance cost of the required infrastructure are also conversed in the chapter. These challenges and mentioned future works can be taken as the subject of research for building flawless IDMSs for safeguarding user's identity.

5.6   Future Scope

Computerized character is related with the financial prosperity of residents and gradually turns out to be fundamental for them getting the privilege to cast a ballot, open a financial balance, and access medical services and, furthermore, instruction. A World Economic Gathering distributed report in 2016 named "A Blueprint for Digital Identity", laying out the requirement for the production of advanced character frameworks and related advantages for partners [24], likewise emphasizes why blockchain is most appropriate for computerized character frameworks.

Having said this, it is likewise significant to take note that blockchain cannot be seen as the panacea for computerized character issues. It gives the system and going with benefits; by and by, similar to each framework, it accompanies its own aces and also cons: first, being the developing nature of the actual innovation, and second, the absence of normalization of information trades. Numerous foundations are put resources into the innovation and persistent endeavours are on to make blockchain-based frameworks secure.

Utilizing the advantages of straightforwardness and trust given by blockchain systems, numerous associations, and countries are holding hands to guarantee interoperability across their lines. Siloed individual character frameworks are offering approach to decentralized computerized personality frameworks that are rising above borders. Along these lines, public digital identities are expected to prompt "Global Identifiers" subsequently making a difference in battle digital psychological oppression and cash washing. While it is a given that no system can be totally secure and without weaknesses, ceaseless specialized advancement and mindfulness can altogether help in cutting down the danger and help us move toward a more secure world.

References

1. Liu, Y., He, D., Obaidat, M.S., Kumar, N., Khan, M.K., Choo, K.K.R., "Blockchain-based identity management systems: A review". *J. Netw. Comput. Appl.*, 166, pp. 102731, 2020.
2. Zhu, X. and Badr, Y., "Identity management systems for the internet of things: a survey towards blockchain solutions". *Sensors*, 18, 12, 1–18, 2018.
3. Liu, J., Li, B., Chen, L., Hou, M., Xiang, F., Wang, P., "A Data Storage Method Based on Blockchain for Decentralization DNS". *2018 IEEE Third International Conference on Data Science in Cyberspace (DSC)*, Guangzhou, China, pp. 189–196, 2018.
4. Dunphy, P., Garratt, L., Petitcolas, F., "Decentralizing Digital Identity: Open Challenges for Distributed Ledgers,". *IEEE European Symposium on Security and Privacy Workshops (EuroS&PW)*, London, UK, pp. 75–78, 2018.
5. El Haddouti, S. and El Kettani, M.D.E.C., "Analysis of identity management systems using blockchain technology". *2019 International Conference on Advanced Communication Technologies and Networking (CommNet)*, IEEE, pp. 1–7, 2019.
6. Molina-Jimenez, C. *et al.*, "Implementation of Smart Contracts Using Hybrid Architectures with On and Off–Blockchain Components". *2018 IEEE 8th International Symposium on Cloud and Service Computing (SC2)*, Paris, France, pp. 83–90, 2018.
7. Jacobovitz, O., *"Blockchain for identity management"*, pp. 1–19, The Lynne and William Frankel Center for Computer Science Department of Computer Science. Ben-Gurion University, Beer Sheva, 2016.
8. Ishmaev, G., "Sovereignty, privacy, and ethics in blockchain-based identity management systems.". *Ethics Inf. Technol.*, 23, 239–252, 2021.
9. Zhu, X. and Badr, Y., "A survey on blockchain-based identity management systems for the Internet of Things". *2018 IEEE International Conference on Internet of Things (iThings) and IEEE Green Computing and Communications*

(GreenCom) and IEEE Cyber, Physical and Social Computing (CPSCom) and IEEE Smart Data (SmartData), IEEE, pp. 1568–1573, 2018.

10. Lim, S.Y., Fotsing, P., Musa, O., Almasri, A., "AuthChain: A Decentralized Blockchain-based Authentication System". *Int. J. Eng. Trends Technol.*, 70–74, 2020.

11. Tobin, A. and Reed, D., *"The inevitable rise of self-sovereign identity"*, vol. 29, The Sovrin Foundation, Salt Lake City and Zug, Switzerland, 2016.

12. Kalamsyah, S.A., Barmawi, A.M., Arzaki, M., "Digital contract using block chaining and elliptic curve based digital signature". *6th International Conference on Information and Communication Technology (ICoICT)*, IEEE, pp. 435–440, 2018.

13. Kuperberg, M., "Blockchain-based identity management: A survey from the enterprise and ecosystem perspective". *IEEE Trans. Eng. Manage.*, 67, 4, 1008–1027, 2019.

14. Kshetri, N., "Can Blockchain Strengthen the Internet of Things", *IT Professional*, IEEE. 19, 4, 68–72, 2017.

15. Angin, P. *et al.*, "An Entity-Centric Approach for Privacy and Identity Management in Cloud Computing," *2010 29th IEEE Symposium on Reliable Distributed Systems*, New Delhi, India, pp. 177–183, 2010.

16. Sarier, N.D., "Efficient biometric-based identity management on the Blockchain for smart industrial applications". *Pervasive Mob. Comput.*, 71, pp. 101322, 2021.

17. Panetta, R. and Cristofaro, L., "A closer look at the EU-funded My Health My Data project". *Digit. Health Legal*, 10–11, 2017.

18. Maler, E. and Reed, D., "The Venn of Identity: Options and Issues in Federated Identity Management". *IEEE Secur. Priv.*, 6, 2, 16–23, 2008.

19. Panait, A.-E., Olimid, R.F., Stefanescu, A., "Analysis of uPort Open, an identity management blockchain-based solution", in: *International Conference on Trust and Privacy in Digital Business*, Springer, pp. 3–13, 2020.

20. Bertocci, V., Serack, G., Baker, C., *"Understanding windows cardspace: an introduction to the concepts and challenges of digital identities"*, Pearson Education, India. 2007.

21. Bertino, E. and Takahashi, K., *"Identity management: Concepts, technologies, and systems"*, Artech House, New York, USA, 2010.

22. Leiding, B. and Norta, A., "Mapping requirements specifications into a formalized blockchain-enabled authentication protocol for secured personal identity assurance". *International Conference on Future Data and Security Engineering*, Springer, pp. 181–196, 2017.

23. Yao, Y. and Xie, T., "A blockchain based authentication mechanism in wireless local area network." *2019 International Conference on Computer, Network, Communication and Information Systems (CNCI 2019)*, Atlantis Press, pp. 227–231, 2019.

24. Lim, S.Y., Fotsing, P.T., Almasri, A., Musa, O., Kiah, M.L.M., Ang, T.F., Ismail, R., "Blockchain technology the identity management and authentication

service disruptor: a survey". *Int. J. Adv. Sci. Eng. Inf. Technol.*, 8, 4–2, 1735–1745, 2018.

25. Wood, G., "Ethereum: A secure decentralised generalised transaction ledger", in: *Ethereum project yellow paper*, vol. 151, pp. 1–32, 2014.

26. Karuppiah, M. and Saravanan, R., "A secure remote user mutual authentication scheme using smart cards". *J. Inf. Secur. Appl.*, 19, 4–5, 282–294, 2014.

27. Maria, A., Pandi, V., Lazarus, J.D., Karuppiah, M., Christo, M.S., "BBAAS: Blockchain-Based Anonymous Authentication Scheme for Providing Secure Communication in VANETs". *Secur. Commun. Netw.*, 2021, Article ID 667988211, 1–11, 2021.

28. Karuppiah, M. and Saravanan, R., "A secure authentication scheme with user anonymity for roaming service in global mobility networks". *Wirel. Pers. Commun.*, 84, 3, 2055–2078, 2015.

29. Pradhan, A., Karuppiah, M., Niranchana, R., Jerlin, M.A., Rajkumar, S., "Design and analysis of smart card-based authentication scheme for secure transactions". *Int. J. Internet Technol. Secur. Trans.*, 8, 4, 494–515, 2018.

30. Karuppiah, M., Kumari, S., Li, X., Wu, F., Das, A.K., Khan, M.K., Basu, S., "A dynamic id-based generic framework for anonymous authentication scheme for roaming service in global mobility networks". *Wirel. Pers. Commun.*, 93, 2, 383–407, 2017.

31. Kumari, S., Karuppiah, M., Li, X., Wu, F., Das, A.K., Odelu, V., "An enhanced and secure trust-extended authentication mechanism for vehicular ad-hoc networks". *Secur. Commun. Netw.*, 9, 17, 4255–4271, 2016.

32. Karuppiah, M., Kumari, S., Das, A.K., Li, X., Wu, F., Basu, S., "A secure lightweight authentication scheme with user anonymity for roaming service in ubiquitous networks". *Secur. Commun. Netw.*, 9, 17, 4192–4209, 2016.

33. Naeem, M., Chaudhry, S.A., Mahmood, K., Karuppiah, M., Kumari, S., "A scalable and secure RFID mutual authentication protocol using ECC for Internet of Things". *Int. J. Commun. Syst.*, 33, 13, 1–13, 2020.

34. Karuppiah, M., Das, A.K., Li, X., Kumari, S., Wu, F., Chaudhry, S.A., Niranchana, R., "Secure remote user mutual authentication scheme with key agreement for cloud environment". *Mobile Netw. Appl.*, 24, 3, 1046–1062, 2019.

35. Li, X., Niu, J., Bhuiyan, M.Z.A., Wu, F., Karuppiah, M., Kumari, S., "A robust ECC-based provable secure authentication protocol with privacy preserving for industrial internet of things". *IEEE Trans. Industr. Inform.*, 14, 8, 3599–3609, 2017.

6

Insights Into Deep Steganography: A Study of Steganography Automation and Trends

R. Gurunath[1], Debabrata Samanta[1]* and Digvijay Pandey[2]

[1]Department of Computer Science, CHRIST (Deemed to be University), Bangalore, India
[2]Department of Electronics Engineering, Institute of Engineering and Technology, Dr. A.P.J. Abdul Kalam Technical University, Lucknow, India

Abstract

Recurrent neural networks (RNNs) are built on the foundation of feed forward networks. The greatest comparison for RNN is simple writing analysis, where the prediction of the next word is always dependent on prior knowledge of the sentence's contents. RNN is a type of artificial neural network that mimics the human neuron network and is used to recognize a series of data and then analyze the results to anticipate the conclusion. The LSTM is a kind of RNN that comprises of a stack of layers containing neurons. This article also discusses the problems that each technology faces, as well as potential solutions. To reduce losses, optimization algorithms change the characteristics of neural networks, such as weights and learning rates. One of the sections provides optimization algorithms in neural networks. A section devoted to some of the most recent extensive research on steganography and neural network combinations. Finally, we present an analysis of existing research on present study for the previous 5 years (2016 to 2020).

Keywords: Stenography, convolutional, CNN, NLP, RNN, LSTM

Corresponding author: debabrata.samanta369@gmail.com

Sabyasachi Pramanik, Debabrata Samanta, M. Vinay and Abhijit Guha (eds.) Cyber Security and Network Security, (129–156) © 2022 Scrivener Publishing LLC

6.1   Introduction

In text steganography, conventional stenography procedures vary based on the cover objects employed. In conventional steganography, the whole cover objects for hiding the data may be done by changing the structure of the cover file. Modern techniques, on the other hand, produce the cover text depending on the size of the secret message and a stego object built on the fly, such that the stego text's semantics resemble a normal phrase. As a result, there is no reason for mistrust [1, 2]. The majority of contemporary data concealment solutions rely on automatic cover creation using artificial neural networks (ANNs), payload capacity, robustness, and undetectability are all issues with older techniques. Artificial intelligence (AI)–based techniques are particularly good at handling steganographic characteristics. In this chapter, we will look at how AI is being utilized in current steganography to solve problems of traditional steganography. Data concealing may be accomplished using a variety of techniques in ANNs. Recurrent neural networks (RNNs), convolutional neural networks (CNNs), multilayer perceptron (MLP), neural network, feed forward neural network, and long short-term memory (LSTM) are just a few examples.

Neurons get information from the first layer, which is transmitted to the next layer through weights, and so on, until it reaches the last layer. The expected result is compared to the model's output, and the weights are adjusted. The basic example of a neuron is the perceptron, which accepts inputs and processes them into outputs. It is a binary classification approach. MLP starts with at least three layers or more. MLP is a classification algorithm that solves issues when classes are not differentiable. Back propagation is used for training, which is based on gradient descent (GD) [3].

Another prominent neural network is CNN, which works similarly to but not identically to any other neural network. CNN is used to extract features from pictures, and it is responsible for grouping, classification, and image recognition. It will be guided by supervised deep learning. Similar to CNN, feed forward networks learn features. Two or more layers are possible. There will be no hidden layer if there are two layers (input and output layers). It travels up to the output layer and produces output provided, if there are any hidden layers. "Feed forward" is the phrase for this. As is customary, the weight updation, bias, and activation functions are all used. CNNs work in a similar fashion, but if a neuron has a back propagation link, then it is referred to as a RNN. The rest of the paper provides details of the following sections: types of neural network, back propagation in neural networks, literature survey on neural networks in steganography,

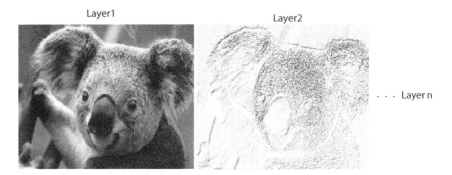

Figure 6.1 An example of extraction of image feature in convolution neural networks.

optimization algorithms in neural networks, and analysis of neural network steganography [4].

Multiple layers of neural networks are used in convolutional networks. Each layer is made up of numerous nodes known as neurons, and their behavior is determined by their weights. When an image is put into a convolutional network, each layer creates numerous activation maps, which identify the image's needed features. Each node accepts a set of pixels as input, multiplies their pixel color coordinates values by weights, adds them together, and feeds them to the activation functions. After feeding a particular image into a convolutional network, the first hidden layer determines the photo's essential features, such as diagonal, horizontal, and vertical edges [5]. The result is sent to the next layer, which extracts further characteristics from the input, such as corners and combined edges. As it progresses to the following layers, it extracts more details to the image, such as objects, faces, and so on, as shown in Figure 6.1.

Convolution is the technique of computing the product from pixel values and weights and then adding them up; hence, it is a CNN. Other layers, such as a classification layer, which is generally the last layer, accept input from the last CNN layer in order to detect more complicated characteristics from the image. The classification layer results in terms of values between 0 and 1, which reflects the confidence ratings, with the final activation map from CNN. The outcome indicates how probable the image is to belong to a "class" [6].

6.2   Convolution Network Learning

The process of weight adjustment in a neural network is known as "training". It is the most difficult aspect of any neural network. When the weights of

Figure 6.2 Training model with MINST database.

the neurons or nodes of the layers are modified, the characteristics of the pictures may be extracted. Essentially, CNN is utilized to identify the picture and extract the characteristics based on a label match. In the beginning, CNN is given random weights, and throughout training, it is given data sets of photographs divided into distinct classes. When the network's output does not match, it changes the weights of its neurons, bringing the image's characteristics a little closer to the match in successive outputs. Iteration generates an error, which is then corrected through back propagation by modifying the weights. Back propagation improves the process and makes it easier for the network to determine which units require change. An "epoch" is a single run of the whole training data set. During training, CNN goes through numerous such epochs and modifies weights in modest increments. The network's learning improves with each completed epoch. When the training is finished, the output will be checked against the test data set [7]. Testing is not a component of the training process. Obviously, the test data set is a way to assess the neural network as a whole. The output value is good during training, but when it is tested, it scores worse. This circumstance is referred to as "over-fitting". This is due to a shortage of training data or the CNN going through too many epochs on the training data set at particular points.

Of course, the greatest CNNs are usually trained on enormous data sets. As a result, data sets in the scale of tens of thousands are required for training. Figure 6.2 shows training model with MINST database.

In order to train such a large data set, a prepackaged library of data sets is available, one of which is MNIST (Figure 6.6), which has roughly 70K pictures. In a method known as "transfer learning", AlexNet, a pre-trained model, may be used to train CNN [8].

6.2.1   CNN Issues

When evaluating the parameters for CNN, such as learning rate, weight, decay, batch size, and type of activation, it is clear that a large quantity of data is required for training. A great deal of validation was required in order to adjust these parameters to an ideal level. When images are submitted, CNN always performs well; nevertheless, text and numbers do not function well for CNN. RNN is, of course, the ideal option for such data. It is exceedingly difficult to obtain adequate training data that allows for significant learning. Even when data is accessible, a slew of restrictions and security issues must be solved before the data may be used. Detecting medical disparities, unlike identifying an image, necessitates a high level of precision [9].

6.3   Recurrent Neural Networks

RNNs were first presented in the 1980s. For the study of character strings, numerous scholars contributed to RNN, including Rumelhart, Hinton, and Williams. Virtual reality systems, wind turbine power estimates, financial prediction, music synthesis, natural language processing (NLP), and other applications are among them. RNN is available in both fully linked and partly connected networks. There is no discrete input layers of nodes in fully connected, and each node works as an input node for all other nodes [10].

A few nodes in the partly connected RNN belong to a feed forward network (Figure 6.3), while others give semantics and get input from other nodes. RNNs transmit input from their output to a layer, enabling the network to "remember" from the past and recognize characteristics in time sequence patterns. RNNs are especially helpful in NLP, and it is more crucial to grasp the entire meaning of a phrase than just one word at a time. RNNs are a type of neural network that uses a feedback network to feed output from one process into the current process [11, 12]. In terms of RNN, recurrent meaning that it repeats the same procedure for each element in a sequence. The information from the previous phase is stored in RNN's

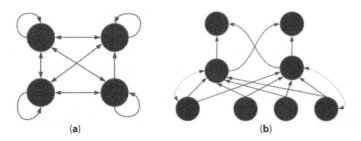

Figure 6.3 (a) Fully connected RNN and (b) simple, partially connected RNN.

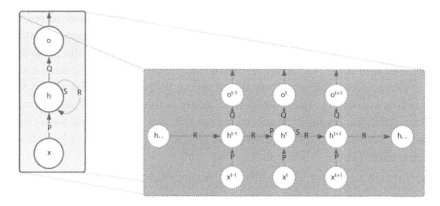

Figure 6.4 Abstraction and the detailed process of recurrent neural network.

memory. In general, neural networks' input and output are independent, but RNNs are required to predict the next word in a sentence using the previous word's link. Figure 6.4 shows abstraction and the detailed process of RNN.

RNN was created specifically to process a sequence of character/word data. RNN is ideally suited to handle any data belonging to voice or language in a series. The prediction of the following word in a series in NLP necessitates knowledge of the terms. As a result, RNNs utilized to repeat the same task using feedback mechanisms. Whatever knowledge is gained is kept in the memory allotted to it.

The RNN network is depicted in Figure 6.4 as an abstraction of the whole process on the left that erupts into a complete architecture with hidden layers and nodes on the right. The number of hidden layers in a sequence is determined by the number of words, where x(t) is the input at time step "t" and h(t) is the hidden state that serves as a network storage buffer. The current input and the previous time step hidden state are used to compute h (t):

$$h(t) = f(Px(t) + Rh(t-1)) \qquad (6.1)$$

Non-linear transformations or activation functions such as sigmoid, tanh, and ReLU (Rectified Linear Unit) are represented by "f". The weight matrix P is used as the input to the RNN hidden connections, the matrix R is used for hidden to hidden connections, and the matrix Q is used for hidden to output connections. All of these PQR weights are distributed across time.

When the network has additional layers downstream, o(t) reflects the network's output, which can be exposed to non-linearity.

6.3.1   RNN Forward Propagation

The fundamental purpose of RNN operation is forward propagation over time. Any dimension can be used for input (x_i) and hidden layers. Normal output and output (o_t) with regard to time are two components of the RNN output. A sentiment analysis for a social media message, for example, might be favorable or negative. Let us say a sentence has four words. $x_i \leq x_{11}, x_{12}, x_{13}, x_{14}$. It processes the first word at time t = 1, the second word at time t = 2, and so on. Preprocessing occurs at the hidden layer as soon as the first word is sent to RNN, and output is produced. Aside from the following word, the initial word's output is also transmitted to the RNN. Because of this, sequence of data is stored in the RNN [13]. Propagation in the forward direction and the procedure for completing the aforementioned four-word sequence is as follows. The number of neurons in the RNN hidden layer varies depending on the situation. Activation is a function of each neuron. The first word is entered into a hidden layer at time t = 1. Each hidden layer has a weight that is multiplied by the input to produce an output. Then, for the first output, the output function may be expressed as $o_1 = f(x_{i1} w)$.

The hidden layer receives the first output calculated. Then, second word is sent to the second hidden layer at time t = 2, and the same weight is applied as previously. The weight is multiplied by the input and then passed to the hidden layer. It is worth noting that the weights will only be changed in back propagation, not forward propagation. Figure 6.5 shows process of

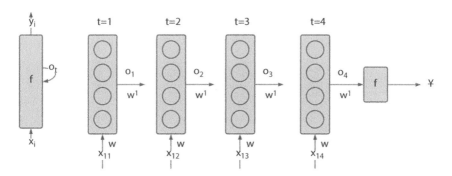

Figure 6.5 Process of RNN forward propagation.

RNN forward propagation. The prior output is then transferred to a second layer with a different weight at the same time (w1). The second and subsequent output equations as follows:

$$\text{At time } t = 2, \ o_2 = f(x_{12} \, w + o_1 \, w_1)$$

$$\text{At time } t = 3, \ o_3 = f(x_{13} \, w + o_2 \, w_1)$$

$$\text{At time } t = 4, \ o_4 = f(x_{14} \, w + o_3 \, w_1)$$

The last hidden layer's output is sent to the sigmoid activation function, which is also given a new weight (w^{11}). The classification layer then produces the result, y, which is the expected output value. The primary goal of RNN is to lower the loss value. Once this is completed, backward propagation can begin. RNN is a bidirectional system that may be utilized in both directions. RNN may propagate both forward and backward. Backward RNN captures backward patterns, while forward RNN captures forward patterns. Bidirectional RNNs are used to incorporate sequential patterns in both forward and backward directions.

6.4   Long Short-Term Memory Networks

It is a special case RNN network that is superior to the RNN itself. When LSTM was first used in conjunction with RNN, it produced incredible results. Why utilize LSTM? Because RNN has a problem with long-term

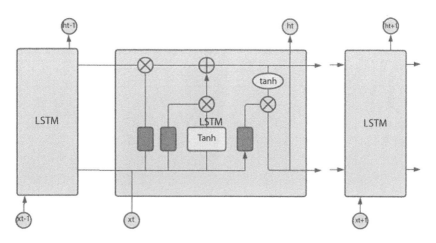

Figure 6.6 Basic LSTM structure for RNN.

dependencies, it is tough to learn to link to information when there is a lot of context given to it. LSTM was created to address this RNN flaw. The capacity to store information for lengthy periods of time is a natural characteristic of LSTM networks. Figure 6.6 shows basic LSTM structure for RNN.

The repeating model of LSTM differs from that of RNN since it follows a chain system. The LSTM model is depicted in Figure 6.10. Each LSTM node is connected and receives an input and produces an output. One LSTM's internal circuit is illustrated. Vector addition and multiplication are indicated by the circular objects inside LSTM. The trained neural network layers are shown by the blue squares. The top horizontal line connects all of the nodes and frequently performs linear transformations; it also contains gates for adding and removing data from the LSTM state. The sigmoid neural network layer is used to create these gates. Sigmoid outputs either 0 or 1, with 0 indicating "stopping the path" and 1 indicating "allow everything" [14]. Input, output, and forget are the three gates of the LSTM. For each number in the cell state Ct-1, the forget gate outputs a number between 0 and 1, as determined by the sigmoid layer, and decides to discard some data that is not necessary. One indicates "keep the data", whereas zero "throw it away". The input gate determines whether fresh data should be stored in the cell state. The tanh layer generates a new candidate value (ct), which is then added to the state. Then, input xt and Ct are updated to the "state". The old cell state, Ct-1 updated to the new cell state Ct. Then, the product of new cell state and the old cell state and updated. The sigmoid layer determines which elements of the cell state should be output [15].

6.4.1 LSTM Issues

Leaving aside the good elements of LSTM, it also has drawbacks, and it requires a lot of time and memory to train, which it frequently tends to be over-fitted, causing the classification to be somewhat erroneous, and which it impacts the model with significant mistakes, lowering the prediction efficiency. Dropout is more difficult to handle, as it involves excluding input and recurring links to LSTM modules from activation and weight adjustments when training a network. In order to discover the number of precise weights for a given learning algorithm from input to output data, neural network algorithms are frequently provided with random initialization. This is a common occurrence and a characteristic, however, because LSTMs are sensitive to even small changes. Therefore, random weight initialization is one of the issues. Gated recurrent unit (GRU) is similar to LSTM, which is simple and faster and can handle issues like vanishing gradient. GRU has less number of gates than LSTM [16].

6.5   Back Propagation in Neural Networks

The back propagation method is an optimization approach (iterative) for bringing a network from a non-learned state to a fully learnt state. The following is pseudo code for the back propagation in neural networks. Figure 6.7 shows back propagation in neural networks.

Intialialize the weights with small random values
Repeat
    Repeat
        Select desired pattern from the training set
        Fed the pattern to Input layer
        Compute predicted output of the network
        Compare predicted output with target value
            If (predicted value <> target value)
            Then update the weights
            Else
                Accept the value
    Until *all patterns selected from the training set*
Until *total error< criterion*
	Pseudo code for back propagation in neural networks

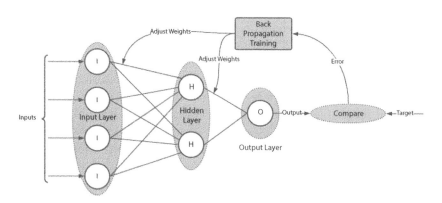

Figure 6.7 Back propagation in neural networks.

Back propagation (Figure 6.11) aims to approach the global minimum condition by optimizing or lowering the neural network's prediction error. This is given by the formula

$$E = \frac{1}{2} \sum_{i=1}^{n} (y_i - d_i)^2 \tag{6.2}$$

where n is the number of network outputs, y_i is the ith output, and d_i is the ith output required. Back-propagation learning is essentially an optimization approach for determining weight coefficients and thresholds for a chosen neural network and training data. The network is expected to be made up of neurons whose behavior is characterized by the following equation:

$$y = S\left(\sum_{i=1}^{N} w_i x_i + b\right) \tag{6.3}$$

The output of the nonlinear function [shown in Equation (6.8)] is provided as follows in the preceding equation S:

$$S(\varphi) = \left(\frac{1}{1 + e^{-\gamma\varphi}}\right) \tag{6.4}$$

where denotes the slope of the curve, and coordinates are expected to be in the range of 0 to 1.

The steps of the back propagation algorithm are as follows:

Step 1: All of the network's weights are initialized at random within a predetermined range, like <−0.2, 0.2>

Step 2: In the input layer of the network, a pattern from the training set is chosen. Following that, Equations (6.6) and (6.7) are used to compute in following hidden layers of matching nodes.

Step 3: The output of the network is compared to the target in this stage, and the error for the output is calculated using the equation:

$$\delta_i^{output} = \left(d_i - y_i^{output}\right) y_i^{output} \gamma \left(1 - y_i^{output}\right) \tag{6.5}$$

where "output" refers to the output layer, while "i" refers to the index.

Step 4: The following equations are used to calculate back-propagation of an error and weight adjustment in this phase. The values are calculated for each of the layer's neurons, where "h" is hidden layer and ij are indexes,

$$\Delta W_{ij}^l(t) = \eta \delta_i^l(t) Y_j^{l-1}(t) + \alpha \Delta W_{ij}^l(t-1) \qquad (6.6)$$

$$\Delta b_i^l(t) = \eta \delta_i^l(t) + \alpha \Delta b_{ij}^l(t-1) \qquad (6.7)$$

$$\delta_i^{h-1} = Y_i^{h-1}(1 - Y_i^{h-1}) \sum_{k=1}^{n} W_{ki}^h \delta_k^h \qquad (6.8)$$

An error determined after the final hidden layer is back propagated to the immediate layer behind it. To modify the weights, use the following equations:

$$W_{ij}^l(t+1) = W_{ij}^l(t) + \Delta W_{ij}^l(t) \qquad (6.9)$$

$$b_i^l(t+1) = b_i^i(t) + \Delta b_i^l(t) \qquad (6.10)$$

The above step is applied for each layers of the network.

Step 5: For the next pattern from the training set, repeat steps (2) through (4). This method is performed in a similar manner for all of the patterns.

Step 6: When the neural network forecast value of the last computation is smaller than the target value, the procedure is complete [17].

6.6   Literature Survey on Neural Networks in Steganography

The following section contains a comprehensive literature review on the use of ANNs in steganography. On the topic of steganography, we investigated the use of RNNs, CNNs, multilayer neural networks, MLP, and LSTM-based networks [18, 19].

6.6.1   TS-RNN: Text Steganalysis Based on Recurrent Neural Networks

A text steganalysis-based method uses TSteg data set was used to train the RNN model, which included Chinese and English texts. By altering the amount of bits per word in both ways, the steganographic sequence may be reduced at a different rate. Three RNN hidden layers and 300 LSTM are utilized in this technique, with a detection threshold of 0.5. The neurons employ the tanh activation function, which is a non-linear activation function. The learning rates are set to 0.001 with a batch size of 128. The authors compared the algorithm to three other methods: methods. Precision, recall, F1-score, and accuracy are some of the classification models used to assess the model's capabilities. To avoid the radiant descent issue, the RNN method employs LSTM in the hidden layers. According to the authors, the detection value increases as the rate of embedding increases [20].

6.6.2   Generative Text Steganography Based on LSTM Network and Attention Mechanism with Keywords

Huixian Kang *et al.* [36] Proposed a steganography technique based on LSTM and attention mechanism. The steganalysis resistance is provided via an LSTM-based steganographic technique of producing steganographic

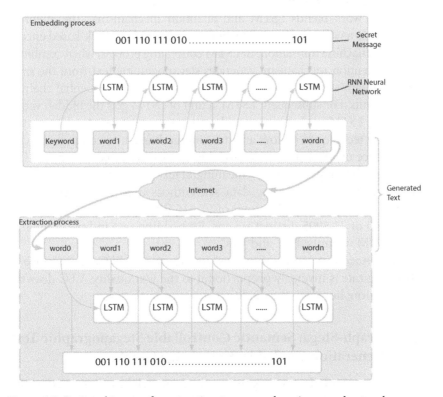

Figure 6.8 Basic architecture for generative steganography using neural networks—embedding and extracting of message based on LSTM networks.

texts and embedding the secret on them. Because the text it generates is semantically qualified and raises no suspicions. By integrating a large database of words for the goal of training the network, LSTM networks are used to produce automatic text creation for steganography (Figure 6.8). Several researches have shown that this is an excellent topic for the future [21].

Embedding process: Using either FLC (fixed length coding) or VLC (variable length coding), the embedding procedure converts the message words into a quantity, integer d (d ≥ 0). The candidate words are chosen from the corpus and sorted by probability frequency in decreasing order. The picked (d + 1) word is presumed to be a created word, and the process continues until the last number is reached. LSTM processes words based on feedback mechanisms and outputs a meaningful stego text at the conclusion of the process. The extraction takes place in a reverse manner. Figure 6.8 gives the general idea of steganography using neural network. Figure 6.8 shows basic architecture for generative steganography using neural networks—embedding and extracting of message based on LSTM Networks.

Attention mechanism: For generating semantically accurate stego sentences, this work blends LSTM and attention mechanisms. The attention mechanism is a well-known NLP technique for neural network-based encoder-decoder machine translation. In LSTM concealing process, when combined with the attention mechanism, generates steganographic text from the message bits stream and key words. LSTM always employs a sequential chain of repeating units. For subsequent LSTM, a unit of LSTM gets the hidden vector from earlier LSTM, a word vector, and creates a new word vector. During this process, the technique employs an attention mechanism to compute the correct sequence of words from a keyword list, as well as a hidden vector. This procedure will be repeated until a meaningful text has been created [21].

Data sets: For the training data set, authors used two types of data: "ZhiHu", a paraphrase with a total of 97,616 different phrases, and essays with a total of 23,8905 distinct tokens. Embedding rate in bpw compared to two LSTM variants: FLC and VLC.

Result: According to the findings, in the case of FLC, an increase in embedding rate is inversely proportional to the text quality. VLC does the same function; however, the quality is superior in this case.

6.6.3   Graph-Stega: Semantic Controllable Steganographic Text Generation Guided by Knowledge Graph

The authors provided a text steganography approach based on a text generating algorithm, with the usage of a knowledge graph to guide the process.

Google released the knowledge graph in 2012. It is the technique of extracting similar semantic terms based on their frequency of occurrence. The main concept is to make use of knowledge graphs. In the knowledge graph, every path is a sub-graph. The secret text is represented by these sub-graphs, which are then coded [22].

Embedding: The embedding process begins with the creation of a knowledge graph, which is then utilized to extract a mini-Graph based on the secret message input. The secret bits are hidden based on the path chosen, and after data hiding, we get a full graph. The graph is then used to generate the stego text.

For sub-graph embedding, RNN with GRU is employed. RNN with LSTM is used to generate sentences.

Data sets: The authors of the algorithm utilized an automotive review data set to train the system, and an appropriate knowledge graph was created. The levels of semantic nodes are recorded as triplets in the knowledge graph. Entity, attribute, and sentiment are the three. The graph is made up of 36,373 triplets and 100,000 natural phrases in total. The embedding rates of the model with the data sets are assessed using a few common metrics, including BLEU, METEOR, CIDEr, and ROUGH-L.

Result: To protect against steganalysis, the model contains certain anti-detection capabilities. The semantic significance of the created texts exhibits a very thin marginal improvement with various embedding rates, according to the generated findings and there is scope for research.

6.6.4   RITS: Real-Time Interactive Text Steganography Based on Automatic Dialogue Model

RITS, proposed by Yan *et al.*, a RNN version of text steganography based on reinforcement learning, is proposed in this work. Based on an input sentence, a real-time interactive text generates semantically, consistent and syntactically accurate word sequences. While generating the semantically right phrase, the data hiding procedure was merged. This is accomplished by choosing the most semantically correct word.

Data hiding: Text feature extraction is aided by the use of a RNN, which is a power characteristic. The model was trained using reinforcement learning to guarantee that the generated text is reliable. The problem of RNN's "gradient disappear" was solved using RNN and the LSTM method, because RNN cannot handle long texts or words on its own. Bidirectional RNN, i.e., forward and backward propagation strategies to minimize the loss function value, is used for model learning [23, 24].

The message's embedding bits, as well as any potential word space data, are given to the RNN module. RNN selects words from the input layer that are semantically accurate, and as the model learns, it produces a meaningful phrase including the hidden message bits.

Data sets: There are 5,808 conversations in the training sample data. Bidirectional RNN with 256 neurons in the hidden layer and 128 neurons in the RNN sentence generation layer. For clip gradients learning rate greater than 1.0, the learning rate in the model is set to 0.1. The value of the Mini Batch size is 16.

Results: Authors have tested and assessed the model in terms of the time it takes to create a particular volume of words in real time. The following are the different sets having numbers of words generated against the time taken: (4 words, 21.946 ms), (6 words, 30.336 ms), (8 words, 38.122 ms), and (14 words, 67.215 ms). The study provides minimal information on how long it takes to produce a set of words, but the test data regarding the volume of secret embedded is unclear [25, 26].

6.6.5   Steganalysis and Payload Estimation of Embedding in Pixel Differences Using Neural Networks

PVD (Pixel Differencing Method) is proposed for steganalysis. The difference between the cover image and the stego image is determined using the histogram approach in this proposal. Because the approach employs a multilayer neural network with five unique MLP, the system is capable of detecting many layers of embedding. The network's voting algorithm receives input images and distinguishes them as cover or stego pictures [27, 28].

6.6.6   Reversible Data Hiding Using Multilayer Perceptron–Based Pixel Prediction

Author proposed a novel reversible data concealing, using a MLP neural network. The suggested approach employed the stego image to extract both the cover picture and the message. Because the data bits are obscured in the extended prediction error, pixel value prediction was utilized [29, 30]. Using its eight neighbors, the neural network is trained to predict pixel values. According to the authors, they tested the algorithm by altering the number of hidden layers and neurons. An adaptive method was employed to embed the message in the image.

6.6.7 Neural Network–Based Steganography Algorithm for Still Images

For data concealing, a MLP with three layers and two input units, one unit in the hidden layer, and one output unit is used. Message bits, cover image, and selected cover image bits are first taken for the purpose of conceal-ment. The message bits and k image bits are serially entered one bit at a time for the training module. It is decided on the number of input neurons, hidden neurons, and output neurons. Then, begin inputting the secret bits into the trained network, and the output created is then encoded in the image's LSB [30, 31].

6.7   Optimization Algorithms in Neural Networks

Optimization algorithms modify the properties of neural networks, such as weights and learning rates, to decrease losses. The word "loss" in neural networks refers to how well our model is doing at any given time. It is pos-sible that the performance may fall short of expectations or that it will meet them. The loss value is used to train our network. The main aim is to keep the loss to a bare minimum so that the model's performance improves. When the loss is increased, the model tends to provide undesirable results [32].

Choosing an appropriate weight value is part of the process of lowering the loss value. In the early phases of network learning, selecting the proper value is quite challenging. As a result, a random weight value is always initialized, and the weights are adjusted depending on trial and error on the loss function. This procedure will continue until a consistent weight is achieved. Modifying the weights and learning rates is critical for low-ering the loss value, but how can this be done? The optimizers or proce-dures used to optimize the loss values are referred to as such. We employ a number of different optimizers, namely, GD, Stochastic Gradient Descent (SGD), Mini Batch SGD, SGD with momentum, and Adaptive Gradient (AdaGrad) [33].

6.7.1   Gradient Descent

It is an optimization technique that can train a model with an underlying convex function by iteratively reducing a cost function to its local mini-mum or minimum cost. For back propagation, this approach may be used

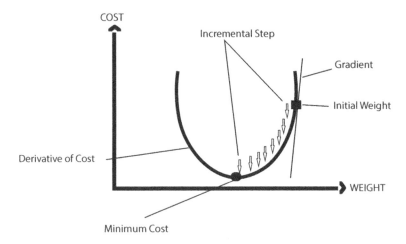

Figure 6.9 Illustration of gradient descent optimization technique in neural network.

on neural models such as RNN, CNN, and others [34]. Figure 6.9 projects illustration of GD optimization technique in neural network.

As illustrated in Figure 6.9, the minimum cost is the point at the bottom of the curve, which is the end destination, after calculating weights and learning rates iteratively. The following is the loss function for GD method. Where "ŷ" is predicted value and "y" is actual value, and $i=1$ to n, indicates that the GD takes all samples at once.

$$loss_{GD} = \sum_{i=1}^{n}(y - \hat{y})^2 \tag{6.11}$$

The learning rate is a measure of how fast or slow the GD algorithm moves in the direction of the lowest cost or local minima; we can visualize how quickly or slowly the algorithm moves in the direction of optimal weights. For this, the learning rate is set to a reasonable number that is neither too high nor too low. Otherwise, it may fail to achieve local minimum and instead alternate between radiant descents. If the learning value is reduced, then it slowly reaches the goal. However, it takes an excessive amount of time [35].

6.7.1.1   GD Issues

When compared to other approaches, the GD optimizer is the simplest and can simply devise. However, if the data sets are too large, reaching local minima might take a long time, and the memory requirements for this approach are rather high. The quantity of data points that GD requires is all, which implies that if we have lakhs of data points to feed, the amount of computation and resources required is tremendous. Non-differential loss functions are difficult to produce since this function is reliant on derivatives. Although this technique is defined as a convex function, non-convex functions suffer. It can get trapped in local minima at times, and the only way to pull it out is to restart it arbitrarily [36].

6.7.2   Stochastic Gradient Descent

SGD is a GD add-on that has helped to solve a few GD problems. Because the GD technique requires a large amount of buffer space to load all of the data points at the same time in order to compute the loss function differentiation, it demands a large amount of buffer space. SGD is a basic algorithm that takes a single data point and applies it to an instance. SGD requires several oscillations to attain convergence compared to GD. However, it just takes a short amount of time to complete one step. GD, on the other hand, takes a long time [37]. Figure 6.10 shows differential process of (a) SGD and (b) GD methods.

In terms of convergence to local minima, Figure 6.10 depicts the differences between two techniques: (a) SGD and (b) GD. As in (b), it shows a straight line to the local minimum with no variation. SGD, on the other hand, has zigzag lines that lead to local minima and reaches faster than GD.

The following is the loss function for GD method. Where "ŷ" is predicted value and "y" is actual value, since SGD takes one data point at a time, therefore no summation required.

$$loss_{SGD} = (y - \hat{y})^2 \tag{6.12}$$

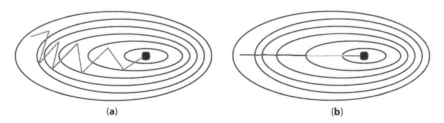

(a)   (b)

Figure 6.10 Differential process of (a) stochastic gradient descent and (b) gradient descent methods.

The zigzag movement is known as "noise". This, of course, may be reduced by employing a technique known as "Stochastic Gradient Descent with Momentum". In SGD, the gradient is calculated and the weights are adjusted one by one for each training data set. The whole set of training data is uploaded at once, and the gradient is computed in GD [38, 39].

6.7.2.1   SGD Issues

Regular updates in the SGD technique for attaining local minima causes zigzagging and noisy movement, and it can take a long period at times. For one data point, frequent weight change consumes a lot of computing resources. Only one training sample is processed at a time, and the system is unable to handle numerous samples at the same time [40].

6.7.3   SGD with Momentum

With the aid of the approach "Stochastic Gradient Descent with Momentum", the disadvantage in SGD with noises may be smoothed out. The main concept is to utilize a technique termed "exponential weight average" to reduce noise to some extent. This method lowers the variances on the way to convergence. The smoothed path in SGD with momentum is shown in Figure 6.11 as contour graph [41]. Figure 6.11 shows convergence techniques in SGD with momentum.

This technique converges more quickly than GD. The main drawback to this technique is the "γ" value computation for each update. On the plus side, the "γ" symbolizes momentum, which helps to decrease fluctuations

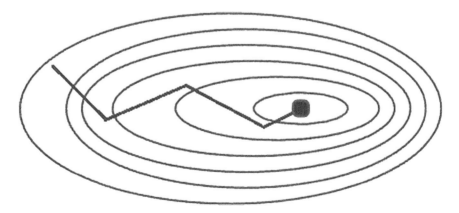

Figure 6.11 Convergence techniques in SGD with momentum.

produced by the GD approach. The "γ" value is generally set to a very low number, such as 0.9 or something close. The "γ" is calculated using all of the previous adjustments and produces a weight that is utilized in the current updates. As a result, the convergence process accelerates [42].

6.7.4   Mini Batch SGD

It is a version of the GD algorithm that calculates the error for each sample in a given batch. This is to address the issue of GD, which processes the entire population at once in a given time and necessitates a large amount of computer resources to process a large number of samples at once. The Mini Batch technique is a better way to tackle the problem. Instead of storing all of the data in one place, it stores it in batches of "k" samples (as shown in the following equation), requiring less resources and requiring fewer weight modifications [43].

$$loss_{MiniBatchSGD} = \sum_{i=1}^{k}(y - \hat{y})^2 \tag{6.13}$$

Because of the lower update frequency, the error gradient is more stable. These characteristics have an impact on the model, resulting in more consistent convergence.

6.7.4.1   Mini Batch SGD Issues

Because there are fewer updates, a consistent error gradient may result in early convergence. Memory issues may develop as the batch size grows.

6.7.5   Adaptive Gradient Algorithm

AdaGrad is a distributed adaptive gradient method that has shown impressive outcomes on sizable machine learning problems such as training deep neural networks. AdaGrad is a popular optimization approach for fine-tuning learning rates while doing gradient optimization. AdaGrad is designed for situations of greater complexity, and it automatically changes weights for each dimension. Additional features that the AdaGrad addresses are the, difficulties, such as sparse gradients, forward and backward splitting, and duel averaging. The optimizers mentioned before are widely utilized in the implementation of neural network issues including ANN, CNN, and RNN. To decrease the loss function with regard to weights, techniques like as GD, SGD, and Mini Batch SGD are employed [44].

Updating function used in as follows:

$$w_{new} = w_{old} - \eta \frac{\delta L}{\delta w_{old}},$$

and can be changed to

$$w_t = w_{t-1} - \eta \frac{\delta L}{\delta w_{t-1}},$$

where t, is current time, and $t - 1$ is previous time.

In the prior approaches, all neurons and hidden layers had the same learning rates. The core principle of AdaGrad is that, for each neuron, hidden layer, and iteration, various learning rates are employed. This is done in order to tackle the problem of DENSE and SPARSE features in neural networks. SPARSE features have primarily zeroes and few nonzero, but DENSE features always function with nonzero values. As a result, there is no way to establish a similar learning rate for both characteristics, which necessitates distinct learning rates.

Then, AdaGrad equation becomes

$$w_t = w_{t-1} - {}_t^1\eta \frac{\delta L}{\delta_{t-1}},$$

where ${}_t^1\eta$ specifies learning rate at each iteration

The ${}_t^1\eta$ value is given by

$${}_t^1\eta = \frac{\delta}{\sqrt{\alpha_t + \in}},$$

where $\in$ is a positive integer

Where α_t is

$$\alpha_t = \Sigma_{i=1}^t \left(\frac{\delta L}{\delta w_i} \right)^2 \tag{6.14}$$

Let us take a closer look at the equations. Squaring α_t produces a large number, which when substituted into the $\frac{1}{t}\eta$ equation yields a very tiny number, $\frac{1}{t}\eta$ drops as α_t grows as the iteration progresses. The learning rate is higher in the beginning phases. The weights (w_t) decline slowly as the $\frac{1}{t}\eta$ decreases, and then it converges well [45].

6.8   Conclusion

As a result, the learning rate in AdaGrad changes as the process progresses in terms of features, layers, and iterations. Because we employ DENSE and SPARSE features in AdaGrad, it necessitates various weights and learning rates in order to effectively reach global minima. Because the derivative is squared, α_t can occasionally reach a very large value. It becomes too high as the repetition progresses. We utilize the RMSprop technique to address this problem. Another disadvantage of GD is that it requires all data sets to be processed at the same time, whereas SGD just requires one at a time. SGD makes a lot of noise while reaching local minima. The method SGD with momentum is used to flatten the noise. Mini Batch SGD is a great technique since it accepts a batch of data sets at a time, as opposed to GD and SGD; however, it has an early convergence problem that can be solved by using the AdaGrad method. In the last part, the number of publications on steganography methods based on neural networks published in the past 5 years was examined. The most papers were published by CNN tops the table, then followed by RNN, deep neural networks, generative adversarial networks, and others. Another finding of the study revealed that image-related publishing is more common than text or other forms of steganography.

References

1. Biswal, A.K., Singh, D., Pattanayak, B.K., Samanta, D., Yang, M.-H., "IoT-Based Smart Alert System for Drowsy Driver Detection". *Wirel. Commun. Mob. Comput., vol*, 2021, 21, 2021.
2. Poovendran, R., Sangeetha, M., Saranya, G.S., Vennila, G., "A video steganography using Hamming Technique for image Processing using optimized algorithm," *2020 International Conference on System, Computation, Automation and Networking (ICSCAN)*, pp. 1–5, 2020, doi: 10.1109/ICSCAN49426.2020.9262341.

3. Guha, A., Samanta, D., Banerjee, A., Agarwal, D., "A deep learning model for Information Loss Prevention from multi-page digital documents". *IEEE Access*, 9, 15, 2021.

4. Abdali, N.M. and Hussain, Z.M., "Reference-free Detection of LSB Steganography Using Histogram Analysis," *2020 30th International Telecommunication Networks and Applications Conference (ITNAC)*, pp. 1–7, 2020, doi: 10.1109/ITNAC50341.2020.9315037.

5. Mekala, M.S., Patan, R., Islam, S.K., Samanta, D., Mallah, G.A., Chaudhry, S.A., "DAWM: Cost-Aware Asset Claim Analysis Approach on Big Data Analytic Computation Model for Cloud Data Centre". *Secur. Commun. Netw.*, 24, 2021, 2021.

6. Manohar, N. and Kumar, P.V., "Data Encryption & Decryption Using Steganography," *2020 4th International Conference on Intelligent Computing and Control Systems (ICICCS)*, pp. 697–702, 2020, doi: 10.1109/ICICCS48265.2020.9120935.

7. Samanta, D., Karthikeyan, M.P., Banerjee, A., Inokawa, H., "Tunable graphene nanopatch antenna design for on-chip integrated terahertz detector arrays with potential application in cancer imaging". *Nanomedicine*, 16, 12, 1035–1047, 2021.

8. Tiwari, K. and Gangurde, S.J., "LSB Steganography Using Pixel Locator Sequence with AES," *2021 2nd International Conference on Secure Cyber Computing and Communications (ICSCCC)*, pp. 302–307, 2021, doi: 10.1109/ICSCCC51823.2021.9478162.

9. Pramanik, S., Samanta, D., Bandyopadhyay, S.K., Ghosh, R., "A New Combinational Technique in Image Steganography". *Int. J. Inf. Secur. Priv. (IJISP)*, 15, 3, 48–64, 2021.

10. Lopez-Hernandez, A.A., Martinez-Gonzalez, R.F., Hernandez-Reyes, J.A., Palacios-Luengas, L., Vazquez-Medina, R., "A Steganography Method Using Neural Networks," *IEEE Lat. Am. Trans.*, 18, 03, 495–506, March 2020. doi: 10.1109/TLA.2020.9082720.

11. Samanta, D. *et al.*, "Cipher Block Chaining Support Vector Machine for Secured Decentralized Cloud Enabled Intelligent IoT Architecture". *IEEE Access*, 9, 98013–98025, 2021.

12. Pan, I.-H., Liu, K.-C., Liu, C.-L., "Chi-Square Detection for PVD Steganography," *2020 International Symposium on Computer, Consumer and Control (IS3C)*, pp. 30–33, 2020, doi: 10.1109/IS3C50286.2020.00015.

13. Khamparia, A., Singh, P.K., Rani, P., Samanta, D., Khanna, A., Bhushan, B., "An internet of health things-driven deep learning framework for detection and classification of skin cancer using transfer learning". *T. Emerg. Telecommun. T.*, 32, 7, e3963, 2021.

14. Rathor, M., Sarkar, P., Mishra, V.K., Sengupta, A., "Securing IP Cores in CE Systems using Key-driven Hash-chaining based Steganography," *2020 IEEE 10th International Conference on Consumer Electronics (ICCE-Berlin)*, pp. 1–4, 2020, doi: 10.1109/ICCE-Berlin50680.2020.9352192.

15. Gurunath, R. and Samanta, D., "A novel approach for semantic web application in online education based on steganography". *Int. J. Web-Based Learn. Teach. Technol. (IJWLTT)*, 17, 4, 1–13, 2022.

16. Govindasamy, V., Sharma, A., Thanikaiselvan, V., "Coverless Image Steganography using Haar Integer Wavelet Transform," *2020 Fourth International Conference on Computing Methodologies and Communication (ICCMC)*, pp. 885–890, 2020, doi: 10.1109/ICCMC48092.2020.ICCMC-000164.

17. Gurunath, R., Alahmadi, A.H., Samanta, D., Khan, M.Z., Alahmadi, A., "A Novel Approach for Linguistic Steganography Evaluation Based on Artificial Neural Networks". *IEEE Access*, 9, 120869–120879, 2021.

18. Thakur, A., Gill, G.S., Saxena, S., "Analysis of Image Steganography Performance Check Using Bit Selection," *2020 7th International Conference on Signal Processing and Integrated Networks (SPIN)*, pp. 1–5, 2020, doi: 10.1109/SPIN48934.2020.9071251.

19. Tavares, J.M.R.S., Dutta, P., Dutta, S., Samanta, D., *"Cyber Intelligence and Information Retrieval: Proceedings of CIIR 2021"*, Springer Nature, Springer Berlin, 2021.

20. Varthakavi, S.S., Mohan, P., Gupta, A., Anurag, M., "A Steganographic Analysis using Batch Steganography," *2020 IEEE International Conference for Innovation in Technology (INOCON)*, pp. 1–5, 2020, doi: 10.1109/INOCON50539.2020.9298191.

21. Raghavendra Rao, A. and Samanta, D., "A Real-Time Approach with Deep Learning for Pandemic Management", in: *Healthcare Informatics for Fighting COVID-19 and Future Epidemics*, pp. 113–139, Springer Berlin, 2022.

22. Podder, S.K. and Samanta, D., "Green Computing Practice in ICT-Based Methods: Innovation in Web-Based Learning and Teaching Technologies". *Int. J. Web-Based Learn. Teach. Technol. (IJWLTT)*, 17, 4, 1–18, 2022.

23. Samanta, D., Karthikeyan, M.P., Agarwal, D., Biswas, A., Acharyya, A., Banerjee, A., "Trends in Terahertz Biomedical Applications", in: *Generation, Detection and Processing of Terahertz Signals*, pp. 285–299, 2022.

24. Althar, R.R., Samanta, D., Konar, D., Bhattacharyya, S., *Software Source Code: Statistical Modeling*, Walter de Gruyter GmbH & Co KG, Springer Berlin, 2021.

25. Wu, Y., Zhuang, S., Sun, Q., "A Steganography Algorithm Based on GM Model of optimized Parameters," *2020 International Conference on Computer Engineering and Application (ICCEA)*, pp. 384–387, 2020, doi: 10.1109/ICCEA50009.2020.00089.

26. Khadri, S.K.A., Samanta, D., Paul, M., "Message communication using Phase Shifting Method (PSM)", *Int. J. Adv. Res. Comp. Sci.* 4, 3, 2013.

27. Ghosh, G., Samanta, D., Paul, M., "Approach of message communication based on twisty 'Zig-Zag'", in: *2016 International Conference on Emerging Technological Trends (ICETT)*, pp. 1–5, 2016.

28. Singh, R.K., Begum, T., Borah, L., Samanta, D., "Text encryption: character jumbling", in: *2017 International Conference on Inventive Systems and Control (ICISC)*, pp. 1–3, 2017.

29. Ghosh, G., Samanta, D., Paul, M., Janghel, N.K., "Hiding based message communication techniques depends on divide and conquer approach", in: *2017 International Conference on Computing Methodologies and Communication (ICCMC)*, pp. 123–128, 2017.

30. Praveen, B., Umarani, N., Anand, T., Samanta, D., "Cardinal digital image data fortification expending steganography". *Int. J. Recent Technol. Eng.*, 8, 3, 163–172, 2019.

31. Guha, A., Samanta, D., Pramanik, S., Dutta, S., "Concept of Indexing and Concepts associated with Journal Publishing", in: *Interdisciplinary Research in Technology and Management: Proceedings of the International Conference on Interdisciplinary Research in Technology and Management (IRTM, 2021)*, 26–28 February, 2021Kolkata, India, p. 17, 2021.

32. Pramanik, S., Samanta, D., Dutta, S., Ghosh, R., Ghonge, M., Pandey, D., "Steganography using Improved LSB Approach and Asymmetric Cryptography," *2020 IEEE International Conference on Advent Trends in Multidisciplinary Research and Innovation (ICATMRI)*, pp. 1–5, 2020, doi: 10.1109/ICATMRI51801.2020.9398408.

33. Gurunath, R., Samanta, D., Dutta, S., Kureethara, J.V., "Essentials of Abstracting and Indexing for Research Paper Writing", in: *Interdisciplinary Research in Technology and Management*, pp. 10–16, CRC Press, ICOIACT, Indonesia, 2021.

34. Indrayani, R., "Modified LSB on Audio Steganography using WAV Format," *2020 3rd International Conference on Information and Communications Technology (ICOIACT)*, pp. 466–470, 2020, doi: 10.1109/ICOIACT50329.2020.9332132.

35. Bhattacharya, A. *et al.*, "Predictive Analysis of the Recovery Rate from Coronavirus (COVID-19)", in: *Cyber Intelligence and Information Retrieval*, pp. 309–320, Springer Berlin, 33-ICOIACT, Indonesia, 2022.

36. Naidu, D., Ananda Kumar, K.S., Jadav, S.L., Sinchana, M.N., "Multilayer Security in Protecting and Hiding Multimedia Data using Cryptography and Steganography Techniques". *2019 4th IEEE Int. Conf. Recent Trends Electron. Information Commun. Technol. RTEICT 2019 – Proc*, pp. 1360–1364, 2019.

37. Samanta, D., Dutta, S., Galety, M.G., Pramanik, S., "A Novel Approach for Web Mining Taxonomy for High-Performance Computing", in: *Cyber Intelligence and Information Retrieval*, pp. 425–432, Springer Berlin, 2022.

38. Ramya, G., Janarthanan, P.P., Mohanapriya, D., "Steganography based data hiding for security applications", in: *Proc. IEEE Int. Conf. Intell. Comput. Commun. Smart World I2C2SW 2018*, pp. 131–135, 2018.

39. Eapen, N.G., Rao, A.R., Samanta, D., Robert, N.R., Krishnamoorthy, R., Lokesh, G.H., "Security Aspects for Mutation Testing in Mobile Applications",

in: *Cyber Intelligence and Information Retrieval*, pp. 17–27, Springer Berlin, 2022.

40. Hegde, D.S., Samanta, D., Dutta, S., "Classification Framework for Fraud Detection Using Hidden Markov Model", in: *Cyber Intelligence and Information Retrieval*, pp. 29–36, Springer Berlin, 2022.

41. Hossain, M.A., Samanta, D., Sanyal, G., "Statistical approach for extraction of panic expression", in: *2012 Fourth International Conference on Computational Intelligence and Communication Networks*, pp. 420–424, 2012.

42. Khadri, S.K.A., Samanta, D., Paul, M., "Novel Approach for Message Security". *Int. J. Inf. Sci. Intell. Syst. (IJISIS)*, 3, 1, 47–52, 2014.

43. Khadri, S.K.A., Samanta, D., Paul, M., "Message Encryption Using Text Inversion plus N Count: In Cryptology". *Int. J. Inf. Sci. Intell. Syst. (IJISIS)*, 3, 2, 71–74, 2014.

44. Khadri, S.K.A., Samanta, D., Paul, M., "Approach of message communication using Fibonacci series: in cryptology". *Lect. Notes Inf. Theory*, 2, 2, 4, 2014.

45. Mukherjee, M. and Samanta, D., "Fibonacci Based Text Hiding Using Image Cryptography". *Lecture Notes on Information Theory*, 2, 2, 172–176, 2014.

7

Privacy Preserving Mechanism by Application of Constrained Nonlinear Optimization Methods in Cyber-Physical System

Manas Kumar Yogi[1]* and A.S.N. Chakravarthy[2]

[1]Computer Science and Engineering Department, Pragati Engineering College (Autonomous), Surampalem, A.P., India
[2]Department of Computer Science & Engineering, JNTUK-University College of Engineering, Vizainagaram, A.P., India

---

Abstract

In the future, cyber-physical systems (CPSs) will be used in most of real time scenarios. To make the world smart, the application of such systems is inevitable. However, with increasing use of such systems, privacy has also to be increased. If privacy aspect is compromised, then the users will not be easily habituated to such systems. CPSs involve multiple heterogeneous sensor data sources, so introducing considerable level of privacy remains an ever growing challenge for the system designers. In this chapter, we are going to present the applicability of exact penalty function and its benefits to increase the privacy level of CPSs. We will compare this with other techniques of privacy preservation in CPSs and throw light on the future enhancements of our proposed privacy framework.

Keywords: Cyber-physical system, privacy, penalty, barrier, security

7.1 Introduction

Cyber-physical systems (CPSs) are becoming an increasingly important component of modern life. One of the most well-known CPS operations,

---

**Corresponding author*: manas.yogi@gmail.com

Sabyasachi Pramanik, Debabrata Samanta, M. Vinay and Abhijit Guha (eds.) Cyber Security and Network Security, (157–168) © 2022 Scrivener Publishing LLC

Table 7.1 Popular privacy preservation schemes pertaining to CPS.

Sl. no.	Approach	Strength	Limitations
1	Cryptographic methods	High level of integrity, safe, trustworthy, and computations are possible on encrypted datasets	Increase in communication complexity; scalability is an issue
2	Data mining methods	High level of privacy and efficiency	Linking attacks cannot be faced
3	Statistical methods	High level of privacy, improvement in data analytics due to data projection	Degradation in data utility due to disturbance in data, difficulty in balancing between privacy and data correction
4	Authentication-based models	Third party authentication is possible; degree of data integrity can be controlled without much effort	Poor system reliability, processing overhead, and data storage cost is also high
5	Blockchain-based methods	No single point of failure, high degree of data transparency and traceability, and high level of user confidentiality	High operation and customization costs, blockchain literacy, adaptability challenges, and scalability challenges
6	Machine learning and deep learning–based methods	Easy application of randomization techniques, learns from large datasets, and data analytics becomes easy	Cost of parameter setting becomes high, data utility becomes costly, and overhead in computational resources

which span smart homes, smart transportation systems, smart energy systems, and smart urban communities, is that data obtained from individuals or elements is an essential part of the dynamic and control buried inside the systems' operation [1]. The advancement in CPSs opens a rising field of multi-disciplinary participation, connecting software engineering and control hypothesis with a few designing regions, innate sciences, and medication [2]. Progressively, CPSs are further developing execution, usefulness, and energy productivity in the control of physical cycles. Specialists and professionals are planning and prototyping independent vehicles with more significant levels of robotization and network. Also, the medical care area is creating novel clinical applications to all the more likely help and treats patients, including independent implantable gadgets and framework structures for checking patients in clinics or at home. Other important CPS applications remember mechanical control systems for assembling and interaction plants, mechanical technology, control systems in basic frameworks offering fundamental types of assistance to networks (e.g., shrewd lattices, water, and wastewater systems), and independent military safeguard rockets, among others [3]. Thinking about the promising turns of events and the basic utilizations of CPSs, government organizations and mechanical associations respect the exploration endeavors in CPSs as a need [4]. Table 7.1 enumerates the different approaches for privacy preservation in CPS and brings out their relative strengths and limitations. Table 7.1 shows popular privacy preservation schemes pertaining to CPS.

7.2 Problem Formulation

In this part of our chapter, we will formulate a privacy problem as a constrained nonlinear optimization problem where privacy loss has to be minimized.

In our objective of minimizing the privacy loss, sources emitting private data might be required to remove PII from the dataset. Let x_j be the amount of PII (Personally Identifiable Information) to be removed at source j. Our proposed mechanism tries to minimize the privacy loss:

$$\text{Minimize} \sum_{i=1}^{n} fj(xj) \tag{7.1}$$

Subject to:

$$\sum_{j=1}^{n} aijxj \geq b_i (i = 1, 2, \ldots, m)$$

$$0 \leq x_j \leq u_j (j = 1, 2, \ldots, n),$$

where

$f_j (x_j)$ = Cost of removing x j amount of PII at source j,

b_i = Minimum desired improvement in privacy loss at point i in the CPS,

a_{ij} = Quality of Privacy loss, at point i in the system, caused by removing PII at source j,

u_j = Maximum degree of PII that can be removed at source j.

7.3   Proposed Mechanism

We have observed that the penalty function is playing a crucial role in determining multiple constrained optimization issues in the factory design domains. It is conventionally developed to work out nonlinear functions by integrating some degree of penalty factor or barrier factors with respect to the limitations applied related to the objective function. Then, using unconstrained or bounded constrained optimization mechanisms or sequential quadratic programming (SQP) techniques, it can be optimized. Regardless of the technique used, the penalty function is always dependent on a small parameter. As 0, the punishment function's minimizer, such as a barrier function or a quadratic penalty function, merges with the original problem's minimizer. When applying an exact penalty function like the l1 penalty function, the minimizer of the related penalty problem must be a minimizer of the original problem when. The privacy loss in our situation will be indicated by ε, which must be reduced using the precise penalty function.

In principle, our problem of minimizing the privacy loss can be expressed as

$$\text{Minimize } f(x^\varepsilon) \text{ subject to } x \leq u_j \text{ and } x > b_j \qquad (7.2)$$

Assume that P(x) denotes a penalty for being infeasible, given by

$$P(x) = + \infty \text{ if x is infeasible (that is, } x > u_j \text{ or } x > b_j),$$
$$= 0 \text{ if x is feasible (that is, } b_j \leq x \leq u_j). \qquad (7.3)$$

Then, our constrained optimization problem can be rehashed in unconstrained state as

$$\text{Minimize } \{f(x^{\varepsilon}) + P(x)\} \tag{7.4}$$

Because our objective function with the penalty term is in line with the original objective function for any feasible point and is equal to $+\infty$ for every infeasible point.

Although we are able to represent the privacy loss minimization function in terms of penalties, the implementation of the method is rendered difficult due to presence of $+\infty$. Moreover, even if a large penalty $K > 0$ is used to replace the $+\infty$ penalty, the objective function becomes discontinuous at the boundary of the feasible region.

We can work to overcome this barrier by using a smooth function to approximate the penalty term. Now, if we replace $P(x)$ with $2P(x)$, $3P(x)$, $4P(x)$, or, more generally, $rP(x)$ for $r > 1$, then the penalty increases for each infeasible limit. As the penalty factor r increases, the penalty associated with any single infeasible point increases as well, resulting in a solution to the modified penalty issue.

Minimize $\{f(x^{\varepsilon}) + r P(x)\}$ is driven in spitting distance to the feasible region.

Consider a situation where $r > 1$, the solution to the penalty problem occurs to the left of $f(x^{\varepsilon}) = 1$, where the penalty term is $r(1 - f(x^{\varepsilon}))^2$. In this area, the penalty problem of minimizing

$$\{f(x^{\varepsilon}) + r P(x)\} \text{ reduces to}$$
$$\text{Minimize } \{f(x^{\varepsilon}) + r (1 - f(x^{\varepsilon}))^2\}. \tag{7.5}$$

Setting the first derivative of this objective function to zero gives

$$d(f(x^{\varepsilon})) - 2r(1 - d(f(x^{\varepsilon}))) = 0 \tag{7.6}$$

$$d(f(x^{\varepsilon})) = 2r(1 - d(f(x^{\varepsilon}))) \tag{7.7}$$

Now, applying the barrier methods on (7.7), so that we obtain the absolute values for $f(x^{\varepsilon})$.

We can easily observe that the barrier term $1/(f(x^{\varepsilon}) - b_j)^2$ tends to be infinite as x moves to the boundary of the constraint, where $f(x^{\varepsilon})) = b_j$, if the function originates with an initial feasible point, the minimization function will not let it overpass the boundary, if it passes the boundary, then it becomes infeasible. As value of r becomes huge, the barrier term reduces near the boundary and the terms in (7.7) begin to appear like the penalty function with $P(x) = 0$ when x is feasible and $P(x) = +\infty$ when x is infeasible.

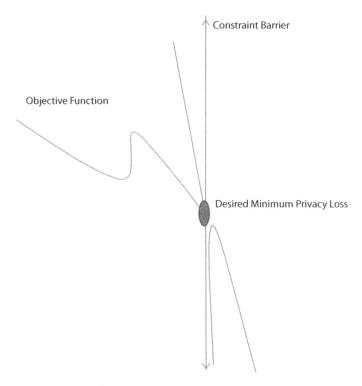

Figure 7.1 Minimization of privacy loss using barrier function.

If α denotes the optimal solution for (7.7), then r ≥ ε solves the original objective function. Figure 7.1 shows minimization of privacy loss using barrier function.

Hence, we can observe that the privacy loss at a node j can be reduced to a great extent by modeling the functionality of a node in CPS as a constrained nonlinear function. We know that a CPS environment is dynamic in state, and its functionality can be modeled with respect to time series equation also [5]. This feature adds value to our proposed mechanism because by applying the exact penalty function and barrier methods our approach fits directly into the CPS ecosystem where we focus on the privacy loss factor.

7.4   Experimental Results

In this part, we will validate our model applicability with an example study of smart health management system where the privacy of the patients is absolute necessary. Quite possibly the most alluring operation of interlacing physical and digital world is medical and health care frame works [6]. This association has a colossal impact in CPSs, and it brings about multiple applications related to generic healthcare, for example, real-time health monitoring, work out schedules, far off health monitoring, and old care [7]. Another potential application of this association is treatment medication and from places remote in nature. In the same sense, health-related record storage using enormous data and implementing the concerned realizations of data analytic reviews for improved diagnosing of illness at initial stage is also being worked on phase. We have observed during our study that, in CPSs related to healthcare, technologies like ultra-narrow band (UNB), 4G long-term evolution (LTE), low and power wide area are used to carry out communication [8]. The majority of these popular and reliable standards send real-time health data with the shortest possible delay. Because they are directly linked to a user's personal life, the inherent health records have data that contains special arrangements for real-time or e-health checked data, and these arrangements should be secured with a certain degree of privacy control. Consider, for example, a diagnosis of a specific illness, the expiration date of health insurance, a specific level of glucose in the body, the date of a doctor's appointment, and so on. If an intruder gains access to sensitive data, then it can directly or indirectly have an impact on the patient's life [9]. With the swift expansion of remote gadgets in our day-to-day lives, the way we handle our health-related aspects keeps changing dynamically. Data related to health is being accounted for to databases or medical experts in real-time to monitor client conduct and movement; for example, data of heart rate rest conditions and circulatory strain; walk steps can be shared with insurance companies and hospital authorities [9]. Nonetheless, the divulgence of data which seems unnecessary can lead to extreme concerns of privacy.

During the context of data sharing related to health records, two aspects are considered as primary goal:

1. Utility (handiness of data) and
2. Privacy (divulgence of minimum private data).

Wearable medical gadgets act as prominent sources of real time health data; these gadgets are non-invasive, and autonomous gadgets intended to play out any specific medial capacity, for example, monitoring data related to person's health. The integral indications of patients, for example, blood oxygen level, blood pressure, body fat, heart rate, and state of respiration, are monitored continuously and observed to know about future undesirable ailments. Also, athletes utilize gadgets in speed and heart rate, calories burn in the course of exercise, and the concerned coaches gets a specialized report on them. Now, this data includes specific arrangements, which may give important inference data regarding. Notwithstanding, imagine the person gets in the control of any bandit user, and then, the concerned user may have to experience serious health circumstances.

Figure 7.2 shows (1) the useful information collected from smart wearable devices from the users that are stored in a central database, (2) denotes the data collected from the hospital records are also directed toward the central database, and (3) represents the proposed mechanism that applies exact penalty barrier function to the health records and removes the sensitive PII from the data set so that the query analyst gets only the minimum information which can be used for further processing. We used a cancer patient's data set downloaded from Kaggle, which had 1,000 rows and over 20 features based on which their treatment was undertaken. Figure 7.3 shows sample of the dataset on which we applied our proposed mechanism. Figure 7.3 shows portion of cancer patients' dataset used in our study. Table 7.2 show age ranges of cancer patients based on dataset obtained from Kaggle with the application of exact barrier-penalty function applied at $\varepsilon = 0.11$.

Over few years, the enticing practice of medical clinics embracing electronic method of saving patient sensitive data has increased drastically. This approach is popularly called as e-health technique, which integrates advanced communication mechanisms. This health information includes PII, like blood pressure level, disease pre-existence, and heart rate monitoring on either weekly or monthly, medical symptoms, date of birth.

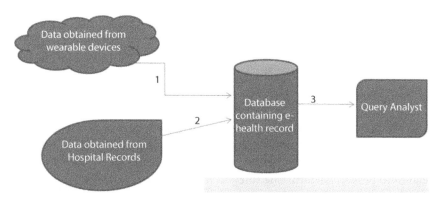

Figure 7.2 Illustrative mechanism for smart health management system.

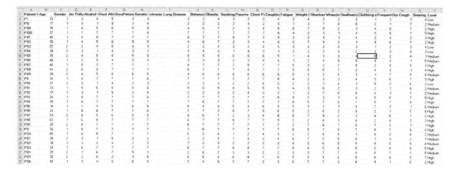

Figure 7.3 Portion of cancer patients' dataset used in our study.

Table 7.2 Age ranges of cancer patients based on dataset obtained from Kaggle with the application of exact barrier-penalty function applied at ε = 0.11.

Age range of patients	Real value of number of cancer patients	Value of number of cancer patients (after application of exact barrier-penalty function mechanism)
15–25	166	94
26–35	333	80
36–45	277	128
46–55	157	14
56–65	62	219
66–75	11	27

This sensitive information is extremely private, which gets stored in datasets and shall not be divulged outsiders else except the doctor and patient.

As we can observe from above, the optimal value at ε = 0.11 brings down the privacy loss too nearly 15% compared to ε = 0.50. Hence, we advocate the privacy engineers to work with ε = 0.11 so as to get more than satisfactory results with exact penalty-barrier function method. Values less than 0.11 produce infeasible results, and also, computational overhead increases. Ordinarily, the sensitive medical records are protected by utilizing cloud computing mechanisms as well as anonymizing operations amid information cleaning and arrangement. In cloud computing approach, attributes like the keys and personal information keys are disguised; subsequently for

Table 7.3 Results of privacy loss for different ε values used in minimization of the objective function.

No. of iterations	ε value	Privacy loss (in %)
10	0.11	14.68
10	0.20	19.88
10	0.30	24.03
10	0.50	31.51

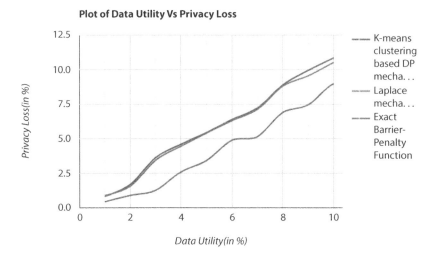

Figure 7.4 Comparative performance between most promising privacy preservation mechanisms in cyber-physical systems.

the purpose of mining, a dataset is constructed which is, in turn, protected in nature. Nevertheless, the masked records are prone to be exposed with respect to few PII when they are investigated and blended in with various other capabilities (Table 7.3). Figure 7.4 shows comparative performance between most promising privacy preservation mechanisms in CPSs.

7.5   Future Scope

Much of the success of our proposed mechanism depends on the technique used to solve the intermediate problems, which, in turn, depends on the complexity of the CPS model. One thing that ought to be done preceding endeavoring to address a nonlinear program utilizing a penalty function technique is proportional to the constraints so the penalty produced by each is about a similar magnitude. This scaling activity is expected to guarantee that no subset of the constraints impacts the pursuit interaction. On the off chance that a few constraints are prevailing, the calculation will control toward an answer that fulfils those constraints to the detriment of looking for the base. In a like way, the underlying worth of the penalty boundary ought to be fixed with the goal that the magnitude of the penalty term is not a lot more modest than the magnitude of objective function. In the event that an irregularity exists, the impact of the objective function could guide the calculation to head toward an unbounded least even within the sight of unsatisfied constraints. Regardless, convergence might be incredibly lethargic.

7.6   Conclusion

Privacy issues are very critical for CPS ecosystem because people are becoming more and more aware regarding how their personal data is being used and monitored in public domain. The very success of CPS functionality depends on minimum amount of privacy loss of the users. As agreed that many CPS designers still do not take privacy as a quality while designing a robust CPS architecture, the rate of success of a CPS will surely depend if the CPS become even more trust worthy. In this direction, an intuitive privacy preservation scheme must be put into practice. The CPSs have to face different privacy attacks to access basic information or records from public or private datasets by the malicious attackers. In this chapter, we have robustly advocated a novel approach to identify the limit of privacy loss for an entity in CPS ecosystem so that the user may feel no threat to their privacy while operating in the concerned environment. We have tried our best to comprehensively cover the crucial dimensions and aspects of differential privacy with preservation of private and other sensitive data during system implementations in major CPSs areas. Penalty and barrier methods are among the most powerful class of algorithms available for tackling general nonlinear advancement issues. This statement is supported by the way that these techniques will converge to something like a nearby least as a rule, regardless of the convexity characteristics of the objective function and constraints. Our proposed approach will reduce the loss of privacy to a substantial degree and will help the privacy mechanism to hide sensitive details of a user in the CPS ecosystem.

References

1. Jia, R., Dong, R., Sastry, S.S., Sapnos, C.J., "Privacy-enhanced architecture for occupancy-based hvac control, in: *ACM/IEEE 8th International Conference on Cyber-Physical Systems (ICCPS)*, pp. 177–186, 2017.

2. Ghayyur, S., Chen, Y., Yus, R., Machanavajjhala, A., Hay, M., Miklau, G., Mehrotra, S., "Iot-detective: Analyzingiot data under differential privacy,", in: *Proceedings of International Conference on Management of Data. ACM*, pp. 1725–1728, 2018.

3. Lee, A., "Guidelines for smart grid cyber-security,". *Tech. Rep.*, 1, 2, 2010.

4. Kreutzmann, H., Vollmer, S., Tekampe, N., Abromeit, A., *"Protection profile for the gateway of a smart metering system,"*, German Federal Office for Information Security, Transactions on Emerging Telecommunications Technologies, John Wiley & Sons, Inc., 26, 5, 876–891, 2011.

5. Jawurek, M., Kerschbaum, F., Danezis, G., "Sok: Privacy technologies for smart grids–a survey of options,". *Microsoft Res*, Cambridge, UK, 2012.

6. Desai, S., Alhadad, R., Chilamkurti, N., Mahmood, A., "A survey of privacy preserving schemes in IoE enabled Smart Grid Advanced Metering Infrastructure,". *Cluster Comput.*, 22, 1–27, 2018.

7. Anonymization, Josep Domingo-Ferrer, David Sánchez, and JordiSoria-Comas Synthesis Lectures on Information Security, Privacy, and Trust, January 2016, 8, 1, 1–136, 2020. [online] Available: https://github.com/anonymized.

8. Ye, H., Liu, J., Wang, W., Li, P., Li, J., "Secure and efficient outsourcing differential privacy data release scheme in Cyber–physical system". *Future Gener. Comput. Syst.*, 108, 1314–1323, July 2020.

9. Xu, J., Wei, L., Wu, W., Wang, A., Zhang, Y., Zhou, F., "Privacy-preserving data integrity verification by using lightweight streaming authenticated data structures for healthcare cyber–physical system". *Future Gener. Comput. Syst.*, 108, 1287–1296, July 2020.

8

Application of Integrated Steganography and Image Compressing Techniques for Confidential Information Transmission

Binay Kumar Pandey[1], Digvijay Pandey[2*], Subodh Wairya[2], Gaurav Agarwal[3],
Pankaj Dadeech[4], Sanwta Ram Dogiwal[5] and Sabyasachi Pramanik[6]

[1]Department of Information Technology, College of Technology, G B Pant University
of Agriculture and Technology Pantnagar, Uttrakhand, India
[2]Department of Electronics Engineering, Institute of Engineering and Technology,
Dr. A.P.J. Abdul Kalam Technical University, Lucknow, India
[3]Department of Computer Science and Engineering, Invertis University, Bareilly, India
[4]Computer Science & Engineering, Swami Keshvanand Institute of Technology,
Management & Gramothan (SKIT), Jagatpura, Jaipur, Rajasthan, India
[5]Department of Information Technology, Swami Keshvanand Institute
of Technology, Management & Gramothan (SKIT), Jagatpura, Jaipur,
Rajasthan, India
[6]Department of Computer Science and Engineering, Haldia Institute of Technology,
Haldia, West Bengal, India

Abstract

In the present day, images and videos account for nearly 80% of all the data transmitted during our daily activities. This work employs a combination of novel stegnography and data compression methodologies. So that the stego image generated while using stegnograpghy to the source textual image could be further compacted in an efficient and productive way and easily transmitted over the web. The initial inputs, textual images and images, are both pre-processed using spatial steganography, and the covertly content images are then extracted and inserted further into the carrier image picture element's least significant bit. Going to follow that, stego images were condensed in order to offer an elevated visual while

Corresponding author: digit11011989@gmail.com
Pankaj Dadeech: ORCID https://orcid.org/0000-0001-5783-1989
Sabyasachi Pramanik: ORCID https://orcid.org/0000-0002-9431-8751

Sabyasachi Pramanik, Debabrata Samanta, M. Vinay and Abhijit Guha (eds.) Cyber Security and Network Security, (169–192) © 2022 Scrivener Publishing LLC

conserving memory space just at sender's end. Nevertheless, it has been found that, throughout steganographic compression techniques, the wavelet transform is generally favored over the discrete cosine transform because the reassembled picture using the wavelet transformation seems to be of greater resolution than the discrete cosine transform. As pictures might not have been properly rebuilt given the limited bandwidth, the regions of interest method is often utilized to analyze the important area first, allowing the relevant portion of the image to be rebuilt even on a limited bandwidth network. The stego image would then have been sent to the recipient through a network connection. Now, at the receiver's end, steganography and compression are reciprocated. The performance of the suggested methods using different wavelet filters is examined to determine the best feasible outcome. So far, all efforts have been focused on creating a technique with a significant PSNR value and low data rates. Additionally, stego pictures can be effectively broadcasted, and textual visuals might well be easily recreated using a deep learning model over just a limited bandwidth connection.

Keywords: Steganography, image compression, HAAR wavelet, biorthogonal transform, PSNR

8.1   Introduction

The confidentiality of communications has always been a significant issue. Since only relevant users get privy to sensitive data [1], this must be maintained secure at any times. The volume of information getting exchanged via a web from one place to another has increasing rapidly, well beyond the fevered imagination. As a result, the need for data security increases, and this will need for collaborative information. Obfuscation techniques serves critical in the transmission of secret facts. Steganography provides a technique of concealing data [24] within normal transmission. Steganographic techniques are often used to conceal content [5]. With terms of the security, attackers should prioritize unique revealed encrypted content, irrespective as to how impenetrable it really is. Steganography could be a viable alternative enabling concealing [19] in authoritarian circumstances when implementing encryption might generate unwanted attention. The utilization of digital communication and digitalization to encode information and afterward hide this in digital material [18] is known as contemporary steganography [6]. Approaches for encrypting and decrypting appear to be the two most essential components of the any modern steganographic system. The implanted technique takes into account concealed information, confidential keys, and also the covered items [25], which will be utilized to communicate information. The stego picture was created via an embedding technique. The steganographic picture can also be utilized as that of an input to an images compression technique, resulting inside a compressed stego image [20] that can be easily transmitted more than a web. Authors in [1] discovered a compression method that lowers the total amount of content by eliminating superfluous data while preserving security of information. Morse codes have been used as initial compression method in [30], with shorter code words assigned to characters like "e" and "t". Authors in [21] proposed a technique for transmitting cipher words based on symmetric probability [2]. With that kind of restricted range of vague language, the compression of stego pictures is controlled using rigorous code and technology, requiring a compromise between compression ratio and error rates. Compressing technologies is becoming increasingly helpful as online storing is becoming more prevalent. Data compression seems to be an important component of the system technology since it lowers the cost of transmitting information as well as storage via the web. The goal of compressing would have been to diminish the quantity of bits necessary to describe content, thus lowering communication speeds [3]. The deployment of technology such as streaming media with informational minimization will be virtually difficult. Some other terminology for compression methods includes source encapsulation. Compressed is indeed a technique of plummeting the quantity with one or more artifacts to make them simpler to handle [4]. The main purpose of information compression is to minimize redundancy in information stored or sent across a link, thus decreasing resource usage and improving effective information density. As illustrated in Figure 8.1, the two most popular kinds of information compression methods are lossless and lossy reduction. During such a multilayered procedure, comprising insertion, a stego image would also have been transmitted to an opposite end of the range via the protected channel. The calculation indicated that the suggested methodology outperforms

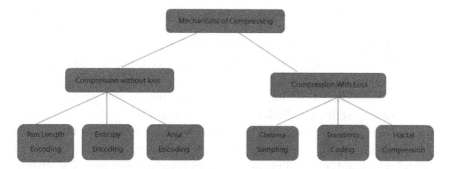

Figure 8.1 Various compression techniques.

a traditional procedure in accordance with the performance metrics like peak signal-to-noise ratio (PSNR) and structural similarity index-based evaluations.

8.2   Review of Literature

The identification of bending and multifarious text information in a coherent kind from complicated deteriorated image frames using a new-mask region-based fully convolution network-based textual information detection technique is described in [37].

Authors in [38] gave a novel methodology for data recognition and identifications, thus according to the authors [39], it is a linked element method that uses maximally stable extreme areas. The text recognition procedure is difficult because of the numerous blurs generated by motion and defocus.

The goal of this research [40] is to distinguish and locate medical face masks artifacts in real-life photos. In public settings, wearisome a health face mask may help prevent the spread of COVID-19. There are two main components to the framework that has been created. The ResNet-50 deep transfer learning system is being used in the initial component to feature extracted. The second component, which is based on YOLO v2, is used to identify medical surgical masks. For this research, two databases of medical face masks were combined into a single dataset. As detection, an Adam optimizer received a high average accuracy percentage of 81 percent, according to the results. A comparative result utilizing focused activities has also been given at the end of the study. In respect of exactness, the proposed detector surpassed previous actual research.

Modeling of textural pictures utilizing functional and partial differential equations was suggested by [41].

The image is deconstructed in this work into a total of two processes denoted by u+v, where u denotes a limited variation method and v denotes a texture or noise procedure. The suggested method is based on a differential equation and is straightforward to implement. This also described how the technique can be applied to texture separation and texture classification.

Authors in [42] proposed a Marr's primitive draft concept with three major components: a texture model, a generative model, picture primitives, and a Gestalt field. Following study and analyzing distinct kinds of models, the comprehensive Markov random field modeling, and the generating wavelet/sparse coding system, it also explains the concept of "stretchability", which aids in the division of images between texture and geometry.

This explored the embedded zero-tree wavelet (EZW) technique for image compressing, as described in [7]. Using wavelet filtering to remove interference even while decoding and creating an appropriate threshold, notably Haar [34], biorthogonal, Coiflets [35], Daubechies, Symlets, and reverse biorthogonal. Since compression methods decrease the quantity of bits necessary to adequately represent an image, they are particularly useful for remote monitoring. So, although the portraiture was already condensed, the electronic data requirements have already been reduced, but the transmission efficiency has been improved.

The EZW technique is a powerful yet effective picture compression approach, and the quantitative results show that Daubechies wavelet group's "db10" wavelet filter produces a better PSNR with much the same number of computations. For just a proper balance of bit rate and also a reconstructed picture, a threshold of 50 has now been found to be the optimal option. Visual information compression has already been achieved using a variety of methods, including sparse representation, subband encoding, and transformation-based techniques, as per [8]. The fact that, although the selection of a visually compression technique is primarily based on compaction proportion variables, the overall quality of the reconstructed image is dependent on the methods used has become a recent problem. Wavelet transform-based coding has emerged as a viable option for compression techniques that is also extremely efficient in terms of total coding efficacy, according to some research. It is well acknowledged that JPEG-2000, a revolutionary wavelet-based image compression technique, has now been officially accepted as a worldwide standard. The implementation of a novel method posited utilizing the EZW encoder, wherein initiatives combine multi-threading techniques which will be fully integrated and managed to accomplish the many core frameworks, which include Epiphany III, and also the findings of this study are stated in this article.

As given in [9], EZW encoding would have been a higher compression method with encoding advantages. Nonetheless, the signal compression proportions are reduced by the multi-layered structured coding of the data employed in EZW. The goal of the study was to optimize an EZW compression method in order to achieve better results. To begin, the authors used elevated wavelet transforms to analyze electrocardiograph (ECG) data, paying special emphasis to a raising approach. Second, the ECG data breakdown was utilized to deconstruct the EZW compression coding technique, which was being used to calculate the values of the features identified. A variability estimated on the basis of the ECG wavelet coefficients has been used to achieve the goal of a greater compressing benefit.

According to [10], the EZW technique outperforms an efficient encoding strategy for low–bit rate image compression in the area of visual compression. The authors recommend a revised EZW (NE-EZW) version of such a strategy, which provides for better compression outcomes in lossy compression methods in terms of PSNR and bit rate while retaining a compact file size. This method relies on increasing the number of coefficients that are not represented by the use of extra signs in order to distribute probability more effectively. Apart from that, it proposes a method for improving binary encoding effectiveness by using compression cell operators. When contrasted to the preceding approaches, the proposed system excelled at conventional EZW and other improved EZW methods in both naturalistic and healthcare visual encoding scenarios. In terms of results, the authors show that the proposed method outperforms other well-known techniques, such as set splitting in hierarchical trees (SPIHT) and JPEG2000.

They proposed a new picture compression technique based on the EZW method and the Huffman coder in [11]. Within the layout, Huffman coder design characteristics improve the structure's speed. The lesser installation complexity of a threshold computing architecture would have been completely incorporated and formally established. The DWT coefficients were determined using a lifting-based paradigm. The architecture may be expanded to support a larger number of levels.

Using the same memories for all estimates, using a unified RAM for DWT coefficient collection helps in the reduction of hardware objects. As a result, when this architecture is combined with the Huffman encoder, the compaction ratio is increased without sacrificing bandwidth economy. For enhanced image analysis, the integration seems to be suitable [27]. Image compression, as per [12], would be used to decrease the quantity of data saved and make it even easier to transfer pictures without sacrificing total image quality. The HAAR wavelet-based Discrete Wavelet Transformation (DWT) is described all through this work for the aim of appropriate and thorough image compression. This is a simple technique of compression since the coefficient of HAAR DWT has either been 1 or −1. Once more, wavelet transformation was utilized for time-frequency analysis. The compression proportions within this work have indeed been proven to be considerably higher after three levels of breakdown. Despite creating substantial damage to the primary image, the disassembled image may be reconstructed.

The authors described visual steganography using a generative adversarial network method in their paper [23]. First, review the fundamentals of steganography, including its concepts and characteristics. Following that, a traditional image obfuscation method approach, as well as its disadvantages, may be explained. They also introduce the idea of generative adversarial networks and also various future models. This article concentrates on generative adversarial networks [29] data concealing methods such as cover image change, cover choosing, and covers synthesis. The diverse and important functions that generative adversarial networks serve in various methods were explored. Based on the mode, a generative adversarial network was utilized to generate whether the cover image or an alteration matrix in the generative adversarial network cover alteration methods. The Generative Adversarial Network Coverage Approach's has a weak insertion capacity and the need for a secret channel to transmit keys.

In [43], a significant proportion of slashing binary visual content concealment techniques concentrate on l-shape sequencing centers for integrating modifications. However, one such inserting condition has an unpredictable effect on border formations. To detect newly developed content-adaptive binary images data stealing, the work presented a steganalysis method that uses the embedded impact associated with both the l-shape sequences embedded criteria and the embedded effects associated with the l-shape sequences embedded standard. Firstly, an examination of how different l-shape arrangements influence the dispersion of a single 4×3–sized design. Depending on the outcomes, a 32-dimensional steganalysis set of features is developed, with four categories of layouts used to represent the proportion of two pixels orientated in the patterns changing course.

Encryption technology is the main technique of information security, as per [44], with steganography capable of serving as a substitute in certain instances. Steganography is the scientific method of private conversation among two people that attempts to keep the communication from being found. There has also been a lot of picture steganography to back up the notion. The majority of elements cause statistically substantial changes in the covers carrier's characteristics, especially only when textual payload is large. Also, authors presented a new transform domain JPEG image steganography method that significantly enhances embedded efficiency while requiring only minimal changes to a cover carrier image. The DCT-M3 technique employs 2 bits of a compact form of a concealed code based on modulus 3, the distinction between two DCT coefficients.

Authors in [45] presented a new technique for image compressing in both the temporal and frequency domains. The wavelet transformation has been used to create distinct picture sub-bands and divide these into multiple stages. For encoding the wavelet, a distortion structuring bit methodology is employed, presuming that features of high-resolution pictures would be less apparent to a human eye.

The author of this work [46] proposed a compression method with the feature of generating embedding code from the bits in the flow. The binary representation structures offered in the embedding code differentiate between a picture of interest and a null image. For standardized test pictures, a visual compressing technique termed as EZW consistently outperforms all those other compressing systems. Until now, similar efficiency has indeed been obtained using a technique which does not need any additional training, pre-stored databases, or prior knowledge of the image's origin. Image compressed methods allowing improved image quality restorations are accessible for such important portions of such a scene, owing to this study [47].

In the case of medical imaging, even the smallest percentage of such an image may be important for medical testing. Nevertheless, the cost of erroneous evaluation is exorbitant. Lossless compression across focus areas could be used to provide fast and reliable image encoding methods for clinical conditions. A new binarization technique of colorful documents has also been described in [48]. Conventional adaptive threshold methods will not provide acceptable binarization findings in documents with blended or mixed foreground and background colors. To begin with, a luminosity distribution is being used to gather data on picture characteristics. Following that, the decision-tree generated binarization method is suggested for binarizing color documents' pictures by choosing various color characteristics. So, considering the colors in the documents' pictures are confined to a narrow range, saturated was employed initially. Secondly, brightness is being utilized since the foreground colors of the picture seem critical. Thirdly, if a picture's backdrop colors have been concentrated inside a narrow range, then brightness is usually employed. Furthermore, saturation gets used if somehow the total quantity of minimal pixels is less than 60; otherwise, all luminance and saturation are used. In experimental research, 519 color images have always been utilized. The vast majority of those were standardized invoicing and name-card documentation images. The proposed binarization technique exceeds previous current methods in shape and connected-component evaluation. Additionally, in commercialized OCR systems, the binarization method outperforms comparable approaches in terms of recognition reliability.

As [49] noted, textual recognition in pictures or video seems to be an important factor in getting multi-media material. This article presents a quick technique for recognizing, categorizing, and retrieving horizontal oriented textual in picture backdrops with complicated backgrounds (and digital videos). A color reduction technique, an edge detection technique, and text area localization utilizing projection profile analyses and geometrical characteristics are all suggested methods.

The method generates textbox with a reduced backdrop that are ready to be sent into an OCR engine for character recognition. The method's effectiveness is shown by encouraging research observations with only a series of images gathered from different video sequences. This study proposed a novel texture-based technique of identifying text in images [50, 51]. A support vector machine is used to evaluate text-based characteristics. Rather than utilizing external features, the brightness levels of a single picture element that primarily constitute a texture characteristic, are delivered directly to the SVMs, which also work extremely well in high-dimensional environments. The texture feature extraction findings will then be used to detect text areas utilizing merely an update mean shift technique. A combination of CAMSHIFTs and SVMs yields flexible word recognition, but time-consuming texture studies with less important pixels are limited, leaving just a tiny part of each input picture texture-analyzed. Recognition, localization, surveillance, excavation, augmentation, and text recognition from input pictures are all components of an extraction method, according to Jung K et al. [53]. Extraction of these data necessitates detection, localization, observation, text extraction, improvements, and recognition of a specific picture. Text data in images and movies provides valuable information in terms of automated annotations, indexes, and image structure. Collecting this content from a particular scene includes identification, localization, tracking, extraction, augmentation, and text recognition. Automatic text extraction is challenging due to text factors such as form, style, position, alignment, and low visual contrast and a complicated backdrop. Despite extensive assessments on similar issues such as face detection, documentary analysis, and audio/video index were provided, textual information retrieval was not very well addressed.

Authors in [52] proposed two local Wiener filtration procedures for the double localized Wiener filtering method. Elliptic directing windows were utilized to estimate the signal variations of noisy wavelet coefficients from various alignment sub-bands as well as the noisy picture. According to the study's results, the suggested method substantially increases de-noising efficacy. For this work, throughout pre-processing, a low pass filter, including a Wiener filter, is being used to give a sensible estimation of fore-ground regions for background outer edge prediction, interpolation of adjoining back-ground intensity levels for back-ground outer edge evaluation, thresholding, besides combining the approximated back-ground surface areas in the main picture while also including image up sampling, and finally post-processing stages for image quality augmentation. Steganography, or the writing of words, has risen to prominence as a major study area in the exchange of information, with many investigations having been performed to improve this subject. Authors also provided an enhanced least significant bit eLSB method for inserting textual data in cover image for "steganography" purposes. The integrity of the cover image is better when compared with the traditional LSB method used during steganography.

According to [26], the main aim of the study was to create an effective health imaging display. A thorough review of the research was performed in order to thoroughly understand the different features as well as objectives of such methods. The findings of this reviewed literature offered a comprehensive knowledge of both enhancement and compression methods, which will be helpful for future research. Apart from just that, researchers investigated how these capabilities functioned with medical monochromatic images. A first step included conducting compacted to use both lossless and lossy methods, followed by a process of optimization. In terms of compression, four methods have already been used: BTC, DCT, DWT, and RLE [32]. BTC [31] was perhaps the most often utilized method. In comparison to a DCT technique [33], lossy compression with DWT improvements based on specified assessment criteria provided better results despite losing any extra data. Aside from losing substantial information, the RLE and BTC techniques effectively compress information. According to the study's findings, the RLE method outperformed the BTC technique in terms of compression rate. Every compressing technique was enhanced further with the assistance of two compressing approaches, AHE and MO. Additionally, the study's overall results showed that a combination of compaction and enrichment methods was successful when applied in tandem. When compared to PSNR and SSIM, the BTC method had more value than excellent image resolution after enhancement, while the RLE approach had more worth and high image lucidity after augmentation. The research showed that when the AHE and RLE processes have been combined, the obtained results were much superior to those gained using other approaches. In contrast to the DWT compressing method, the AHE method greatly improved the condensed image. Instead of increasing or boosting the disparities of the pictures, morphological techniques are utilized in this instance to enhance the backgrounds. Rather than brightening a picture, morphological techniques were employed to improve the clarity of the backgrounds rather than the shot itself. These methods, for instance, have been used to contribute to the improvement of a certain area of interest. It is conceivable to observe advancements in imaging techniques as a consequence of computer vision applications such as image identification, assessment, and augmentation. Image analysis [13] on its own raises the percentage and number of problems identified. Image computation and image enhancement seem to be methods attributed directly to different image analysis settings and improvements using various machine learning variables. Data protection is mainly dependent on cryptography, with steganography providing an additional layer of security in certain instances. Steganography is a scientific technique of concealed communication between two parties attempting to conceal a hidden message. Several methods for image steganography have been proposed. All of these have a measurable effect on a cover carrier, particularly whenever the information payload seems big. The preceding research offers a new transformation entity JPEG steganographic technique with improved detection performance and minimal changes to the cover image. The DCT-M3 technique [22] integrates two bits of a hidden code's compressed manner utilizing modulus 3 of the representation of different DCT coefficients [14]. Text steganography has also evolved as the dominant field of study within the field of content communications, with many studies being conducted to improve such an area. The number of hidden codes that may be concealed in a particular cover picture has always been a critical issue for any steganography used to transmit secret content. The preceding paper describes a steganography implantation method based on a modified Least Significant Bit (eLSB) [15]. The efficacy of a cover image has been increased as compared to the conventional LSB method [28] employed during steganography. The proposed method operates inside the spatial domain and encrypts a concealed message in two stages. The first step involves the creation of meta-data and the incorporation of the first few bytes of a cover picture. The next phase is in charge of processing the hidden message and stashing it in the cover picture in the most efficient way possible, which is made possible by analyzing the strings of a secret message. Because the suggested approach fine-tunes hidden messages during the steganographic phase, one such strategy enables greater volume embedding yield as well as more safety. Information can and will not be correctly recreated attributed to the network's limited bandwidth. As a consequence, the main emphasis is on developing a prioritized encoded, that prioritizes data processing such that essential data is handled first. As a consequence, the area of interest method is utilized to find critical data. As a result, a DWT was used to divide the acquired stego picture into four sub-bands and to concentrate on the low-frequency band. To conserve space, a picture was already condensed immediately as the textual image was hidden. For densification, a Discrete Wavelet Transform (DWT) methodology can be used, and the Opposite Discrete Wavelet Transform (lDWT) procedure would be used to recover the original stego image and obtain a secret code, which was used to retrieve the concealed textual image from the text-based image decoding technique. To securely transmit or recreate textual pictures over low-bandwidth networks, the proposed technique combines steganography, image compression technology, and deep learning. A thorough series of studies was carried out to determine the feasibility of the proposed of the proposed approach and to assess the value of its accomplishment in contrast to the existing methods.

8.3   Methodology Used

The obfuscation techniques technique that has been proposed operates within the spatial realm and is thus split into two phases. The creation of metadata could take place during the first step. The header data was always placed in the first few pieces of data of a cover image and that usually represented the situation. The cover image contains cryptic information that has been saved in the most efficient manner. Following that, the stego picture was flattened, and the cryptographic keys were generated by the implantation procedure, which was then compressed. Image compression methodologies such as the discrete cosine transform, the discrete Fourier transform, and the discrete wavelet transforms are frequently used when an image has indeed been successfully transmitted along a communication system, despite the fact that the frequency range appears to also be confined. The discrete wavelet transform is one of the most well-known because of the exceptional quality of the textual image that is reproduced using it. While performing this task, incorporation of an image compression system that is based on EZW compaction that also includes region of interest coding, also known as region of interest-embedded zero-tree coding is performed, to ensure that the information can be transmitted rapidly over low bandwidth channels while prioritizing the most valuable information. Profitable representation of an important element and the background in a picture is referred to as ROI. This technique allows the important component to

Table 8.1(A) Suggested algorithm at sender side.

At sender side	
1	Construct a cover image which includes picture elements which will be transmitted across the channel throughout the transmission phase and calculate the LSB of each picture element.
2	Each bitwise binary result of a text-based image must be replaced in order to transmit the LSB of every image pixel in the cover picture.
3	The following criteria should be entered: stego picture, deconstruction level, and shifting parameter. The following criteria should be entered: stego picture, decomposition level, and shifting parameter.
4	From 1 to the decomposition_level, in increasing order
5	Perform decomposition of (image)
6	Select Region of Interest (ROI)
7	If dimension (ROI) > dimension (image)
8	Go to step 18
9	Else goto 9
10	Mask region of interest to wavelet domain
11	Choose ROI_Scale
12	If minimum_ROI_coefficent > Maximum_background_coefficent
13	ROI(Region of Interest)_scale = minimum(2^Shifiting_parameter)
14	else Goto 11
15	Down-scale (background_coefficients)
16	Embedded_encoding (ROI_cofficient + background_coefficient)

Table 8.1(B) Suggested algorithm at receiver side.

At receiver side	
1	Reconstruct (stego image) by performing compression in reverse
2	In contrast, marker-based watershed segmentation is used to enhance the stego picture
3	To get textual data from a cover picture, use the inverse of steganography
4	A weighted Naïve Bayes model is used to identify the textual data
5	The efficiency of such a model may be improved substantially by utilizing an adaptive optimization technique such as gradient descent
6	Calculate mean squared error
7	Calculate peak signal-to-noise ratio)
8	end

be reconstructed, although at very low rates, only by detracting from the backdrop's representation.

The compressed stego image will then be decompressed in the same manner as in the reception, and the covert key acquired via the implanted methodology might be given to a textual treatment technique as in the transmitter. A deeply ingrained text-based image has already been recovered using a secret key, and the recovered textual image would have been deduced from the cover image utilizing a mixture of convolution neural network modeling on three wavelet filters, Haar, daubechies, and biorthogonal [36] wavelet filters, that also determine various parameters including bit rate, mean squared error (MSE), and PSNR, among others.

These outcomes of the computations show the biorthogonal wavelet filtering outperforms all other methods, achieving the highest PSNR as well as the least average squared error in the process. Tables 8.1A and B illustrate the procedures for the approaches that have been proposed.

8.4   Results and Discussion

The efficacy of the merging of stegnography and image compression techniques has now been evaluated by means of MSE [17], PSNR [16],

Table 8.2 Values for PSNR at decomposition level = 16.

Name of filter used	Threshold value = 16 Value of PSNR	Threshold value = 20 Value of PSNR	Threshold value = 24 Value of PSNR	Threshold value = 28 Value of PSNR	Threshold value = 32 Value of PSNR	Threshold value = 36 Value of PSNR	Threshold value = 40 Value of PSNR
Haar	11.78	12.019	12.781	12.93	12.01	11.99	12.54
Daub2	11.99	12.516	13.41	13.49	12.43	13.01	13.56
Bior4.4	12.91	13.123	14.24	14.34	13.33	13.50	13.89

and bit rate using various filters during this whole part. In this part, the PSNRs of compressed images and the original image were determined using different wavelet filters at different threshold levels and decomposing methods. The effectiveness of a reproduced image was enhanced. PSNR estimates for the cover image of a Lena 512 × 512 picture for different threshold settings for decomposition level = 16 have been calculated and are shown in Table 8.2. This has been found that increasing the threshold raises the PSNR value. Table 8.2 shows that Bior4.4 has the highest PSNR value when compared to certain other wavelet filters.

Figure 8.2 shows the PSNR for a compressed stego picture in relation to the decomposition level = 16 threshold. The graph indicates that the Bior4.4 wavelet has the highest PSNR value, while the Haar wavelet has the lowest value as threshold value increases.

Table 8.3 shows the PSNR values of compressed stego images of Lena 512 × 512 images with various parameters and decomposition level = 4. This has been found as decreasing the amount of the level of decomposition from 8 to 4 leads to the value of PSNR becoming negative, and its values decrease as the thresholds are increased.

Figure 8.3 shows the PSNR for a compressed stego picture in relation to the decomposition level = 4 threshold. The graph indicates that the Bior4.4 wavelet has the highest PSNR value, while the Haar wavelet has the lowest value.

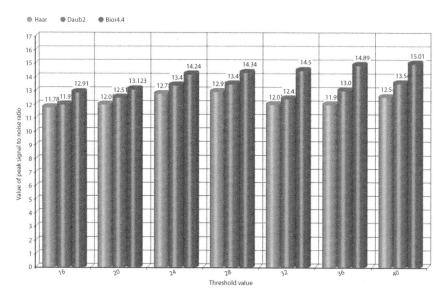

Figure 8.2 PSNR vs. threshold for image at decomposition level = 16.

Table 8.3 Values for PSNR at decomposition level = 4.

| Name of filter used | Threshold value = 16 | Threshold value = 20 | Threshold value = 24 | Threshold value = 28 | Threshold value = 32 | Threshold value = 36 | Threshold value = 40 |
	Value of PSNR	Value of PSNR	Value of PSNR	Value of PSNR	Value of PSNR	Value of PSNR	Value of PSNR
Haar	−7.77	−7.98	−7.93	−7.96	−7.85	−7.96	−7.99
Daub2	−7.74	−7.89	−7.90	−7.86	−7.87	−7.97	−7.88
Bior4.4	−7.44	−7.68	−7.83	−7.83	−7.86	−7.98	−7.96

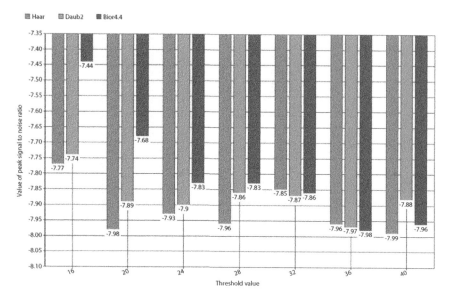

Figure 8.3 PSNR vs. threshold for image at decomposition level = 4.

8.5   Conclusions

Over the past few decades, there has been an increase in the need for the preservation and transmission of multi-media information. Videos and images, for example, contribute to generating an interactive environment. In today's technically advanced world, data and information should be transferred swiftly and securely, while significant information should be safeguarded from unauthorized people. Throughout this study, a deep convolutional neural network is used to build a clandestine communications system along with a textual document retrieval method based on steganography and image compression. The original source textual images and cover image all seem to be pre-processed utilizing spatial steganography, and then, the concealed text-based pictures are extracted and planted into the least relevant bit of the cover image picture element. Following that, stego images were condensed to provide a higher-quality picture while saving space for storage just at the sender's end. After then, the stego image will be sent to the recipient via a communication channel. Steganography and compression are then inverted at the recipient's end. This work contains a plethora of issues that offer it many opportunities to pursue. By far, the most essential aspect of this effort is determining the best steganography and picture compression method. The proposed technique, which combines image-steganography with compaction, provides higher peak signal-to-noise efficiency.

References

1. Bhattacharya, A., A.Ghosal, A.J., Krit, S., Shukla, V.K., Mandal, K., Pramanik, S., Unsupervised Summarization Approach With Computational Statistics of Microblog Data, in: *Methodologies and Applications of Computational Statistics for Machine Intelligence*, D. Samanta, R.R. Althar, S. Pramanik, S. Dutta, (Eds.), IGI Global, Hershey, United States, 2021, DOI: 10.4018/978-1-7998-7701-1.ch002.

2. Kudeep, P. and Vivek, S., "A Survey of Various Image Compression Techniques". *Indian J. Appl. Res.*, 5, 1, 47–49, Special Issue ISSN - 2249- 555X, Jan 2015.

3. Bansal, R., Obaid, A.J., Gupta, A., Singh, R., Pramanik, S., Impact of Big Data on Digital Transformation in 5G Era. *2nd International Conference on Physics and Applied Sciences (ICPAS 2021), Journal of Physics: Conference Series*, 2021.

4. Songgang, Z., Gaofeng, Y.F., Liu, X., Research on UAV video compression based on compression algorithm, in: *Integrated circuit applications*, vol. 36, Jacob, J.M. (Ed.), pp. 39–40, 2019.

5. Yang, M., Zhao, W., Xu, W., Feng, Y., Zhao, Z., Chen, X. *et al.*, "Multitask learning for cross-domain image captioning". *IEEE Trans. Multimedia*, 21, 4, 1047–1061, Apr. 2019.

6. Pramanik, S. and Bandyopadhyay, S.K., "Image Steganography Using Wavelet Transform and Genetic Algorithm". *Int. J. Innov. Res. Adv. Eng.*, 1, 1–4, 2014.

7. Pramanik, S., Samanta, D., Ghosh, R., Bandyopadhyay, S.K., "A New Combinational Technique in Image Steganography". *Int. J. Inf. Secur. Priv.*, 15, 3, article 4, 48–64, 2021.

8. Alvarez-Cedillo, J.A., Alvarez-Sanchez, T., Aguilar-Fernandez, M., Sandoval-Gutierrez, J., "Many-Core Algorithm of the Embedded Zerotree Wavelet Encoder,", in: *Coding Theory*, S. Radhakrishnan and M. Sarfraz, (Eds.), IntechOpen, Rijeka, 2020, doi: 10.5772/intechopen.89300.

9. Ziran, P., Guojun, W., Huabin, J., Shuangwu, M., Research and improvement of ECG compression algorithm based on EZW. *Comput. Methods Programs Biomed.*, 145, 157–166, 2017, ISSN 0169-2607. https://doi.org/10.1016/j.cmpb.2017.04.015.

10. Boujelbene, R., Boubchir, L., Jemaa, B.Y., An enhanced Embedded Zerotree Wavelet algorithm for lossy image coding. *IET Image Process.*, 13, 1364–1374, 2019, doi: 10.1049/iet-ipr.2018.6052.

11. Aishwarya, S. and Veni, S., Hardware Implementation of EZW based Image Compression with Huffman coding. *Int. J. Eng. Sci. Innov. Technol. (IJESIT)*, 2, 5, 437–445, September 2013.

12. Pramanik, S., Singh, R.P., Ghosh, R., Bandyopadhyay, S.K., "A Unique Way to Generate Password at Random Basis and Sending it Using a New Steganography Technique". *Indones. J. Electr. Eng. Inform.*, 8, 3, 525–531, 2020.

13. Pandey, D., Pandey, B.K., Wairya, S., Hybrid deep neural network with adaptive galactic swarm optimization for text extraction from scene images. *Soft Comput.*, 25, 1563–1580, 2021. https://doi.org/10.1007/s00500-020-05245-4.

14. Kanchanadevi, B. and Tamilselvi, Dr. P.R., Post Processing Using Enhanced Discrete Cosine Transform for Image Compression. *Int. J. Adv. Sci. Technol.*, 29, 06, 9372–9386, 2020. Retrieved from http://sersc.org/journals/index. php/IJAST/article/view/34743.

15. Al-Momin, M., Abed, I., Leftah, H., A new approach for enhancing LSB steganography using bidirectional coding scheme. *Int. J. Electr. Comput. Eng. (IJECE)*, 9, 5286, 2019, doi: 10.11591/ijece.v9i6.pp5286–5294.

16. Bandyopadhyay, S., Goyal, V., Dutta, S., Pramanik, S., Sherazi, H.H.R., "Unseen to Seen by Digital Steganography", in: *Multidisciplinary Approach to Modern Digital Steganography*, S. Pramanik, M.M. Ghonge, R. Ravi, K. Cengiz, (Eds.), IGI Global, Hershey, United States, 2021, https://doi. org/10.4018/978-1-7998-7160-6.ch001.

17. Pramanik, S. and Singh, R.P., "Role of Steganography in Security Issues". *International Conference on Advance Studies in Engineering and Sciences*, pp. 1225–1230, 2017.

18. Pandey, B., Mane, D., Nassa, V., Pandey, D., Dutta, S., Ventayen, R., Agarwal, G., Rastogi, R., Secure Text Extraction From Complex Degraded Images by Applying Steganography and Deep Learning, IGI Global, Hershey, United States, 2021, doi: 10.4018/978-1-7998-7160-6.ch007.

19. Pandey, D., Nassa, V., Jhamb, A., Mahto, D., Pandey, B., George, A.S.H., George, A.S., Bandyopadhyay, S., An Integration of Keyless Encryption, Steganography, and Artificial Intelligence for the Secure Transmission of Stego Images, IGI Global, Hershey, United States, 2021, doi: 10.4018/978-1-7998-7160-6.ch010.

20. Pandey, B.K., Pandey, D., Wairya, S., Agarwal, G., An Advanced Morphological Component Analysis, Steganography, and Deep Learning-Based System to Transmit Secure Textual Data. *Int. J. Distrib. Artif. Intell. (IJDAI)*, 13, 2, 40–62, 2021. http://doi.org/10.4018/IJDAI.2021070104.

21. Gallager, R., Claude E. Shannon: A retrospective on his life, work, and impact. *IEEE Trans. Inf. Theory*, 47, 2681–2695, 2001, doi: 10.1109/18.959253.

22. Pramanik, S., Bandyopadhyay, S.K., Ghosh, R., "Signature Image Hiding in Color Image using Steganography and Cryptography based on Digital Signature Concepts,". *IEEE 2nd International Conference on Innovative*

Mechanisms for Industry Applications (ICIMIA), Bangalore, India, pp. 665–669, 2020, doi: 10.1109/ICIMIA48430.2020.9074957.

23. Liu, J., Ke, Y., Zhang, Z., Lei, Y., Li, J., Zhang, M., Yang, X., Recent Advances of Image Steganography With Generative Adversarial Networks. *IEEE Access.*, 8, 1–1, 2020, doi: 10.1109/ACCESS.2020.2983175.

24. Pramanik, S. and Bandyopadhyay, S.K., "Hiding Secret Message in an Image". *Int. J. Innov. Sci. Eng. Technol.*, 1, 553–559, 2014.

25. Liu, M.M. *et al.*, *"Coverless Information Hiding Based on Generative adversarial networks"*, Cornell University's, Ithaca, NY 14850, United States, 2017, ArXiv e-prints: 1712.06951.

26. Pourasad, Y. and Cavallaro, F.A., Novel Image Processing Approachto Enhancement and Compression of X-ray Images. *Int. J. Environ. Res. Public Health*, 18, 6724, 2021. https://doi.org/10.3390/ijerph18136724.

27. Połap, D., An adaptive genetic algorithm as a supporting mechanism for microscopy image analysis in a cascade of convolutionneural networks. *Appl. Soft Comput. J.*, 97, 106824, 2020.

28. Gupta, A., Pramanik, S., Bui, H.T., Ibenu, N.M., "Machine Learning and Deep Learning in Steganography and Steganalysis", in: *Multidisciplinary Approach to Modern Digital Steganography*, S. Pramanik, M. Ghonge, R.V. Ravi, K. Cengiz, (Eds.), IGI Global, Hershey, United States, 2021, DOI: 10.4018/978-1-7998-7160-6.ch004.

29. Zhang, R., Dong, S., Liu, J., "Invisible steganography via generative adversarial networks". *Multimed. Tools Appl.*, 78, 7, 8559–8575, Apr. 2019.

30. Gong, L., Deng, C., Pan, S., Zhou, N., Image compression-encryption algorithms by combining hyper-chaotic system with discrete fractional random transform. *Opt. Laser Technol.*, 103, 48–58, ISSN 0030-3992, 2018. https://doi.org/10.1016/j.optlastec.2018.01.007. https://www.sciencedirect.com/science/article/pii/S003039921730957X).

31. Pramanik, S., Samanta, D., Dutta, S., Ghosh, R., Ghong, M., Pandey, D., "Steganography using Improved LSB Approach and Asymmetric Cryptography". *IEEE International Conference on Advent Trends in Multidisciplinary Research and Innovation*, 2020.

32. El-Sharkawey, A. and Ali, M., *Comparison between (RLE & Huffman and DWT) Algorithms for Data Compression*, Tadepalligudem, India, 2019.

33. Zhou, X., "Research on DCT-based image compression quality,". *Proceedings of 2011 Cross Strait Quad-Regional Radio Science and Wireless Technology Conference*, pp. 1490–1494, 2011, doi: 10.1109/CSQRWC.2011.6037249.

34. Pramanik, S., Singh, R.P., Ghosh, R., "A New Encrypted Method in Image Steganography". *Int. J. Electr. Comput. Eng.*, 14, 3, 1412–1419, 2019.

35. Majumdar, S., Comparative Analysis of Coiflet and Daubechies Wavelets Using Global Threshold for Image De-Noising. *Int. J. Adv. Eng. Technol.*, 6, 2247–2252, 2013.

36. Pramanik, S., Singh, R.P., Ghosh, R., "Application of Bi-orthogonal Wavelet Transform and Genetic Algorithm in Image Steganography".

Multimed. Tools Appl. 79, 17463–17482, 2020. https://doi.org/10.1007/s11042-020-08676- 2020.

37. Huang, Z., Zhong, Z., Sun, L., Huo, Q., Mask R-CNN with pyramid attention network for scene text detection, in: *IEEE Winter Conference on Applications of Computer Vision (WACV)*, IEEE Publications, pp. 764–772, 2019.

38. Pramanik, S., Ghosh, R., Ghonge, M., Narayan, V., Sinha, M., Pandey, D., Samanta, D., A Novel Approach using Steganography and Cryptography in Business Intelligence", in: *Integration Challenges for Analytics, Business Intelligence and Data Mining*, IGI Global, pp. 192–217, 2020, DOI: 10.4018/978-1-7998-5781-5.ch010.

39. Baran, R., Partila, P., Wilk, R., Automated text detection and character recognition in natural scenes based on local image features and contour processing techniques, in: *Advances in Intelligent Systems and Computing International Conference on Intelligent Human Systems Integration*, Springer, Cham, Germany, pp. 42–48, 2018, doi:10.1007/978-3-319-73888-8_8.

40. Loey, M., Manogaran, G., Taha, M.H.N., Khalifa, N.E.M., Fighting against COVID-19: A novel deep learning model based on YOLO-v2 with ResNet-50 for medical face mask detection. *Sustain. Cities Soc*, 65, 102600, 2021. DOI: 10.1016/j.scs.2020.102600.

41. Vese, L.A. and Osher, S.J., Modeling textures with total variation minimization and oscillating pattern in image processing. *J. Sci. Comput.*, 19, 1/3, 553–572, 2003. doi:10.1023/A:1025384832106.

42. Guo, C., Zhu, S., Wu, Y., Towards a mathematical theory of primal sketch and Sketchability, in: *Proceedings of the Ninth IEEE International Conference on Computer Vision (ICCV)*, Nice, France, 2003October 2003.

43. Pramanik, S. and Bandyopadhyay, S.K., "Application of Steganography in Symmetric Key Cryptography with Genetic Algorithm". *Int. J. Eng. Technol.*, 10, 1791–1799, 3, 2013.

44. Pramanik, S. and Bandyopadhyay, S.K., "An Innovative Approach in Steganography". *Sch. J. Eng. Techn.*, 2, 276–280.9, 2014.

45. Antonini, M. and Barlaud, M., Image coding using wavelet transform. *IEEE Trans. Image Process.*, 1, 2, 205–220, 1992.

46. Shapiro, J.M., Embedded Image Coding Using Zerotrees of Wavelet Coefficients. *IEEE Trans. Signal Process.*, 41, 12, 3445–3462, 1993, December.

47. Pramanik, S. and Ghosh, R., "Techniques of Steganography and Cryptography in Digital Transformation", in: *Emerging Challenges, Solutions, and Best Practices for Digital Enterprise Transformation*, K. Sandhu, (Ed.), IGI Global, Hershey, United States, 2020, DOI: 10.4018/978-1-7998-8587-0.ch002.

48. Bandyopadhyay, S., Goyal, V., Dutta, S., Pramanik, S., Sherazi, H.H.R., "Unseen to Seen by Digital Steganography", in: *Multidisciplinary Approach to Modern Digital Steganography*, S. Pramanik, M.M. Ghonge, R. Ravi, K. Cengiz, (Eds.), IGI Global, Hershey, United States, 2021, https://doi.org/10.4018/978-1-7998-7160-6.ch001.

49. Gllavata, J., Ewerth, R., Freisleben, B., A robust algorithm for text detection in images, in: *IEEE Proceedings of the 3rd International Symposium on In Image and Signal Processing and Analysis. ISPA*, vol. 2, pp. 611–616, 2003, September.

50. Pramanik, S. and Suresh Raja, S., "A Secured Image Steganography using Genetic Algorithm". *Adv. Math.: Sci. J.*, 9, 7, 4533–4541, 2020.

51. Pramanik, S. and Das, T.S., "A Framework for Digital Image Steganography". *Int. J. Adv. Trends Comput. Sci. Eng.*, 2, 26–30, 2013.

52. Angelopoulos, G. and Pitas, I., Multichannel Wiener filters in color image restoration based on AR color image modeling, in: *ICASSP-91, 1991 International Conference on IEEE Acoustics, Speech, and Signal Processing*, 1991, pp. 2517–2520, 1991.

53. Jung, K., Kim, K., Jain, A., Text information extraction in images and video: A survey. *Pattern Recognition*, 37, 977–997, 2004. 10.1016/j.patcog.2003.10.012.

9

Security, Privacy, Risk, and Safety Toward 5G Green Network (5G-GN)

Devasis Pradhan[1]*, Prasanna Kumar Sahu[2], Nitin S. Goje[3],
Mangesh M. Ghonge[4], Hla Myo Tun[5], Rajeswari R[1] and Sabyasachi Pramanik[6]

[1]Department of Electronics & Communication Engineering, Acharya Institute of Technology, Bangalore, Karnataka, India
[2]Department of Electrical Engineering, National Institute of Technology, Rourkela, Odisha, India
[3]Department of Management & Technology, Webster University, Tashkent, Uzbekistan
[4]Department of Computer Engineering, Sandip Institute of Technology and Research Center, Nashik, India
[5]Department of Electronic Engineering, Yangon Technological University, Yangon, Myanmar
[6]Dept. of Computer Science & Engineering, Haldia Institute of Technology, West Bengal, India

Abstract

The prevalence of mobile network–associated gadgets keeps on growing dramatically. 5G network will give the hypothetical speed of 20 Gbps so that clients will get 100 Mbps of access data rate. An expected 5 billion gadgets exist around the world. With the development of wearable gadgets, an ordinary client can convey up to two network-associated gadgets or D2D communication. The 5G network draws in clients by publicizing low inertness information correspondence with faster access and transfer data rate with more secure nature. With the quantity of endorsers on the scaling, the sudden concerns of information and computerized assurance would increment to organize with the uprightness of data security. Likewise, with any type of data security, there are consistently protection worries of clients and their delicate information. This chapter will give an idea to secure the versatile structures associated networks, where these networks are helpless to

Corresponding author: devasispradhan@acharya.ac.in

Sabyasachi Pramanik, Debabrata Samanta, M. Vinay and Abhijit Guha (eds.) Cyber Security and Network Security, (193–216) © 2022 Scrivener Publishing LLC

be compromised, well-known attack strategies, and the alleviation against technical discrepancy.

Keywords: 5G, green network, privacy and security, cyber security, NSA, SA, cloud

9.1   Introduction

The 5G communication is presently at the focal point of consideration of industry, the scholarly community, and government around the world. 5G drives numerous new necessities for various organization capacities. As 5G targets using many promising organization innovations, such as SDN, NFV, ICN, NS, CC, and MEC, additional support toward a colossal number of associated gadgets incorporating previously mentioned trend setting innovations and enhancing new strategies will most likely carry gigantic difficulties to security, protection, and trust. The five primary security and protection issues are recorded underneath the outline. Most parts of this chart are powerless against validation, access control, and malevolent conduct. Nonetheless, a few innovations are especially touchy to specific issues. Sub-atomic communication and the THz development both assist the futuristic cellular environment. The sub-atomic communication is the progression toward the data transfer in more secure manner and assures the issues toward affirmation, encoding/decoding, and correspondence, while the THz development mainly encounters the situation to secure information exchanged and vindictive lead. Blockchain innovation and quantum correspondence cross-over with conveyed man-made reasoning and astute radio. The principle security and protection worries here identify with validation, access control, information transmission, and encryption. In like manner, secure network designs, instruments, and projections are required as the justification for 5G in order to identify the issues and follow up by plan toward secure of information with mainlining rules and regulations/protocols. Finally, as in 5G network, altogether, more number of users, data, and traffic conjunction due to heterogeneous network will be moved, the tremendous secrecy of data or information going to be exchange by the end users which will be incorporated with AI systems. This plays a vital role in order to search for address, the size of the data volume and to ensure secrecy with assurance being referred to best utilization in 5G green network (5G-GN).

9.2 Overview of 5G

In February 2017, the ITU delivered a report that set up key necessities which are least prerequisites identified with specialized execution for IMT-2020 for 5G portable correspondence innovation [1–3]. This report mentioned 1 GHz of least transfer speed, 20 Gbps of most extreme information transmission rate, and 1 ms of the briefest inactivity time for cutting edge administrations. These are specialized necessities to understand the vital motivations behind 5G: super-connection, super quick, and super low inertness, and furthermore, the negligible prerequisites to acknowledge different 5G services. 5G communications is more about creatively progressed contrasted with 4G communications toward overall including speed, utilizing the convention, and network setups.

5G is designed in a software-define network (SDN) with a speed of 20 Gbps, multiple times faster than existing LTE, while the 5G network has been transformed from a unified kind to a decentralized sort to limit traffic transmission delay. 5G-specialized guidelines are driven by Third-Generation Partnership Project (3GPP), and discharge 15 frozen in March 2019 characterizes the designs of non-standalone (NSA) and standalone (SA) and covers LTE framework movement. What is more, discharge 16 frozen in July 2020 covers 5G-based assembly industry support including 5G vehicle-to-everything communication (V2X) and 5G Internet of Things (IoT), alongside execution improvements in 5G framework [3].

Furthermore, as deals of 5G-related enterprises are on the ascent, deals of 5G network frameworks are relied upon to arrive at USD 6.8 billion out of 2021 as per reports distributed by Gartner [2, 3], as shown in Figure 9.1. In this unique situation, the voices of clients requiring a safe 5G assistance climate are developing, and many audits are needed prior to dispatching the administrations in light of the chance of intrinsic security dangers in the current LTE correspondence organization. Also, new 5G security dangers should be recognized ahead of time because of specialized changes separated from 4G, and safety should be fortified by creating security innovation devoted to 5G, if essential [4–6]. For phone allies, 5G helps toward fastest exchange rates of data or information, minimize defer calls, and increase the limit of uploading/downloading of data. For 5G, heterogeneous network scaled down the usage of network to record and impart the delivery mechanism in more secure manner using beamforming techniques, Let us consider a situation in a scenario of a network where around 30,040 cameras all imparting live to a single association—this can be easily tackled by 5G system in a better way through which efficiency

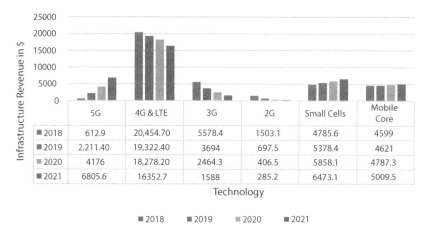

	5G	4G & LTE	3G	2G	Small Cells	Mobile Core
■ 2018	612.9	20,454.70	5578.4	1503.1	4785.6	4599
■ 2019	2,211.40	19,322.40	3694	697.5	5378.4	4621
■ 2020	4176	18,278.20	2464.3	406.5	5858.1	4787.3
■ 2021	6805.6	16352.7	1588	285.2	6473.1	5009.5

■ 2018   ■ 2019   ■ 2020   ■ 2021

Figure 9.1 Cellular infrastructure revenue forecast, Worldwide, 2018–2021 (Millions of Dollars) (Source: Gartner).

and utilization of power is also lower due to which network can be energy efficient. By 2035, 5G is projected to bring $10 trillion up in bargains.

9.3   Key Enabling Techniques for 5G

5G wireless networks are a long ways past the 4G wireless network. These Next-Generation Mobile Networks Alliance (N-GMNA) gives altogether higher limit and supports various sorts of arising applications that have tough quality-of-service (QoS) prerequisites [7–10]. This segment depicts the 5G empowering innovations that advance effectiveness and improve protection as referenced in Figure 9.2.

The key innovations are depicted underneath as follows:

a)   **mm-Wave (millimeter wave):** mm-Wave band basically used to transmit tremendous data/information at a rate of 30–300 GHz (1–10 mm frequency) maintains GBs of data transfer through the network, for example, super superior quality TV additionally extremely rapid web access. The mm-Wave experience the inconsistency with microwaves, i.e., due to a development in repeat, they got impact is lessened to low. The mm-Wave profoundly use less amount of energy for feasible communication but at the same time challenges faced due to different circumstance which may

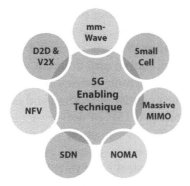

Figure 9.2 Key enabling techniques for 5G.

deteriorate or block the placed calls [11]. In order to manage the limited bar sufficiently, mm-Wave systems provide highly directional antenna through which tremendous number of information/data can be exchanges between UE and base station (BS) appropriately for short-distance communication. The advantage of 5G systems is that it can use both mm-Wave and microwave signals on account of confined spatial incorporation of mm-Wave. In 5G, various small cells are overlaid on macrocells, and each cell contains its BS interconnecting each with fiber interface ends up being much expensive. Thus, the association can be composed with mm-Wave, which will be monetarily wise, mm-Wave is used for quick WLAN and WPAN indoor administrations in macrocells.

b)   **Small Cell:** These cells are minified BSs, put 250 m or more far off separated, and require less ability to work. They are utilized to broaden network inclusion and limit indoor or open air by portable administrators. The little cell might make out of femtocell, picocell, and microcell. As mm-Wave cannot travel bigger distances so little cells are utilized to go about as a hand-off. Little cells decrease call drop issues and help in quick exchanging however require security as information transferring is a danger to information security. By conveying huge number of low force smaller than normal BSs gathered intently framing a group to send signals around the impediments [11–13].

c) **Massive MIMO:** Utilizing progressed enormous MIMO, the range proficiency can be improved and the information rate additionally gets upgraded. MIMO alludes to numerous information and different yield. The organization limit of any remote framework can be improved by expanding the quantity of sending and getting antennas to the framework [14, 15]. To deal with a lot of information traffic, numerous transmission and getting antennas can be utilized all the while. In a 4G network, the quantity of ports on a BS for dealing with cell traffic is 12 (MIMO). In 5G, this number develops to around 100 ports in a BS, which makes it gigantic MIMO.

d) **Beam Forming:** In cellular network, the BSs send motioning every which way yet in the beamforming idea, and it distinguishes the User Equipment (UE) and communicates flags just toward the client. With this idea of beamforming, BSs become more productive in following the most ideal course of information conveyance to a specific client. Beamforming works with huge MIMO in settling on the best choice of picking the right way for transmission [14–16]; in this way, range is too productively used.

e) **NFV:** Network Function (NF) is the practical structure block in a network with various exclusive equipment gadgets. These equipment gadgets give outside interfaces and different functionalities. Be that as it may, the organization capacities are reason assembled genuinely introduced, which makes it hard to overhaul after changes [15]. Each time another NF is to be added to the help, it makes an overhead to make changes in the entire interface. In this way, there is another method of managing such changes through network function virtualization (NFV). NFV alludes to the decoupling of organization capacities from equipment based parts like switches, load adjusts, firewalls, and moving these capacities to run on cloud-based servers and data center.

f) **D2D Communication:** With direct D2D communication (device-to-device), the load on the BS gets decreased. The most extreme transmission distance in D2D is in the scope of 10–1,000 m. It offers an information pace of around 1 Gbps. The D2D correspondence is essentially ordered into two significant classifications as inband and outbound. Inband, as the name recommends works in the band dispensed to cell network, for example, authorized radio range [14–16]. Then, again, outbound works outside the band designated to cell network, for example, unlicensed range. Authorized or inband range is additionally ordered into overlay and underlay mode. In the overlay mode, there are discrete committed recurrence assets both for cell clients and D2D clients. In underlay mode, there are normal assets that are imparted to cell and D2D clients.

g) **SDN:** It permits the organization administrators to deal with the organization and control them with the assistance of programming by programming application support. The organization turns out to be shrewder and can undoubtedly be robotized. In SDN, the information and control planes are decoupled as referenced in the SBA design of 5G [13].

h) **NOMA:** It is a method where various clients are served by utilizing similar time and recurrence assets however unique force assets. Multiplexing of a similar recurrence is finished with various force transmission levels. NOMA helps in expanding ghastly proficiency and association thickness. It additionally gives adaptability between the feeble and solid client; alongside this, it likewise lessens different access impedance [1–5].

i) **V2X:** With the benefit of higher traffic data frameworks, independent vehicles, and more solid security administrations utilized for the advancement of innovation for vehicles with low lethargy, amount of exchange of data is more, and enduring quality is known as vehicle-to-everything (V2X) correspondence which consolidates vehicle-to-passerby (V2P), vehicle-to-establishment (V2I), and vehicle-to-vehicle (V2V) communication. In order to enable the V2X communication for cell networks, gadgets play a vital role for D2D communication which is more sensible due to transmission of information for longer distance as 5G helps to incorporate the whole system for shorter distance too.

9.4 5G Green Network

5G gives some innate energy upgrades contrasted with past ages of versatile innovation, and to amplify the impacts, a multifaceted methodology can be taken to its sending. This incorporates upgraded power the board at the hardware level; new sitting arrangements like fluid cooling, to decrease the requirement for cooling; and adaptable utilization of assets like range. The energy productivity of 5G networks are relied upon to increment 100 times from 1000 mW/Mbps/s to 10 mW/Mbps/s nearby future [17–19]. The current truth is that general energy utilization by the telecom business needs to descend as the business burns through somewhere in the range of 2% and 3% of worldwide energy right now. Numerous public governments are ordering organizations to stick to energy changes (e.g., EU's 2030 environment and energy system) with the worldwide objective to diminish ozone harming substance outflows, since 2014, by 30% in outright terms by 2020 and half by 2030 [2–5].

The 5G-GN contains countless gadgets that are shaping toward Ultra-Dense Network (UDN). Figure 9.3 discussed about the basic component of 5G-GN. In this network, a large number of contraptions are related, so the prerequisite for staying aware of energy adequacy ought to be a primary enabling feature. Different sorts of techniques have been masterminded in the staggered plan for making the association fast and environment all around

Figure 9.3 Components of 5G green network (5G-GN).

arranged. In the UDN, countless BSs are deployed densely. In this system, the feasible method is to manage lessening energy usage to be in efficient way for the BSs. There is a unique change in customers' situation on either side of the network which is the key feature of UDN [6–8].

In order to make the system more effective and energy efficient, the following methods help to deploy 5G-GN:

a) **UDN:** For 5G super thick cell networks, a spread organization engineering is given. The basic requirement for UDNs area unit is the backhaul energy productivity and the backhaul network cutoff plays a key role to make the dense network more energy efficient through which utilization of energy is less and its helps in deploying the green environment of network.

b) **MU-MIMO:** Multi-User MIMO yield progressions for cellular communication, in the midst of which a social cluster of customers or cellular terminals, each with no less than one gathering devices, speak with each other. In a close to way that OFDMA joins assorted admittance (multi-customer) capacities to OFDM, MU-MIMO fuses different access (multi-customer) abilities to MIMO. It has been an important technique to which is basic requirement while deploying the multiple antenna for short-distance communication. This is an enabling key for 5G system.

c) **Hardware Solution:** The equipment for wireless network frameworks is a strategy for energy productivity, to roll out significant improvements in engineering, similar to cloud base execution in radio access network (c-RAN) [20].

d) **RF Harvesting:** It is the concept of harvesting energy from RF which is the abundant source to provide DC source in order to run the network in more energy efficient for proper communication. In order to harvest the energy, the main requirement is highly directional antenna and RF circuits through which the source is converted into AC signals and then to DC signals. This technique is also one basic pillar for the deployment of 5G-GN.

e) **Resource Allocation:** With the help of the technique the RF signals were used to raise the necessity of energy requirement in effective way for the wireless network to be green and the system incorporate for reasonable outputs. This also helps the network and the devices to work in more reliable manner with quite upgrade in energy utilization; indirectly, it strengthens the 5G ecosystem [21].

f) **MBCA:** In this technique, instruments used to upswing the degree of available data transmission to clients for the heterogeneous network in the 5G deployment [21–23]. Beforehand, it was simply engaged to expand the network reasonableness and limit; however, presently, in the current situation, it also restricts the unused energy to be wasted, and it preserves for making the 5G ecosystem toward energy efficient.

g) **Cell Zooming:** It is a productive energy-able procedure in which energy is saved by zooming the light discharge station to give the assistance of the clients which are in the fuse of the other BS, and the BS of these clients will go into rest mode [24].

h) **IoT:** It is a technique through which a large number of devices can communication and exchange huge amount of data without human intervention in a wireless network. This plays a vital role to connect numerous devices in a common platform which is a key enabler for D2D communication 5G ecosystem. There are some other enablers that are available such as Bluetooth Low-Energy in Personal Area Networks (PAN) and Zigbee in household structures; Wi-Fi, LAN, Low-Power Wide-Area Network (LPWAN), and convenient exchange of information (for instance, 3GPP-4G machine-sort trading data, or MTC) have undeniably more broad extension [25].

i) **Deployment and Planning:** The main objective is to connect numerous gadgets with various undoubtedly tremendous developments have been anticipated for the orchestrating, sending, what is more, cycle of 5G frameworks [8–9]. The chance of UDN is to change the perilously extending measure of gadgets to help by growing the idea of passed on foundation instrumentality [25–27].

9.5 5G Technologies: Security and Privacy Issues

5G network has high steadfast quality, low inactivity, and secure and useful transmission administrations. In any case, as furthermore referred to in the past fragment, an enormous piece of these advances come to the detriment of new security and assurance concerns.

9.5.1 5G Security Architecture

The 5G security configuration involves distinctive organization limits, shows, and parts that are liable for getting end to end communication. Specifically, security capacities are getting the entrance of clients inside the Radio Access Network (RAN), meeting the level of secrecy of data/information in the 5G-GN and line components (Edge Computing), and giving security limits in network limit virtualization [8–10, 26–29]. Likewise, a bunch of components is covering security the executive's capacities, review, and examination. In order to implement the 5G, security designing is displayed in Figure 9.4. In particular, the principle 3GPP 5G security parts are as follows:

a) **Dependability of 3GPP and Network Elements (NEs):** IPsec is used between 3GPP and NEs in order to ensure the data/information is more secure and no intruder can access the information; Security Edge Protection Proxy (SEPP) is arranged among HPLMN and VPLMN; and HTTPS is used between separated 5G core network administrations [30].

b) **Secrecy and Trustworthiness of the Air Interface:** Encryption in the computation that uses a 256-digit key; Subscription Concealed Identifier (SUCI) as home

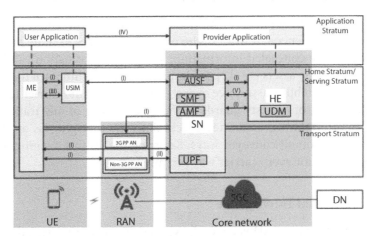

Figure 9.4 Overview of 5G security architecture (source: 5G America White paper 2018).

affiliation identifier and blended Mobile Subscriber Identity Number (MSIN) to ensure client security, and uprightness affirmation is added to the client plane [30–33].

c) **UE Access Control:** In this, there are approvals that were performed between the UE and the association to preserve the presence of effective utilization of BSs.

9.5.2 Deployment Security in 5G Green Network

All organization areas, aside from explicit RAN capacities, may run on cloud frameworks. The equipment at the far edge has the focal and conveyed capacities. This is the locale where dynamic/disengaged antenna systems, radio remote, and base band units may be passed on [10]. The edge and neighborhood cloud, working with the CN, users, and MEC limits are separated from the far edge zone, for instance, the RAN, by the standardized NSA RAN (S1) or SA RAN (NG, for instance, N2 and N3) interface, which guarantees an obvious reasonable and different radio signal access techniques used for the core network [11].

Network services have full control of the induction to the 5G RAN EMS. The 5G-RAN EMS administers RAN parts through its elite South-Bound Interface (SBI), which is, at present, not standardized by the 3GPP [12]. Also, an outsider EMS cannot be utilized for taking care of provider explicit RAN equipment and programming arrangements. The 5G-RAN EMS can be presented and works simply on submitted dealer gave hardware.

9.5.3 Protection of Data Integrity

In 5G-GN, the RAN encodes the data sent between the client and the radio. While it is encoded in LTE, the organization does exclude honesty checking for the concealed information, so invalid information can burn through unearthly assets [11, 12]. 5G improves the uprightness of the RAN by giving respectability assurance over the committed radio carrier (DRB). 5G's affirmation of honesty guards traffic by disposing of any traffic that bombs the uprightness assurance check. Since the uprightness approval is not required on all conveyor ways, Samsung makes this a configurable alternative on a for every carrier way premise.

9.5.4 Artificial Intelligence

Artificial intelligence (AI) is generally viewed as one of the critical pieces of the future organization framework. It is putting it mildly to say that man-made consciousness has drawn in a ton of consideration for the network [13–15]. In spite of the fact that AI in the 5G organization is apparently worked in disconnected regions where gigantic measures of preparing information and amazing however private registering center points are accessible, AI advancements assert that more explicit profound learning may be utilized to distinguish dangers in edge registering. Notwithstanding, this thought requires further investigation.

9.6   5G-GN Assets and Threats

In 5G system, basic assets can be as follows:

- Equipment, programming, and communication components.
- Link between them.
- Data that control the capacity of the framework are delivered and devoured it, or stream inside it.
- The physical and progressive system inside the 5G ecosystem data has been sent safely and more precise manner.
- The technical specialist sort out system requirement and also play a genuine role whose impact reflects on its movement (e.g., customers and structure chiefs).

Because of its worth, a computerized assets turn into an objective for threats specialists. Threats experts are human or programming trained professionals, which may wish to misuse, compromise, or possibly hurt assets [16, 17]. Threats specialists might perform attacks, which make dangers that posture risk to assets in 5G network. Table 9.1 gives brief threats with respect to the assets that belong to 5G green environments [18].

The meaning of the perceived asset gets together, with regard to the CIA term particle that indicates the work of NFV, the leaders of various networks, and game plan (Profoundly 5GC) and programming characterized as organizing, which are the most pivotal resource classifications for keeping up with the CIA security properties [34].

9.7   5G-GN Security Strategies and Deployments

Teleco Partners should foster systems that, freely or then again co-capably, permit decrease of openness to digital attacks. The basic components on which security strategies needs to focus are as follows:

Table 9.1 Threats and assets toward 5G green network (5G-GN).

Sl. no.	Assets	Features	Threats
1	User Equipment (UE)	• eMBB • uRLLC • mMTC	• Malware • Data cloning • Bot commandeering • BTS • Convention downsize • FW/HW/SW (inventory network) harming • IMSI
2	Air Interface		• Pantomime • Information altering • Sticking • BTS • SON attack
3	Mobile Edge Computing (MEC)	• Network Function Virtualization (NFV) • COTS • User Plan Function (UPF)	• DDoS UPF • Spyware • Virtualization discrepancy • Application tampering • API tampering • Untrusted third APP
4	Transport	• Optical Link • Microwave Link • Software-Defined Network (SDN)	• Protocols adjustment and downsize • SDN attacks • Tampering of data
5	Operation and Maintenance	• Equipment, • OSS and EMS programming, • O&M information	• O&M threats • Unapproved authentication • Information spillage • Spyware • API tampering • OSS

a) **Providers** should focus on network safety adequately (for example, regard laws, guidelines, principles, ensure their items, what is more, guarantee quality in their inventory chains).

b) **Telecos'** administrators are liable for surveying hazards and going to fitting lengths to guarantee consistence, security, and, furthermore, versatility of their organizations.

c) **Specialist** co-ops and clients are liable for the execution, organization, backing, and actuation of all fitting security systems of administration applications.

d) **Governments** have the commitment of going to the essential lengths for ensuring the secrecy and precaution toward the communication process to be work in effective way through which the point of interests, the necessity of network, and independent thing testing to be assisted to make green network.

e) **SDO** guarantees that there are appropriate determinations/ principles for security affirmation and best practices set up.

All partners should cooperate to advance security furthermore, flexibility of basic foundations, frameworks, and gadgets. Sharing experience and best works on after examination, relief, reaction, and recuperation from network attack, compromises, or interruptions ought to be advanced [14–16]. The cloud computing basically works with core network and application server, and MEC limits are secluded from the far edge zone, for instance, the RAN, by the standardized NSA RAN (S1) or SA-RAN (NG, for example, N2 and N3) interface, which ensures an unmistakable coherent and actual detachment of the hardware working for accessing the data from the core network components [17].

Between-area interfaces (radio, internet, network wandering, extranet access affiliation, and an authentic square undertaking) and intra-space interfaces (between NEs, intra-NE modules, and O&M) and gear are ensured utilizing security tunnels, for example, IPSec burrows (IPSec encryption and checking to guarantee the portrayal and uprightness of information transmission; IPSec assertion shields information source realness), and firewalls for access control [18]. The 5G RAN EMS coordinates RAN parts through its prohibitive SBI, which is, at this point, not normalized by the 3GPP. Additionally, an outsider EMS cannot be utilized for dealing with provider explicit RAN equipment and programming arrangements. The 5G RAN EMS can be presented and works simply on submitted dealer gave equipment [34, 35].

9.8 Risk Analysis of 5G Applications

Risk analysis can be done on certain scenario with the risk level which was discussed as follows:

a) Disturbance of BSs irregularities: A getting receiving antenna stops working. The attack has affected solely the gear of a given BS. The abutting BSs are not affected.
   Risk level: High

b) Gigantic dysfunctionality of radio helps in a restricted region. Deeply or various receiving antennas are attack in a synchronized manner. Subsequently, various antennas quit working.
   Risk level: Low

c) Enormous dysfunctionality of radio assistance constrained by an outside party focused on a particular region. Radio equipment might be controlled distantly by an outsider, implying that the radio station(s) does not function true to form.
   Risk level: Critical

d) The massive disappointment of network functionalities. An insider assault may cause a colossal disillusionment of the association. This is exceptionally difficult to accomplish by a basic reconfiguration of the data center [15, 16].
   Risk level: Critical

e) Virtualization network dysfunctionality, constrained by an outer party. An outer party (administrator's client) takes advantage of admittance to the organization to assume responsibility for its assets.
   Risk level: Critical

f) Gigantic spillage of individual information. The administrator neglects to guarantee the security of an information base containing basic client information (e.g., through feeble administrator gave encryption of the gathered information submitted to specialist co-ops). Client information (e.g., gadget area) are taken, specifically when another plan of action is presented (e.g., versatile mists) **Risk level:** Significant

9.9 Countermeasures Against Security and Privacy Risks

In view of the framework security and protection arrangements proposed over, the accompanying explicit safety efforts are suggested for 5G application administration engineers and suppliers in various application situations.

9.9.1 Enhanced Mobile Broadband

Security hazards in the enhanced mobile broadband (eMBB) situation predominantly incorporate disappointment of successful observing means, and client protection spillage and the countermeasures are as follows:

i. The optional confirmation and key administration component are utilized to perform auxiliary character validation and approval between the terminal and the eMBB application administration stage to guarantee the genuineness of the terminal and stage personality and the lawfulness of the application [18].
ii. In applications with high-security necessities, the client plane of the 5G organization can be ensured by actual confinement or encryption to ensure the secrecy of data transmission and reception in efficient manner [19].
iii. The network slicing is utilized between the service provider and 5G core network and the eMBB application administration stage to set up a safe information transmission channel to guarantee the security of client business information transmission.

9.9.2 Ultra-Reliable Low Latency Communications

Ultra-reliable low latency communication (uRLLC) situation predominantly incorporates the DDoS assault and the information security hazard, and the comparing countermeasures are as follows:

i. Convey against DDoS capacities to forestall network blockage, remote impedance, and correspondence connect disturbances [19, 20].

ii. Set up a two-way personality confirmation instrument between the client terminal and the application server to keep counterfeit clients from setting up associations.

iii. Through the security capacities sent at the edge processing, just as information trustworthiness assurance, timestamp, chronic number, and different components, to keep application information from being altered/distorted/replayed and guarantee the dependability of information transmission [20, 21].

9.10   Protecting 5G Green Networks Against Attacks

a) DoS attacks by flooding the network with demands (in the control plane) or basically with traffic (in the client plane) such that the organization turns out to be mostly or totally inaccessible for ordinary clients [36, 37]. A particular variation of such a DoS attack against portable organizations is radio interface sticking, for example, making radio assets inaccessible by sending commotion. Flooding assaults might come in the kind of appropriated DoS assaults, where an immense number of sources might be coordinated to create the message floods [21, 22].

b) Creating and taking advantage of secondary passages or malignant capacities inside networks: Such capacities might be embedded by "vindictive insiders" into network components at various pieces of the production network. Refined malware that works subtly might be extremely difficult to identify [23].

c) Exploiting the defects in functional strategies utilized for dealing with the organization: It is accepted that such imperfections will consistently exist, because of people engaged with these techniques [23, 24]. In a more extensive sense, this assault classification additionally is intended to cover assaults by vindictive insiders in the organization activity staff and others with information on and admittance to the organization.

d)   Network accessibility: It guarantees that the organization is consistently accessible in ordinary and surprisingly in debacle recuperation tasks [25]. Occasions affecting the organization, like gadget disappointments, catastrophic events, and security compromise, the organization must accessible to the clients and gadgets [38–40].

e)   Non-renouncement: In this process, data transmission and reception took place between specific users with a private key shared between them so that no other intruder can hamper the whole process. If the private key was wrongly shared, then the safe exchange of information would not carry forward and users loose the utilization of feasible network [26, 27].

9.11   Future Challenges

Each new season of organization development brings new and different applications. Although, a couple of uses from past network ages will, regardless, be applied to 5G-GN, the future application.

a)   **AUV Drone System:** Despite the fact that it has not been conceivable so far to completely send an independent robot framework inferable from the impediments of 5G network could open the maximum capacity. The security and protection issues in independent driving frameworks include a few distinct components, for instance, framework level protection and security issues, area protection, and weak energy utilization frameworks [20–26].

b)   **Quantum Communication:** Quantum correspondence is one more correspondence innovation with incredible application potential in 5G-GN. One of its fundamental advantages is that it can essentially improve the security and dependability of information transmission [21–25].

c)   **VLC:** It is a promising methodology that could be utilized to settle the developing requests for remote availability. A long way from being in its beginning stage stages, VLC has been scrutinized for various years and has now been passed on in different spaces, as indoor masterminding frameworks and the Vehicular Ad Hoc Network (VANET). Separate RF signals have been block with high inactivity, and VLC has higher data transmissions and can conflict with EM impedance. The improvement of strong state lighting has additionally assisted with progressing VLC innovation [1–6].

d) **Blockchain:** Since blockchain innovation imparts information to all included partners [24], it is probably going to be utilized for range and information sharing, in this manner, altogether, improving the security of 5G-GN [5–7].

9.12   Conclusion

5G may be seen as formative with respect to cell development ages. Key limits and constructions express to past ages (3G and 4G) continue to work inside the all around 5G umbrellas. Profoundly, a backward likeness feature did not exist for either 3G or 4G radios similarly as agree with 4G radios as a part of the overall association. Additionally, 5G thinks about a development of access developments of arranged kinds with data speeds from Gbps to Kbps, approved and unlicensed, that relies upon wide spaces of reach gatherings and fuse head ways controlled by standards bodies other than 3GPP. As seen starting here, 5G has every one of the reserves of being a constant update that joins past periods of cell/remote advances. Regardless, when seen by a more broad perspective, 5G is tremendously noteworthy.

To work on the security of business and networks and, simultaneously, guarantee the future thriving of a country, the public authority ought to the following:

a) Should ensure a considerably more aggressive, maintainable, and various telecom production network, to drive better caliber, advancement, and, particularly, boost more ventures in network protection.

b) Should guarantee that there are conformance programs set up and free thing testing for stuff, systems, and programming, and sponsorship express evaluation strategies.

c) Should foster public modern limit as far as programming improvement, hardware producing, research facility testing, congruity assessment, and so forth, seeing start to finish digital protection framework confirmation; new engineering and plans of action; and apparatuses for hazard relief and straightforwardness.

d) Should ensure to diminish the danger of public over-dependence on any one supplier, paying little heed on 5G and fiber networks flexibility for effective usage of energy in order to make ecosystem green.

New advancements in all cloud, AI, IoT, and programming character-ized helps while presenting extraordinary difficulties to the digital protec-tion of ICT framework. The absence of agreement on digital protection, specialized guidelines, confirmation frameworks, and administrative help further worsens these difficulties. Reliable hardware (all inventory net-works) and strong framework and checking will furthermore be totally founded on the principles. This ought to be a communicant effort between private (industry, SME, and examination) and public (policy-makers and regulators) parties, as no single dealer, executive, or government can do it solitary.

References

1. Gartner, Gartner Forecasts Worldwide 5G Network Infrastructure Revenue to Reach $4.2 Billion in 2020, Gartner, Inc. 56 Top Gallant Road Stamford, CT 06902 USA, EGHAM, U.K., August 22, 2019, Available online: https://www.gartner.com/en/newsroom/press-releases/2019-08-22-gartner-forecasts-worldwide-5g-networkinfrastructure (accessed on 17 August 2021).

2. International Telecommunication Union Radio communication, Detailed Specifications of the Terrestrial Radio Interfaces of International Mobile Telecommunications-2020 (IMT-2020); Recommendation ITU-R M.2150-0, 2021.02, International Telecommunication Union Radio communication, Geneva, Switzerland, 2021.

3. Third Generation Partnership Project. 5G System; Technical Realization of Service Based Architecture. Stage 3, TS 29.500. 29 June 2021. Available online:https://portal.3gpp.org/desktopmodules/Specifications/Specification Details.aspx?specificationId

4. UK Department for Digital, Culture, Media & Sport, "UK Telecoms supply chain review report", Telecommunication (Security) Bill, 2019-21 UK, July 2019.

5. The Prague Proposals, "The chairman statement on cyber security of com-munication networks in a globally digitalized world," Prague 5G Security Conference, May 2019.

6. The Intelligence and Security Committee of Parliament, "Statement on 5G suppliers," July 2019.

7. The Science and Technology Select Committee, "Letter to the Secretary of State for Digital, Culture, Media and Sport about Huawei's involvement in the UK's 5G network", July 2019.

8. European Commission (EC), "EU coordinated risk assessment 5G cybersecurity", October 09th 2019.

9. Australian Signals Directorate (ASD), *Cyber supply chain risk management – practitioners guide*", Australian Cyber Security Centre (ACSC) guide, July 2019.

10. European Commission (EC), "Commission recommendation – Cybersecurity of 5G networks", Mar. 2019.

11. European Commission (EC), "ENISA and cyber security certification framework," EUCybersecurity Act, June 2019.

12. Hong, T., Liu, C., Kadoch, M., Machine learning based antenna design for physical layer security in ambient backscatter communications. *Wirel. Commun. Mob. Comput.*, 2019.

13. Nawaz, S.J., Sharma, S.K., Wyne, S., Patwary, M.N., Asaduzzaman, M., Quantum machine learning for 6g communication networks: state-of-the-art and vision for the future. *IEEE Access*, 7, 46317–46350, 2019.

14. Ahmad, I., Shahabuddin, S., Kumar, T., Okwuibe, J., Gurtov, A., Ylianttila, M., Security for 5g and beyond. *IEEE Commun. Surv. Tutorials*, 21, 4, 3682–3722, 2019.

15. Huang, T., Yang, W., Wu, J., Ma, J., Zhang, X., Zhang, D., A survey on green 6g network: architecture and technologies. *IEEE Access*, 7, 175758–175768, 2019.

16. Tomkos, I., Klonidis, D., Pikasis, E., Theodoridis, S., Toward the 6g network era: opportunities and challenges. *IT Prof.*, 22, 1, 34–38, 2020.

17. Ahmad, I., Kumar, T., Liyanage, M., Okwuibe, J., Ylianttila, M., Gurtov, A., Overview of 5G Security Challenges and Solutions. *IEEE Commun. Stand. Mag.*, 2, 36–43, 2018.

18. Using Side Channel Information, in: *Proceedings of the 26nd Annual Network and Distributed System Security Symposium (NDSS)*, San Diego, CA, USA, 24–27 February 2019.

19. Rupprecht, D., Kohls, K., Holz, T., Pöpper, C., Call me maybe: Eavesdropping encrypted LTE calls with ReVoLTE, in: *Proceedings of the 29th USENIX Security Symposium, Online Conference*, 12–14 August 2020.

20. Park, S., Cho, H., Park, Y., Choi, B., Kim, D., Yim, K., Security Problems of 5G Voice Communication, in: *Information Security Applications*, I. You, (Ed.), WISA, Jeju Island, Korea, 2020.

21. Cui, J., Chen, J., Zhong, H., Zhang, J., Liu, L., "Reliable and Efficient Content Sharing for 5G-Enabled Vehicular Networks,". *IEEE Trans. Intell. Transp. Syst.*, 2019. DOI: 10.1109/TITS.2020.3023797.

22. Loghin, D. *et al.*, "The Disruptions of 5G on Data-Driven Technologies and Applications,". *IEEE Trans. Knowl. Data Eng.*, 32, 6, 1179–1198, 1 June 2020. DOI: 10.1109/TKDE.2020.2967670.

23. Agiwal, M., Roy, A., Saxena, N., "Next Generation 5G Wireless Networks: A Comprehensive Survey,". *IEEE Commun. Surv.Tut.*, 18, 3, 1617–1655, 2019.

24. Lin, J.C.W., Srivastava, G., Zhang, Y., Djenouri, Y., Aloqaily, M., "Privacy Preserving Multi-Objective Sanitization Model in 6G IoT Environments,". *IEEE Internet Things J.*, 2020. DOI: 10.1109/JIOT.2020.3032896.

25. Lin, J.C.-W., Srivastava, G., Zhang, Y., Djenouri, Y., Aloqaily, M., "Privacy Preserving Multi-Objective Sanitization Model in 6G IoT Environments." *IEEE Internet Things J.*, DOI: 10.1109/JIOT.2020.3032896.

26. Huang, J., Qian, Y., Hu, R.Q., "Secure and Efficient PrivacyPreserving Authentication Scheme for 5G Software Defined Vehicular Networks,". *IEEE Trans. Veh. Technol.*, 69, 8, 8542–8554, Aug. 2020. DOI: 10.1109/ TVT.2020.2996574.

27. Huang, J., Qian, Y., Hu, R.Q., "Secure and Efficient Privacy Preserving Authentication Scheme for 5G Software Defined Vehicular Networks." *IEEE Trans. Veh. Technol.*, 69, 8, 8542–8554, Aug. 2020, DOI: 10.1109/ TVT.2020.2996574.

28. Thakur, K., Qiu, M., Gai, K., Ali, Md L., "An investigation on cyber security threats and security models.", in: *2015 IEEE 2nd International Conference on Cyber Security and Cloud Computing*, IEEE, pp. 307–311, 2015.

29. Saleem, K., Alabduljabbar, G.M., Alrowais, N., Al-Muhtadi, J., Imran, M., Rodrigues, J.J.P.C., "Bio-Inspired Network Security for 5GEnabled IoT Applications,". *IEEE Access*, 8, 229152–229160, 2020. DOI: 10.1109/ ACCESS.2020.3046325.

30. Khan, R., Kumar, P., Nalin, D., Liyanage, M., A Survey on Security and Privacy of 5GTechnologies: Potential Solutions, in: *Recent Advancements and Future Directions*, IEEE, 2019.

31. Verizon Wireless, 2018 Data Breach Investigations Report, Verizon Wireless, New York, 2018.

32. Hou, J., Zhang, M., Zhang, Z., Shi, W., Qin, B., Liang, B., On the fine-grained fingerprinting threat to software-defined networks. *Future Gener. Comput. Syst.*, 2020.

33. Yang, S., Yin, D., Song, X., Dong, X., Manogaran, G., Mastorakis, G., Mavromoustakis, C., Batalla, J.M., Security situation assessment for massive MIMO systems for 5G communications. *Future Gener. Comput. Syst.*, 2020.

34. Hussain, R., Hussain, F., Zeadally, S., Integration of VANET and 5G security: Design and implementation issues. *Future Gener. Comput. Syst.*, 2020.

35. El-Latif, A.A., Abd-El-Atty, B., Venegas-Andraca, S.E., Mazurczyk, W., Efficient quantum-based security protocols for information sharing and data protection in 5G networks. *Future Gener. Comput. Syst.*, 2020.

36. Yang, T.-W., Ho, Y.-H., Chou, C.-F., Achieving M2M-device authentication through heterogeneous information bound with USIM card. *Future Gener. Comput. Syst.*, 110, 629–637, 2020.

37. Behrad, S., Bertin, E., Tuffin, S., Crespi, N., A new scalable authentication and access control mechanism for 5G-based IoT. *Future Gener. Comput. Syst.*, 2020.

38. Rost, P. *et al.*, "Network Slicing to Enable Scalability and Flexibility in 5G Mobile Networks,". *IEEE Commun. Mag*, 55, 5, 72–79, May 2017.

39. Al-Dulaimi, A. *et al.*, "Orchestration of Ultra-Dense 5G Networks,". *IEEE Commun. Mag.*, 56, 8, 68–69, Aug. 2018.

40. Al-Dulaimi, A. *et al.*, "Orchestration of Ultra-Dense 5G Networks." *IEEE Commun. Mag.*, 56, 8, 68–69, Aug. 2018.

10

A Novel Cost-Effective Secure Green Data Center Solutions Using Virtualization Technology

Subhodip Mukherjee[1], Debabrata Sarddar[2], Rajesh Bose[3] and Sandip Roy[3]*

[1]Department of MCA, Techno International Newtown, Kolkata, India
[2]Department of Computer Science & Engineering, University of Kalyani, Kalyani, India
[3]Department of Computational Science, Brainware University, Kolkata, India

Abstract

Modern information technology environment demands augmentation of the worth for money devoid of adjusting on the potency of the accumulated components. The growing claim for repository, networking, and reckoning has controlled the rise of huge intricate data centers, the giant server companies which administer several present internet operations, economic, trading, and business operations. Several thousands of servers can be stored by a data center, and a data center is able to consume the same energy that a small city can. The huge quantity of calculation ability needed to control such server systems manages several confrontations such as energy exertion, coming out of greenhouse gases, and substitutes and resumption affairs. This is virtualization that signifies a number of technologies, which include a vast area of uses and pursuits. This can be implemented to the fields of hardware and software and the technologies under the periphery of the rise of virtualization. This research shows how we have suggested such virtualization technology for the transformation of a customary data center framework bit by bit to a green data center. This research focuses on the explanation of the price profits of endorsing virtualization technology, which is admonished by almost each dominant enterprise in the market. This is such a technology that can entirely lessen capital prices in our environment, whereas, at the same time, it almost commits small running prices for the upcoming 3 years, pursuing the finance. Here, we discuss the value in terms of cost and space, where space, too, translates to eventual cost.

*Corresponding author: sandiproy86@gmail.com

Sabyasachi Pramanik, Debabrata Samanta, M. Vinay and Abhijit Guha (eds.) Cyber Security and Network Security, (217–232) © 2022 Scrivener Publishing LLC

Keywords: Cloud computing, green computing, green data center, information technology (IT), Network Address Translation (NAT), virtualization technology

10.1 Introduction

Information technology (IT) has radically changed our job and life and upgraded our yield, finance, and civil subsistence over time. At present, different companies, governments, and countries on the run have a novel salient program, that is, controlling the affairs related to our environment. IT has been providing us with the support for the confrontations related to the environment, but the majority of people do not understand it. Momentous quality of electricity is engrossed by computers and other IT groundwork. This consumption is growing by degrees, creating a huge load on our power grids and causing greenhouse gases (GHG). This has been indicated that, by upgrading the applications of data centers through virtualization, it saves up to 20% of exertion of energy in data centers [1].

For making less energy exertion, virtualization is a vital policy nowadays. A single physical server acts as a host of several virtual servers in the process of virtualization. This empowers the data center to invigorate their physical server framework, being the host of several virtual servers on a few more competent servers, applying less power consumption and making a less complicated data center. Not only it receives superior hardware utilization, but also it lessens data center floor volume, creates finer utilization of calculating potency, and diminishes the power consumption of data centers pretty well. Several companies now implement virtualization to diminish the power consumption of the data center. Instead of the holding up of a sole OS, which in succession hosts a server operation such as web server and mail server, a virtualized procedure empowers a sole hardware machine. That executes the identical OS. It empowers a sole host machine that executes the identical OS. It empowers a sole host machine executing several virtual machines. It is virtualization that offers the scopes to measure the service facilities in a data center, offers superior application of hardware assets, diminishes running prices, and lessens power exertion.

Virtualization is assigned to the formation of a virtual edition of an asset which splits up the asset into sole or server application ambience [2, 3]. But, it is problematic in cloud computing because it increases the flexibility as all the servers are assigned to an adequate repository and calculating potency that a customer requires. The growing requirement for consumer function needs more power and volume. In this situation, virtualization is swapping the IT ambience in which the majority of the enterprises have been facilitated to endorse the changes as a means which permits for superior application of hardware and curtailment of prices [4, 5]. It is observed that one of the vital utilities of virtualization is green computing.

It is also observed that virtualization enhances the potency and accessibility of IT expedients and operation that starts with eradicating the former "one server, one operation" prototype and executes several virtual devices [6, 7]. The prime attributes of virtualization are as follows:

(a) Confirms business operations and carry out with the highest availability;
(b) Curtail running prices by using power sources with superiority;
(c) Curtail capital prices by using power sources well.

If anyone means fewer servers, then it practically means less IT-associated procedures that signifies diminished real estate and less energy and cooling needs [8, 9]. It replies to the transformation of the production and takes on novel means with vigorous resource management, swifter server amenities, and advanced operation implementation.

The cause of the integration and virtualization IT framework is that the server is comprehensive. Very often, IT administrators aim at only the price of the physical IT framework. In spite of that, there are supplementary utilities, which can be obtained from server integration as follows:

(1) Suitable exploitation of servers
(2) Appropriate power consumption
(3) Lessening of exertion of power
(4) Lessening of coming out of GHG
(5) Lessening of global warming consequences
(6) Acquiring sustainable commerce
(7) Easy management
(8) Modified data safety
(9) Modified resource exploitation
(10) Simpler amendment management and suppleness

This research aims at curtailing price on cost which upholds via support virtualization to lay beyond each resource on hardware, which is expensive and it also creates power consumption in the customary data centers. It is termed as green cloud computing. In this paper, we talk about the business profits via virtualization and a few virtualization methods such as server virtualization for storing power which are favorable for our atmosphere to keep it green.

10.2   Literature Survey

Virtualization is such a mechanization that remains for a certain time. It is IBM that developed such an idea initially, in the 1960s, to offer a simultaneous bilateral approach to a mainframe computer IBM 360 that upholds several examples of Oss getting executed on the same hardware podium [10].

This mechanization upholds several Oss getting executed on a sole hardware podium and offers a beneficial way of controlling the Oss. The OS and applications getting executed on the virtualization management podium are regarded as VMs [11]. As server virtualization offers a simple technique to flawlessly split up physical servers, permitting the execution of several applications in seclusion on a sole server, it has turned out to be noteworthy in data centers. Virtualization classifies volume servers into distinct resource pools based on the workloads of them. After that, server integration is used. This method breaks up software from hardware and separates microprocessor servers to more self-reliant virtual hosts for more suitable use of the hardware resources, permitting the dissemination of overhauls in one processor. In server integration, several portable physical servers are restored by a huge physical server to augment the use of costly hardware resources, decreasing the exertion of energy and coming out of CO_2 [12].

It is difficult to proceed with energy-apprehensive resource management for a HPC data center. Authors displayed power-apprehensive multicore scheduling and FindHostForVm to prefer what host gets slightest augmenting power loss for authorizing a VM [13]. Nevertheless, the FindHostForVm is akin to the PABFD's disallowing that they bother with memory exploitation in a course of predicted runtime for speculating the energy of the host [14]. It offered a procedure, too, to choose flawless operating frequency for a (DVFS-empowered) host and construct the number of virtual cores for VM.

10.2.1   Virtualization

It is such a technology that is a move toward green computing. It is a customary feature of green IT. Virtualization offers a stage of abstraction termed as hypervisor that remains on the computer hardware. Hypervisor is nothing but a software program, which aims at a rational outlook of computing instead of physical outlook. Hypervisor permits a computer to execute several Operating Systems on a sole device. We can implement virtualization to core computing equipment, such as CPU (processor), storage (Hard Disk), networking (connection), and memory (RAM). The customarily implemented virtualization method is server virtualization, but the aim has also been converted into Desktop Virtualization. server virtualization is full-fledged, whereas Desktop Virtualization is now under survey. Commercial fields consider virtualization as a fund reduction policy. Server Integration has a significant part in commercial fields and 80% of companies are covering projects which uphold Server Integration [15, 16].

Server virtualization is decreasing the quality of servers needed and augmenting the use of servers. Server virtualization stores almost 60% to 90% of energy. In spite of the reality, in hypothesis, practically, just 60% is achievable. If we decrease the server track, then it lessens the energy exertion, and so, it lessens the cooling necessity. An additional utility of virtualization is load balancing that makes harmony of the load among the accessible servers. Server virtualization is acquired via superfluity. A substitute server supports each server. At the beginning, the substitute server count was huge. Afterward this was decreased to 3, and at present, this number is only 1. Now, the well-known and experienced enterprises use just 1 substitute server which is enough for them. Such 1 substitute server is dependable. Server virtualization is the agreeable spot and a preference of the commercial grounds.

10.3   Problem Statement

Data centers are afflicted with several thousands of servers which carry out the processing for trades and end users to assist and bring about hefty target of commercial benefits. But, this is the crisis with these servers that they very often lock to their End-of-Service (EoS) life span. These make an end of a significant segment of our computing requirements. Since the producer will no longer uphold the safeguarding and other attributes of such servers ahead of the EoS point, restoring with virtualization technology, these are our concern and significance for the objectives of this research work and also lay by capital and get ready for a prospective green data center.

Inclination in virtualization is developing all the time. Besides, novel mechanizations are swiftly accessible for execution [17]. As a few IT experts are not able to take up virtual technologies productively; it is observed that a major dilemma subsists [18]. It is now a customary IT crisis that several IT experts are unable to execute novel virtualization technologies. The explicit IT dilemma is that a few IT project managers do not have proper information of the connection between industrial or institutional customs and the thriving agreement of novel virtualization technologies.

It is firmly necessary to comprehend the real ambient and industrial profit of this mechanization for data centers so that customary data centers can with ever rising requirements from trades.

10.3.1   VMware Workstation

Virtualization is verified software mechanization. It is promptly changing the IT scenario. It is also radically amending the procedure folks calculate. At present, with dominant processing skills of X86 computer hardware which only executes a sole operating system and a sole application, that is responsible to make most computer support systems partially used. Virtualization is a firmly secluded software vessel. VMware Workstation Virtualization Software delineates the physical hardware support system to virtual device support systems. That is why, all virtual machines possess their own CPU, memory, disk, and network juncture cards. Moreover, the virtual machine is able to link with the physical network adapter, CD-ROM equipment, hard drives, and USB equipment. VMware Workstation is able to copy other hardware. We can install OS for virtual machines (VM) from ISO image in VMware workstation without using CD ROM. We can also install networks in such a way by using the ESXI console. Besides, we are able to host a virtual network adapter constituted to implement Network Address Translation (NAT) instead of administering an IP address in each virtual machine [19].

10.4   Green it Using Virtualization

Since enterprises have begun to comprehend the significance of green IT in storing energy and feasible improvement, the energy productive and green data center is accumulating strength. This is executed to novel technologies which are able to assist in reducing the energy price of data centers, and it is done for making less expense. Green IT plays a great part in lessening energy exertion in the data center [20, 21]. The suggested work assists

IT trade companies too, especially data center companies to be guided by virtualized green IT infrastructure to lay by a lot of money displaying ROI computation thoroughly and simultaneously decrease coming out of CO_2 that finally mitigates global warming impacts [22]. The suggested green IT infrastructure applying virtualization and green benchmarks ought to be applied and obeyed by data center officials to execute green approaches in their data center with the intention of making it more energy methodical and green. Such data center comprises in the five forms as follows:

(1) Improve plan for green data centers;
(2) Classify data center into scalable equipment;
(3) Categorize green metrics and set yardsticks;
(4) Categorize and apply virtualization kind;
(5) Calculate the presentation in terms of energy effectiveness and CO_2 giving out.

10.5 Proposed Work

We apply VMware server virtualization technology in our suggested work. It is dependent on our suggested framework. After that, we survey the ROI computation and the outcome displays a lot of profit. In the beginning, we selected seven servers to amend. Table 10.1 displays the server name with application specifications, kind of server, and hardware applied for our suggested framework. Compute the volume of the physical server in the customary data center that is displayed in Tables 10.1 to 10.4.

Table 10.1 Server name and type with application details.

Sr. no.	Server name with application details	Server type
1	Tivoli Storage Manager For Mail	PowerEdge 2850
2	Blackberry Enterprise Server	PowerEdge 2850
3	IBM ICC Server	PowerEdge 2850
4	Citrix and Primavera Server	PowerEdge 2850
5	TSM For Content Manager	PowerEdge 2850
6	McAfee Antivirus Server	PowerEdge 800
7	Ftp Server	PowerEdge 2800

Table 10.2 Server type with available hardware.

Server type	Available hardware				
	CPU	CPU details	Memory	Network	HDD
PowerEdge 2850	2 CPU 2 Core	Intel Xeon 3.2 MHz	2 GB	GBPS	140*6
PowerEdge 2850	2 CPU 2 Core	Intel Xeon 3.2 MHz	4 GB	GBPS	72*2
PowerEdge 2850	2 CPU 2 Core	Intel Xeon 3.2 MHz	4 GB	GBPS	140*6
PowerEdge 2850	2 CPU 2 Core	Intel Xeon 3.2 MHz	4 GB	GBPS	140*5
PowerEdge 2850	2 CPU 2 Core	Intel Xeon 3.2 MHz	4 GB	GBPS	140*6
PowerEdge 800	1 CPU	Intel Xeon 3.2 MHz	2 GB	GBPS	72
PowerEdge 2800	2 CPU 2 Core	Intel Xeon 3.2 MHz	2 GB	GBPS	140*5

Table 10.3 Server type with utilization.

Server type	Utilization %			
	CPU avg./ peak	Memory avg./ peak	Network avg./ peak	HDD used
PowerEdge 2850	5%	80%	10%	80%
PowerEdge 2850	10%	80%	10%	80%
PowerEdge 2850	50%	80%	20%	30%
PowerEdge 2850	70%	80%	15%	30%
PowerEdge 2850	10%	80%	10%	80%
PowerEdge 800	5%	50%	5%	30%
PowerEdge 2800	5%	50%	10%	70%

Table 10.4 Server type with operating system and application.

Server type	Operating system	Application
PowerEdge 2850	RHEL 5 64 bit	Tivoli Storage Manager Server
PowerEdge 2850	Ms Win2k3 standard	Blackberry
PowerEdge 2850	MS Win2k8 standard	IBM Content Collector
PowerEdge 2850	Ms Win2k3 standard	Citrix and Primavera
PowerEdge 2850	RHEL 5 64 Bit	Tivoli Storage Manager
PowerEdge 800	MS Win2k3 Standard	McAfee Antivirus Server
PowerEdge 2800	RHEL 3	FTP Server

This research aims at resolving features of price and liberty that principally gives impact on the form of technology and framework fitted for our suggested state of affairs. Price can be additionally segregated into atomic chunks described with regard to energy and cooling prices and that is paid out to ascertain high availability, or HA since this is alluded to in following segments of this research.

In this paper, initially, our objective was to adapt more than seven servers to virtual Server. VMware is implemented in this research for such an objective. In this research, an approximate return of investment (ROI) is suggested for this elucidation (Table 10.5). The ROI is computed on the subsequent considerations and outcome. A beneficial commercial profit is displayed from Tables 10.5 to 10.8.

1. Power and cooling
2. Data center space
3. Network
4. Storage

10.5.1   Proposed Secure Virtual Framework

In our proposed architecture in Figure 10.1, we are using two servers (ESX1 and ESX2) with two switches and one storage system. To create a secure virtual environment, we use one firewall that has two dissimilar networks constituted in Server Zone passing through identical interfaces. The present servers that are intended to make virtualized are prevailed in chiefly two networks (172.16.1.0/21 and 172.17.1.0/24) and VMware network

Table 10.5 Return of investment (ROI) in power and cooling.

Power and cooling	Before consolidation (Dedicated Servers)	After virtualization
Avg. power consumption of a server in watts	600	920
Per server powered on hours in hours (24 hours × 365 days)	8,760	8,760
Server qty.	7	2
Total watt hours	36,792,000	1,611,8400
Total kilowatt required for 1 year	36,792	1,6118.4
Price per kilowatt hour or 1 unit in rupees	9.00	9.00
Total price for 1 year in rupees	INR 331,128	INR 145,065.6
Total price for 3 years in rupees	INR 993,384	INR 435,196.8
Cooling cost 1 year (industry std. 115% of Power cost) in Rupees	INR 380,797	INR 166,825
Cooling cost 3 years (industry std. 115% of Power cost) in rupees	INR 1142,392	INR 500,476
Power and cooling cost per year in rupees	INR 711,925	INR 311,890.6
Power and cooling cost for 3 years in rupees	INR 2,135,776	INR 935,672.8

(taking in ESXI Servers, vCenter Server, and storage) will be staying in 172.17.3.64/26 network, i.e., in Server Zone solely.

In this paper, we focus on computing the ROI. We also keep an eye at the factors such as focuses on the factors such as power and cooling, space, network, and repository separately in the event of previous and after virtualization ambience. In this research, we compute and juxtapose each factor, and that is why, we are able to spot that, if we have seven servers to transform it into a virtual server with the assistance of VMware, then we are able to put aside almost. Rs. 4681878 (in words forty-six lakh eighty-one

Table 10.6 Return of investment (ROI) in data center space.

Space	Before consolidation (Dedicated Servers)	After virtualization
Avg. rack unit of server (in rack units)	2	3
Total rack units for all servers (in rack units)	14	6
Standard rack size in rack units (in rack units)	42	42
Racks required for all servers (rack qty.)	1	1
Cost of one 42 inch rack space	INR 10,000	INR 10,000
Total rack space cost for all servers for 1 year	INR 10,000	INR 10,000
Total rack space cost for all servers for 3 years	INR 30,000	INR 30,000

Table 10.7 Return of investment (ROI) in network.

Network	Before consolidation (Dedicated Servers)	After virtualization
No. of ports per server	2	6
Total no. of switch ports with redundancy	14	12
Network cabling cost for the entire infrastructure (INR 500 per port)	INR 7,000	INR 6,000
Per NIC and switch port cost (INR 500 per port and NIC card)	INR 14,000	INR 12,000
Total NICs, switch ports, and cabling cost	INR 21,000	INR 18,000
Maintenance charges for 1 year (30% of total cost)	INR 6,300	INR 5,400
Maintenance charges for 3 years	INR 42,000	INR 36,000

Table 10.8 Return of investment (ROI) in storage (*considered zero due to previously procurement).

Storage	Before consolidation (Dedicated Servers)*	After virtualization
No. of HBAs per server	0	2
Total no. of switch ports with redundancy (50% servers considered for SAN)	0	4
SAN FC cabling cost for the entire infrastructure (INR 1,000 per port)	0	4,000
Per HBA and switch port cost (INR 30,000/HBA and INR 15,000/FC port)	0	180,000
Total HBAs, switch ports, and cabling cost	0	184,000
Maintenance charges for 1 year (30% of total cost)	0	55,200
Maintenance charges for 3 years	0	165,600

thousand eight hundred seventy-eight Indian rupees) in 3 years. In this way, we are able to transform the remaining physical server bit by bit into a virtual server. We are able to profit from a massive storage in power and money, and consequently, we obtain green surroundings too. Figure 10.2 displays the economic profit of the entire framework price in INR that takes in upholding for first year between integration at the previous stage of virtualization, committed servers, and post virtualization. Figure 10.1 shows virtual architecture of the proposed architecture. Figure 10.2 shows the entire framework price in INR taking in upholding for first year between before integration of out-and-out servers and after virtualization. Table 10.5 shows ROI in power and cooling. Table 10.6 shows ROI in data center space, Table 10.7 shows ROI in network, and Table 10.8 shows ROI in storage (*considered zero due to previously procurement).

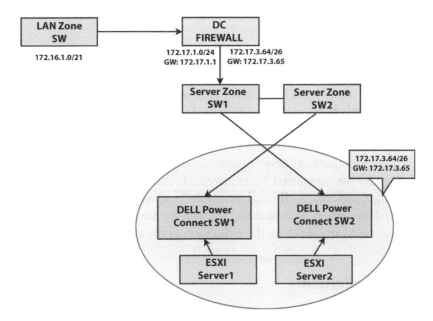

Figure 10.1 Virtual architecture of the proposed architecture.

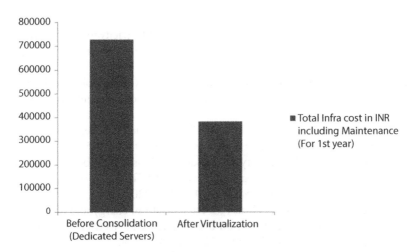

Figure 10.2 Entire framework price in INR taking in upholding for first year between before integration of out-and-out servers and after virtualization.

10.6   Conclusion

In this research, we evaluate several considerations for controlling power and energy in computing systems. For securing the price of power, the former state of integration and virtual environment are compared. We have compared with before consolidation and virtual environment to save the energy cost. Our effort established in this research points to the constant growing attention of researchers in the domain of green computing implementing virtualization. Several green computing procedures for power effectiveness are suggested by researchers; conversely, green computing technology requires additional research as elevated energy exertion is there in data centers. It is summed up with a return of investment or ROI in a virtualized ambience by the evaluation of the significance.

Acknowledgments

Authors gratefully acknowledge to Computational Science and Engineering department of University of Kalyani, West Bengal, India, Techno International New Town, and Brainware University, West Bengal, India, for providing lab and related facilities for doing the research.

References

1. Aslan, J., Mayers, K., Koomey, J. G., France, C., Electricity intensity of Internet data transmission: Untangling the estimates. *Journal of Industrial Ecology,* 22, 4, 785–798, 2018.

2. Bose, R., Roy, S., Mondal, H., Chowdhury, D. R., Chakraborty, S. Energy-efficient approach to lower the carbon emissions of data centers. *Computing,* 103, 1703–1721, 2021.

3. Roy, S., Bose, R., Roy, T., Sarddar, D., Cloud-enabled data center organization using KD tree. *Int. J. Database Theory Appl.,* 8, 69–76, 2015.

4. Mukherjee, D., Chakraborty, S., Sarkar, I., Ghosh, A., Roy, S., A Detailed Study on Data Centre Energy Efficiency and Efficient Cooling Techniques. *Int. J. Adv. Trends Comput. Sci. Eng.,* 9, 1–21, 2020.

5. Morley, J., Widdicks, K., Hazas, M. Digitalisation, energy and data demand: The impact of Internet traffic on overall and peak electricity consumption. *Energy Research & Social Science,* 38, 128–137, 2018.

6. Renugadevi, T., Geetha, K., Muthukumar, K., Geem, Z.W., Optimized Energy Cost and Carbon Emission-Aware Virtual Machine Allocation in Sustainable Data Centers. *Sustainability,* 12, 1–27, August 2020.

7. Garg, S.K. and Buyya, R., Green Cloud computing and Environmental Sustainability, in: *Harnessing Green IT: Principles and Practices*, pp. 315–340, 2012.

8. Ahmed, K. M. U., Bollen, M. H., Alvarez, M. A., Review of Data Centers Energy Consumption And Reliability Modeling. *IEEE Access*, 9,152536-152563, 2021.

9. Sarkar, I., Pal, B., Datta, A., Roy, S., Wi-Fi Based Portable Weather Station for Monitoring Temperature, Relative Humidity, Pressure, Precipitation, Wind Speed and Direction. In: *Information and Communication Technology for Sustainable Development. Advances in Intelligent Systems and Computing*, M. Tuba, S. Akashe, A. Joshi, (eds.), 933, Springer, Singapore, 2020.

10. Rivoire, S., Shah, M.A., Ranganathan, P., Kozyrakis, C., JouleSort: a balanced energy-efficiency benchmark, in: *Proceedings of the 2007 ACM SIGMOD international conference on Management of data (SIGMOD '07)*, pp. 365–376, Association for Computing Machinery, New York, NY, USA, 2007.

11. Abdullahi, M. and Ngadi, M.A., *Hybrid symbiotic organisms search optimization algorithm for scheduling of tasks on cloud computing environment*, 11, 6, e0158229, 1–29, PloS One, USA, 2016.

12. Dhoot, A., Nazarov, A.N., Koupaei, A.N.A., A Security Risk Model for Online Banking System, in: *2020 Systems of Signals Generating and Processing in the Field of on Board Communications*, pp. 1–4, IEEE, March 2020.

13. Anuradha, P., Rallapalli, H., Narsimha, G., Energy efficient scheduling algorithm for the multicore heterogeneous embedded architectures. *Des. Autom. Embed. Syst.*, 22, 1–12, 2018.

14. Singh, A., Juneja, D., Malotra, M., A novel agent based autonomous and service composition framework for cost optimization of resource provisioning in cloud computing. *J. King Saud Univ.-Comput. Inf. Sci.*, 29, 19–28, 2017.

15. Radu, L.-D., Green Cloud Computing: A Literature Survey. *Symmetry*, 9, 1–20, 2017.

16. Furqan, M., Yan, W., Zhang, C., Iqbal, S., Jan, Q., Huang, Y., An energy-efficient collaborative caching scheme for 5G wireless network. *IEEE Access*, 7, 156907–156916, 2019.

17. Lee, H.M., Jeong, Y.S., Jang, H.J., Performance analysis based resource allocation for green cloud computing. *J. Supercomput.*, 69, 1013–1026, 2014.

18. O'Halloran, D., How technology will change the way we work. *World Economic Forum*, Available at: https://www.weforum.org/agenda/2015/08/how-technology-will-change-the-way-we-work/ (Accessed: 18th November 2020).

19. Madni, S.H.H., Abd Latiff, M.S., Coulibaly, Y., Recent advancements in resource allocation techniques for cloud computing environment: a systematic review. *Cluster Comput.*, 20, 2489–2533, 2017.

20. Masanet, E., Shehabi, A., Lei, N., Smith, S., Koomey, J., Recalibrating global data center energy-use estimates. *Science*, 367, 6481, 984–986, 2020.

21. Bose, R., Roy, S., Sarddar, D., On Demand IOPS Calculation in Cloud Environment to Ease Linux-Based Application Delivery, in: *Proceedings of the First International Conference on Intelligent Computing and Communication*, pp. 71–77, 2017.
22. Bose, R., Roy, S., Sarddar, D., A Billboard Manager Based Model That Offers Dual Features Supporting Cloud Operating System And Managing Cloud Data Storage. *Int. J. Hybrid Inf. Technol. (JHIT)*, 8, 229–236, 2015.

11

Big Data Architecture for Network Security

**Dr. Bijender Bansal[1], V.Nisha Jenipher[2], Rituraj Jain[3],
Dr. Dilip R.[4], Prof. Makhan Kumbhkar[5], Sabyasachi Pramanik[6*],
Sandip Roy[7] and Ankur Gupta[1]**

*[1]Dept. of Computer Science and Engineering, Vaish College of Engineering, Rohtak,
Haryana, India*
*[2]Dept. of Computer Science and Engineering, St. Joseph's Institute of Technology,
Semmancheri, Chennai, Tamil Nadu, India*
*[3]Dept. of Electrical and Computer Engineering, Wollega University,
Nekemte, Ethiopia*
*[4]Dept. of Electrical and Electronics Engineering, Global Academy of Technology,
Raja Rajeshwari Nagar, Bengaluru, India*
*[5]Dept. of Computer Science, Christian Eminent College,
Indore, Madhya Pradesh, India*
*[6]Dept. of Computer Science and Engineering, Haldia Institute of Technology,
Haldia, West Bengal, India*
[7]Dept. of Computational Science, Brainware University, Kolkata, India

Abstract

Research is considering security of big data and retaining the performance
during its transmission over network. It has been observed that there have been
several researches that have considered the concept of big data. Moreover, a lot
of those researches also provided security against data but failed to retain the
performance. Use of several encryption mechanisms such as RSA [43] and AES
[44] has been used in previous researches. But, if these encryption mechanisms

Corresponding author: sabyalnt@gmail.com
Dr. Bijender Bansal: ORCID: https://orcid.org/0000-0002-3502-4139
V.Nisha Jenipher: ORCID: https://orcid.org/0000-0002-0518-5599
Rituraj Jain: ORCID: https://orcid.org/0000-0002-5532-1245
Dr. Dilip R: ORCID: https://orcid.org/0000-0002-4316-6532
Prof. Makhan Kumbhkar: ORCID: https://orcid.org/0000-0001-9241-5331
Sabyasachi Pramanik: ORCID: https://orcid.org/0000-0002-9431-8751
Ankur Gupta: ORCID: https://orcid.org/0000-0002-4651-5830

Sabyasachi Pramanik, Debabrata Samanta, M. Vinay and Abhijit Guha (eds.) Cyber Security and Network
Security, (233–268) © 2022 Scrivener Publishing LLC

are applied, then the performance of network system gets degraded. In order to resolve those issues, the proposed work is making using of compression mechanism to reduce the size before implementing encryption. Moreover, data is spitted in order to make the transmission more reliable. After splitting the data contents data has been transferred from multiple route. If some hackers opt to capture that data in unauthentic manner, then they would be unable to get complete and meaning full information. Thus, the proposed model has improved the security of big data in network environment by integration of compression and splitting mechanism with big data encryption. Moreover, the use of user-defined port and use of multiple paths during transmission of big data in split manner increases the reliability and security of big data over network environment.

Keywords: Big data, network security, compression, encryption, RSA, AES, error rate, packet size

11.1 Introduction to Big Data

The term big data has been initialized in starting of 1990. It got the popularity with importance, which is increasing exponentially in following years. At present time, big data is integral task of company's strategy. McKinsey Global Institute has expressed the big data as data sets. The size of these is outside ability to store, manage, data analyze [1], and capture special database software.

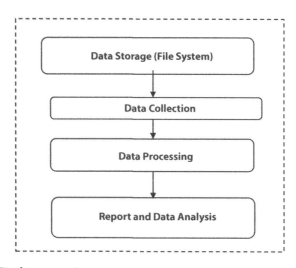

Figure 11.1 Big data processing.

The amount of information generated across the globe is discharged every day. The usage of digital, social, and internet media and stuff adds fire to it. The speed with which information is gained is enormous. Information occurs because it arrives from various devices and it includes a wealth of knowledge that may prove to be a crucial factor in this competitive climate. A large data problem is that data from the same group are more similar than the data from other groups or clusters. In telecommunications, healthcare, bioinformatics, finance, marketing, biology, insurance, city planning, seismic research, and categorization of online documents and in transportation, big data applications [2] are utilized.

11.1.1   10 V's of Big-Data

These are described as data with broader range, increasing volumes and speed. Big data, especially new data sources, is growing in size and complexity. These data sets are so big that traditional technology is incapable of handling them.

The phrase "big data" means a lot of information (terabytes and petabytes). In order to address a specific business case, it is essential to know that the value does not typically contain the full volume, but a tiny portion. This important component cannot, however, be identified without analysis in advance.

Big data means a large quantity of data from which information is gathered. Each second a tremendous amount of data is generated by the companies to be managed. Big data will thus gather, store, and organize the data to be further examined by data analysts. In other words, the big data is an enormous quantity of data, which may be analyzed for valuable information.

Big data, especially new data sources, is growing in size and complexity. Traditional data processing methods cannot handle these massive data sets. This vast quantity of information may nevertheless be utilized to solve business issues that you were unable to handle previously. This is a technology set developed to store, analyze, and manage this bulk data, a macro tool designed in order, in order to provide smart solutions, to discover patterns of this explosion's chaos. It is now utilized in such varied fields as medical, agriculture, gaming, and the preservation of the environment.

There are 10 V's of big data, seven more important characteristics, which everyone needs and wants to know. Conveniently, these characteristics start with V, too; thus, 10 V's of big data are described below:

- **Volume:** Volume was regarded as the greatest large data characteristic. Every minute, 4,000 hours of video material is posted to YouTube. In 2016, the estimated worldwide mobile traffic was 6.2 Exabyte a month, equivalent to 6.2 billion gigabytes. Data volume problems are linked with speed and truthfulness.

- **Velocity:** The word speed refers to the pace at which data has been produced and updated. It seems great to note that the Facebook data warehouse holds up to 4,000 bytes of data.
- **Variety:** It is necessary to deal in the structured data which is used that data in big size. There may be requirement to handle the semi structured and most of the unstructured part of the data.
- **Variability:** Variability in this subject expresses the many things. First, the amount of incoherencies prevailing in the database needs an outside detection method to obtain significant findings. The variability of attribute comes with the various attitudes of data and its dimensions provide outcomes from a range of data and sources.
- **Veracity:** It refers to the authentication and confidence in the data as well its sources.
- **Validity:** Validity in the big data denotes the accuracy with correction related to data.
- **Volatility:** Prolonged life of data is denoted by volatility. Such data has been used in different purposes.
- **Visualization:** Moreover, large data visualization is the other characteristic. Currently, the tools for visualization face technological difficulties because of limits in memory

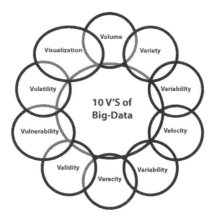

Figure 11.2 10 V's of big data.

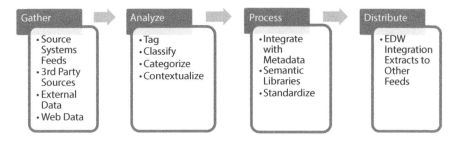

Figure 11.3 Big data technology process.

technology and inadequate scalability, functionality, and reaction time.

- **Value:** Finally, the value characteristic is the most essential. The other characteristics of large data have proven useless if you can extract the business or the actual value from the data. In big data, a significant value has been realized. In this regard, greater knowledge of consumers and subsequently improving procedures for them and company performance are taken into account here.

They are large in volume, high speed, are varied information, which need novel processing techniques for improving decisions, understanding, and optimization of processes. The data set may be termed "big data" if it is difficult for conventional or current technologies to collect, analyze, store, filter, and view data. Generally speaking, "big data" technology [19–21] involves data collection, storage, and useful insights.

11.1.2   Architecture of Big Data

The phrase huge data is a significant volume of data that is defined by a more complicated form of data with an elaborate connection between these data sets. The primary benefit of big data is that it analyzes large data better than traditional techniques of analysis. This is why the big data has become extremely interested in the current generation, which is progress in the gathering of data, storage, and interpretation of data. The usage of digital media has grown in many sectors over the past decades, generating enormous amounts of data, such as medical data, bank data, and social networking [38] data. The cost of data storage is reducing every day, so that the whole data may be saved instead

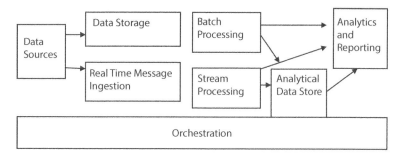

Figure 11.4 Architecture of big data.

being discarded. Many of the data analysis methods are also created; however, only few have successfully analyzed data efficiently. Big data is like the accumulation of enormous resources that can be utilized frequently [4].

11.1.3   Big Data Access Control

Big data typically include huge volumes with a combination of many data types and fast speed. To minimize costs and obtain excellent performance,

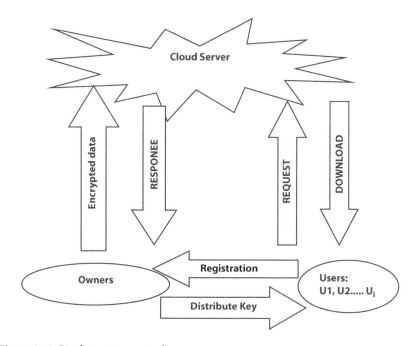

Figure 11.5 Big data access control.

it is most compelling to outsource data to the cloud. Some access mechanisms are necessary to add outsourced data to the cloud for privacy protection and data security [31–34]. Different data sources provide huge quantities of data that is collected via data collection systems such as online transaction, batch processing, or any other sophisticated event data processing. The data generated is most likely externalized to the cloud. Data consumers or users utilize cloud data that the data owner uploads. Some mechanisms for access control must be used for external data in order to prevent illegal use of outsourced data.

Big data framework can be detected and cybernetics [23, 24].

Attribute-based encryption is often used to be outsourced cloud data access control as a framework [6, 7]. Features such as lightweight, access policy enforcement, and encryption supporting encryption are the best option for encryption and access control, attribute-based encryption. It may be flexibly encrypted one-to-many rather than one-to-one. All are depended on performance of big data [8].

11.1.4   Classification of Big Data

Big data classification [3] is a set of technologies designed to store, analyze, and manage this enormous volume as a macrotool for discovering patterns in the chaos of the information explosion and creating smart solutions based on those patterns. Additionally, it is used in the gaming industry and environmental protection, as well as in healthcare and agriculture. In the context of big data, information that is more varied, comes in greater numbers, and does so at a quicker pace is referred to as big. Big data is a phrase used to describe larger and more complex data sets, especially those derived from new sources. The sheer size of these data sets necessitates the use of more traditional data processing methods. Big data is classified in three ways as follows:

- Structured data [6]
- Unstructured data [7]
- Semi-structured data

11.1.4.1   Structured Data

Item reported in lines and columns is defining the meaning of every data. That data kind comprises around 10% of overall data and is easily reached through database management systems. Examples of structured (conventional) data sources contain official records of government agency personal, business, and immovable data and of industrial sensors collecting data processes. Sensor data is one of rapidly growing sectors, especially for movement, temperature, location, liquid and flow monitoring, and financial.

11.1.4.2   Unstructured Data

Item registered with the meaning of each data in rows and columns. This kind of data comprises around 10% of the overall data and is easily reached through database management systems. Examples of structured data sources are consisting official records of government agencies' personal, business, and immovable data, and industrial data processing sensors. Sensor data is one of rapidly growing sectors, especially for movement, light, temperature, location, pressure, vibration, liquid, and flow monitoring in humans as healthcare [13, 22].

11.1.4.3   Semi-Structured Data

Semi-structured data links structured to unstructured data. This usually converts into unstructured data with an attachment of metadata. This may be intrinsic data gathered such as time, location, and device identification stamp or e-mail address [25].

The large diversity of data refers to organized, semi-structured, and unstructured data gathered from different sources. While data can only be used from tablets and databases in the past, data is currently collected in a variety of forms like as e-mail, PDF files, photos, videos, audios, and SM posts [27].

Table 11.1 Big data types based on the level of processing.

Structured data	Unstructured data	Semi-structured data
SQL	User Data	Third Party
Excel, Txt	Likes, Followers, Comments, Tweets	POS
Oracle	Audio	POL
Db2	Video	IR
Main Frame	Geospatial	IMS, MSA

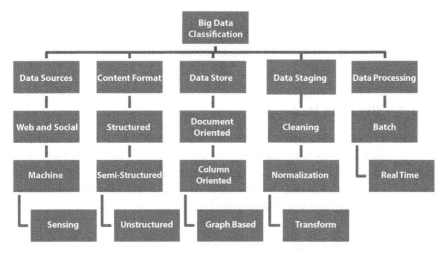

Figure 11.6 Classifications of big data.

Big data supports businesses in generating useful insights. Companies utilize big data to improve their marketing and technology efforts. Companies utilize it for training computers, predictive modeling and other sophisticated analytical applications in machine learning projects. Big data cannot be matched to any particular data volume.

11.1.5   Need of Big Data

Big data helps companies to generate valuable insights. Companies use big data to refine their marketing campaigns and techniques. Companies use it in machine learning projects to train machines, predictive modeling, and other advanced analytics applications. We cannot equate big data to any specific data volume.

11.1.6   Challenges to Big Data Management

The issue and challenges [10–12] in management of big data are as follows:

- Lack of knowledge professionals. To run these modern technologies and large data tools, companies need skilled data professionals;
- Lack of proper understanding of massive data;

- Data growth issues;
- Confusion while big data tool selection;
- Integrating data from a spread of sources;
- Securing data [28].

11.1.7   Big Data Hadoop

Hadoop [7] is open source framework for massive data processing and storage. Hadoop uses simple programming paradigms to handle large data across computer clusters in a distributed setting. Hadoop combines storage with superior processing capability for a huge amount of data. It also enables numerous tasks and jobs to be handled.

11.1.8   Big Data Hadoop Architecture

HDFS is main part of the building design of Hadoop. It gets up for the distributed file systems of Hadoop [9]. This is utilized to collect huge quantity of data and is utilized for this storage by many computers. MapReduce overview is another large data architecture component. The data is processed here on many computers in a distributed way. For data processing resources, the YARN component is utilized. The YARN components are Resource Manager and Node Manager. These two components function as masters and slaves. The Resource Manager is the master, while the slave, i.e., Node Manager, has resources. If the Node Manager starts the job, then it transmits the signal to the master. Big Data Hadoop [26] will be a bonus for you for your thesis.

11.1.9   Security Factors

There have been security [5] treats from viruses and external attacks over big data that is transmitted on network [39–42]. Thus, there are chances of hacking digital content over a network. Hackers are responsible for the access of data without any authentication. On other hand, the cracker is responsible to crack the encrypted content. The encryption techniques and firewalls are frequently used to provide security. But, there have been several attacks that could influence security as follows:

1. Brute force attack
2. Trojan horse attack
3. Man in middle
4. Denial of services
5. SQL injection

11.1.10   Performance Factors

The encryption methods employed to improve the support system's [8] security that is hosting big data are time-consuming and have impact on system's performance. Several variables affect the big data transmission performance, as follows:

- **Transmission Medium:** The kind of transmission media, whether wired or wireless, has an impact on the system's performance. When compared to wired media, wireless systems often operate slowly. In addition, there are many types of wireless and wired systems.
- **Bandwidth:** Bandwidth refers to the amount of data that may be sent in a certain amount of time. More bandwidth allows for the transmission of more data in less time.
- **Data Transmission Protocol:** The data transmission protocol is the set of rules that govern how data travels across the network. In contrast to transmission control protocol, which requires acknowledgement, a protocol like user datagram protocol, which is connectionless and does not need acknowledgment, works quickly.
- **Security Mechanism:** When a security mechanism is used, it may slow down the cloud network's performance since a lot of time is spent determining whether or not the transmission is genuine.
- **Distance:** The performance is influenced by the distance between the transmitter and recipient nodes. The transmission time increases and performance decreases when the distance between the transmitter and the receiver is larger than the distance between the transmitter and the receiver. The transmission time lowers as the distance between the transmitter and the receiver decreases, resulting in better performance.
- **Attenuation:** When a signal travels from one place to another, it loses energy. Distance and transmission medium have an impact on attenuation. To address problems caused by attenuation, a signal regenerator is still required.
- **Compression Method:** To decrease the amount of material utilized in the online learning system, a compression technique is suggested. However, despite the availability of various compression methods, the problem of data loss persists.

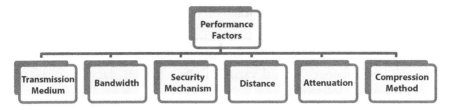

Figure 11.7 Performance factors.

It is necessary to employ a replacement table in which words with a high frequency are replaced with words of smaller size. The size of a packet is reduced when long words are replaced with short ones. As a result, the packet's transmission time is decreased. Furthermore, tiny packets require less time on the network, reducing the likelihood of packet loss. As a result, a compression technique like this may decrease packet transmission time in a big data transmission over network.

11.1.11   Security Threats

Big data security and privacy traditional security and privacy practices cannot manage changes brought forth by big data, from data collection to manipulation, entirely in the digital world. Security mechanisms such as sophisticated encryption algorithms, access restrictions, firewalls, and network security intrusion detection systems may be breached, and even anonymous data can be re-identified and linked for malevolent purpose with a particular user. There are a number of new regulations specifically proposed to deal with challenges big data has introduced in terms of the protection of the individual's privacy, issues like, inference, and aggregation, which allow individuals to be re-identified even when identifying individuals are removed from the data set. However, we face a longstanding dilemma, namely that of a security triangle. This says that because we use harder safeguards, we have a negative impact on system functionality and ease of use, if, for example, a certain regulation limiting the access of companies to raw data analysis and manipulation does not enable corporations to improve their business. In brief, the whole big Data ecosystem, from infrastructure and management to confidentiality rules, integrity, and quality of data, must be reviewed and further investigated in the area of safety and privacy. This section lists some of the big data security and privacy concerns, although extensive study is still needed to fully identify and solve these problems. To ensure that security safeguards are integrated

Figure 11.8 Big data security and privacy areas.

into all big data technologies, such as infrastructure technologies, surveillance and audit procedures, applications, and data origin. Here, we examined big data issues [18] of large data, including framework (Hadoop) [17], infrastructure (Cloud), monitoring and auditing, key management, and data security from five distinct viewpoints (anonymization).

Security of information is threatened in many ways, such as software assaults, intellectual property theft, identification theft, stolen equipment or information, sabotage, and information extortion. Assaults against software mean attacks by viruses, worms, and Trojan horses. Threat may be anything that can exploit security vulnerability and modify, delete, and damage things or objects of interest adversely. Software assaults imply virus, worms, and Trojan horse attacks. Many people think malware, viruses, and worms; bots are all the same stuff. But, they are not the same thing; the only resemblance is that they are all distinct malicious software.

- **Virus**
  You may replicate yourself by connecting them to the host software, such as music and videos, and then through the Internet. ARPANET identified the Creeper virus for the first time. Examples include virus file, macro virus, sector virus boot, and sealth virus.

- **Worms**
  Worms also replicate themselves in nature but do not link up to the software on their host computer. The greatest distinction between viruses and worms is the network consciousness of worms. You may simply go from one computer to another if the network is accessible and you do not cause much damage on the target system, for instance, using hard drive space slowing the device down.

- **Trojan**
  The Trojan idea is quite different from viruses and worms. This is the word Trojan from the Greek mythical "Trojan Horse", which depicts how the Greeks might enter a city in the walls of Troy by hiding their soldiers in a huge wooden horse, which was presented to the Trojans as a gift. The Trojans liked the horses very much and trusted the gift fully. In the night, the soldiers awoke and attacked the city from within.
  Their goal is to hide themselves inside genuine software, and after the program has been implemented, they will either steal information or make a different effort.

11.1.12   Big Data Security Threats

Phrase big data security [14–16] covers all security measures and instruments used in analytics and data operations. Big data systems

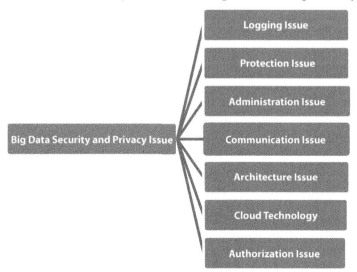

Figure 11.9 Big data security and privacy issue.

assaults—information robbery, DDOS attacks, ransomware, or other harmful actions—may come from offline or online realms, crashing a system.

The effects of robbery may be much greater when businesses keep sensitive or private information such as credit card numbers or customer data. You may face penalties because they have failed to comply with fundamental data security and privacy protection procedures, such as the General Data Protection Regulation.

The difficulties of big data are not confined to on-site systems [29]. They impact the cloud as well. The following list looks at the six most frequent difficulties for big data on site and in the cloud.

11.1.13 Distributed Data

Multiple big data frameworks spread data processing duties for quicker analysis across many platforms. For example, Hadoop is a prominent open-source data processing and storage platform. Originally, Hadoop was built without any safety in mind. Cyber thieves may cause the mapper to display erroneous lists of values or key pairs, rendering the procedure useless. Distributed processing may decrease burden on a system, but additional systems ultimately include more security problems.

11.1.14 Non-Relational Databases

Traditional relational databases utilize row and column tabular schemes. Consequently, they cannot manage large numbers since they are extremely scalable and structurally varied. Non-relational databases, often called NoSQL databases, are intended to circumvent relational database restrictions. Non-relational databases do not utilize the rows and column tabular structure. Instead, NoSQL databases improve data type storage models. NoSQL databases are thus more flexible and scalable than their relational counterparts. NoSQL databases provide security performance and adaptability. Organizations [37] using NoSQL databases must set up the database with extra security actions in a trustworthy environment.

11.1.15 Endpoint Vulnerabilities

Cyber criminals may transmit false data to data lakes on endpoint devices. Safety solutions that analyze logs from endpoints have to check their veracity.

Hackers may, for example, access production systems that utilize sensors to identify process problems. After access, hackers display false findings for the sensors. Such challenges are typically addressed using technology for fraud detection.

11.1.16   Data Mining Solutions

Data mining is at the heart of a huge number of systems. In unstructured data, data mining techniques discover patterns. The issue is that it frequently includes personal and financial information. For this reason, businesses need to incorporate additional safety layers to defend themselves from external and internal dangers.

11.1.17   Access Controls

Companies may want to limit access to sensitive information including personal information, such as medical records. However, individuals who

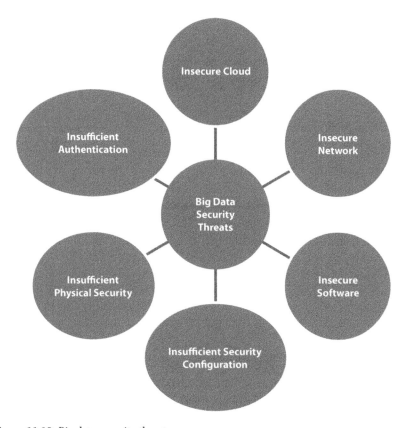

Figure 11.10 Big data security threats.

have no authorization of access, such as medical researchers, nonetheless have to utilize this data. In many companies, granular access is the answer. This implies that people can only access and view the information they need to see.

Big data technologies for granular access are not intended. One option is to transfer necessary data to a second large data storage facility. For example, only medical information without patient names and addresses is copied for medical study.

11.1.18 Motivation

Many kinds of study have been conducted on the big data transmission in network environment [30] via the integration of digital contents. Web technologies have been found to facilitate access to information and resources for remote access of big data. Furthermore, the dynamic web method has shown the most up-to-date technology for exchanging information and applications via the Internet. In the area of big data, the increasing complexity of development objectives and the constant upgrading of technology have created a number of difficulties. Big data has concentrated on the newest technology and tools to explore learning in the contemporary age. Low-cost technology, internet access, and a wealth of instructional material have created a worldwide craze. This phenomenon is assisting in the transformation of big data and communication technologies. To assist academic big data processing, many application tools such as a word processor and spreadsheet tool are provided. The distribution of big data has been found to be unequal among nations. Network environment provides platforms for implementing big data security mechanisms. There are a few security models that have been proposed in previous studies. To protect big data, the RSA, AES, and DES mechanisms, DNA security, and many security protocols have been described. These studies have sparked an interest in securing big data in network. It has been noticed that just a few studies have focused on network performance. As a result, there is a need to increase the speed of big data transmission via the network while maintaining security. Along with DNA security where is need to improve performance using compression mechanism to provide novel approach in order to reduce risk and issues in big data security over network. Such system could help in load balancing and establish significant impact on big data transmission considering challenges. Effectiveness of big data usage could be improved by increasing security of network. In other words, Secure and high performance network that should be capable to manage big data, are supposed to be upgraded.

11.1.19   Importance and Relevance of the Study

When it comes to big data security, the tools and procedures used to protect both data and the analytical processes are referred to as "big data security." In order to safeguard important data from assaults, theft, and other harmful actions, big data security is essential. For cloud-based businesses, big data security issues come in many forms. Theft of online data, ransomware, and DDOS assaults that may bring down a server are all part of this difficult challenge. In the event of these threats being carried out, an organization may suffer significant financial harm in the form of damages, legal expenses, penalties, or punishments.

11.1.20   Background History

A number of studies have been conducted in order to enhance the security and performance of big data. Ularu *et al.* [1] intended to define the concept of Big Data and stress the importance of Big Data Analytics. A larger amount of data gives a better output but also working with it can become a challenge due to processing limitations. M. Agarwal [2] provide guidance to our federal government's senior policy and decision makers, the Tech America Foundation Big Data Commission relied upon its diverse expertise and perspectives, input from government representatives, and previous reports. Suthaharan [3] focuses on the specific problem of Big Data classification of network intrusion traffic. It discusses the system challenges presented by the Big Data problems associated with network intrusion prediction. Shafaque [4] presented a review of various algorithms necessary for handling such large data set is given. These algorithms give us various methods implemented to handle Big Data. Bharvani [5] introduced a research agenda for security and privacy in big data. The paper discusses research challenges and directions concerning data confidentiality, privacy, and trustworthiness in the context of big data.

M. Ke [6] stated the challenges that "Big Data" brings to enterprise aiming to illustrate that only through fostering strengths and circumventing weaknesses can an enterprise remain invincible in "Big Data" era. Bhardwaj [7] implemented of various MapReduce jobs like Pi, TeraSort, Word-Count has been done on cloud based Hadoop deployment by using Microsoft Azure cloud services. D. Asir [8] presented a performance analysis on various clustering algorithm namely K-means, expectation maximization, and density based clustering in order to identify the best clustering algorithm for microarray data. Sum of squared error, log likelihood measures are used to evaluate the performance of these clustering methods.

Verma [9] suggested a Big Data representation for grade analytics in an educational context. The study and the experiments can be implemented on R or AWS the cloud infrastructure provided by Amazon. Minit Arora [10] discourse the possible challenges and security issues related to Big Data characteristics and possible solutions. Naveen [11] proposes the Bayesian classification algorithm of classification mining is suitable for predicting the attack type in the internet worked environment. The forensic aspects of big data issues and challenges are more emphasized in order to help the forensic investigator in case of a network attack. Sivarajah [12] identified relevant BD research studies that have contributed both conceptually and empirically to the expansion and accrual of intellectual wealth to the BDA in technology and organizational resource management discipline. Muhammad [13] gives an insight of how we can uncover additional value from the data generated by healthcare. Large amount of heterogeneous data is generated by these agencies. Ninny [14] utilized to conquer the effectiveness ailing in the space and-time of both ordering and breaking down enormous information. The power of Big Data delivers cost reduction, faster, better decision making and the creation of new products and services. Mohammed [15] researched and developed a security and privacy technique in big data. First, the effects of characteristics of big data on information security and privacy are described. Then, topics and issues on security are discussed and reviewed. Trupti [16] includes some security issues as well as privacy issues in Big data. These issues solved through the creation of a new paradigm: Big Data. Big Data originated new issues related to data security and privacy. Mr. Sharikant [17] presented to utilize ware equipment which is a system show require a solid security instrument, also kerberos utilized for validation it offers get to control rundown and review components, to guarantee the information put away in the Hadoop record framework is secure. Asha [18] was used to fit the proposed model for big data mining. Besides, special features of big data such as velocity make it necessary to consider each rule as a sensitive association rule with an appropriate membership degree. In exiting research Big Data technologies [19] have been introduced with Data Mining Concepts [20] and Techniques. In some researches Big Data Analytics [21] has been made for Wireless and Wired Network Design. While some research focused on Machine Learning Frameworks [22] along with Big Data Framework [23, 24] for building decision support system [25] for big data analysis [26]. Such research has presented utilization of big data and information and communications technology [27]. Researchers have faced several challenges during Big Data, Security [28]. Thus, there remains need to propose mechanism to detect and classify malware efficiently In Big Data

Platform [29, 30]. Secured Image Steganography mechanism [31] could be used for security of big data. Steganography could be performed with support of Wavelet Transform with integration of Genetic Algorithm [32] to provide innovative approach [33] in Steganography [34].

11.1.21   Research Gaps

Several studies have been done on big data and security; however, the research is restricted since the security mechanism employed in the study has reduced the network's performance. Previous researchers have been carried out security of structured data set. Earlier research had drawbacks, such as a high mistake rate, slow speed, and a high packet loss ratio. Structured and unstructured data security, as well as network performance, requires urgent study.

11.2   Technology Used to Big Data

Hardware and software tools used in research have been discussed in this section.

Hardware Requirement

1. CPU above 1 GHz
2. Ram above 4 GB
3. Hard disk 10 GB free space
4. Keyboard and Mouse
5. Monitor

Software Requirement

1. Windows 7/10
2. MATLAB

11.2.1   MATLAB

MATLAB is utilized in a variety of educational settings, including math classes and academies. It is particularly helpful for academic research at universities. In the industrial sector, MATLAB is widely utilized as a simulation tool. It possesses the ability to construct vectors and matrices. Linear algebraic operations are made easier using this program.

Algebra and differential equations are simplified. Numerical integration is carried out with the aid of MATLAB. There are many tools available for dealing with image material. It is possible to make stunning two-dimensional images using MATLAB. It is also useful for creating graphical material that's three-dimensional. Matlab is a well-known programming language that is still in use today. Mathematical program are easier to write with its assistance. It is one of the simplest languages out there to pick up and use.

11.2.2 Characteristics of MATLAB

The characteristics of MATLAB are as follows:

1. It is a high-level programming language.
2. It is capable of being used in technical computing.
3. To manage codes files an environment is given.
4. MATLAB provides interactive features that are useful in many areas like iterating, exploring, and designing. MATLAB tool is used to solve the problems came across while doing various work.
5. To do the activities like Fourier analyzing, filtering, optimizing data MATLAB tool is used. Mathematical functions and equations are also performed in this software. These functions are helpful in solving linear algebraic equations and statically used data, etc.
6. Graphics functions are used as 2D and 3D, which helps in visualising the data.
7. Graphical User Interfaces (GUIs) are customized by the help of the tools present in the MATLAB.

11.2.3 Research Objectives

Objective of research are as follows:

1. To consider current big data research and examining its limits to find security risks to structured and unstructured data, as well as current solutions found in previous studies that have influenced the performance.
2. To proposed work to focus on clustering and encrypting large data, to improve the security of big data while also increasing network speed.

3. To propose model is that is supposed to secure data using encryption mechanism and improve reliability by clustering.
4. To compare of security and performance previous research with the proposed work.

11.2.4   Methodology

The research may be put to use in a variety of ways depending on the methodology used. New problems are organized and identified via exploratory study and gathering information to help solve a problem. To determine if a remedy is viable based on empirical evidence, you will need to do empirical study. Experimental methods, clustering, and encryption mechanisms have all been addressed in this study's findings.

11.3   Working Process of Techniques

Work on implementation and results have been described in this document.

11.3.1   File Splitter

Using a FILE splitter, data would be divided into two distinct files: one for cloud and another for fog. File's name and security code are provided, and file is split and distributed in two locations, one for cloud and another for fog. As a result, transmission is more secure and dependable.

11.3.2   GUI Interface for Client

This is the interface for a file transmitter, which sends data to a server when activated. This is where you will input your username, file path, etc., to send.

11.3.3   GUI Interface for Server

Here, we have a file transmitter interface for sending files to a server. During transmission, factors such as the port number, AES CODE, and file path to be received are taken into account, as well as the security token. To deliver the file to the recipient, the sender must first send it to himself. It is possible that it is a text file saved in notepad. The file would be sent to the recipient's computer. The file's content would be the same as what was delivered from the sender's end.

11.3.4   Encrypted File

The content of the file was shown here while it was being sent. It is illegible since its encoded text. There is no way anybody could understand it if it were stolen from him.

11.4   Proposed Work

11.4.1   Working

During network operations, the work has examined both structured and unstructured information. The simulation tool of choice was Matlab. Data has been grouped using clustering mechanisms and encrypted using encryption methods during the transmission of large amounts of data across networks. Several network ports have been used to transmit the clustered data, ensuring data security while also increasing transmission speed. As a consequence, packet loss and transmission errors are less likely.

11.4.2   Process Flow of Proposed Work

Step 1 Acquire the big data to be transmitted over network.
Step 2 check whether content are structured [36] or unstructured.
Step 3 If contents are unstructured, then make use of map reduce mechanism to create the cluster.
Step 4 If contents are structured, then data set is clustered using normalization technique.
Step 5 Clustered data set is encrypted before transmission.
Step 6 Stop.

11.4.3   Proposed Model

Using the suggested approach, data at the application layer is better protected against active and passive assaults. The proposed model was put up against the existing security model for comparison's sake throughout the study. Packet loss was shown to be less common in the proposed work as compared to traditional work, according to the research.

The use of conventional security measures has been proven unsuccessful. Protecting data using the proposed approach involves utilizing advanced cryptographic methods to separate and encrypt it. With this method, packet loss and congestion are less likely. Active and passive assaults were

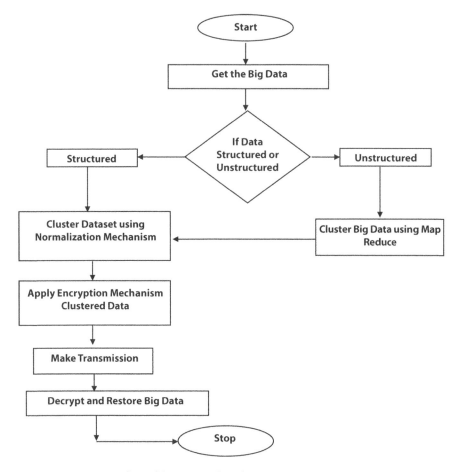

Figure 11.11 Process flow of the proposed work.

examined in this research in order to provide network security at different levels. Packet security is accomplished by dividing them into many parts in the suggested method. New security measures are needed due to limits of current security measures.

Using IP filtering, unauthenticated packets from the server to the client are rejected. If the packet is genuine, then the improved AES ENCRYPTION module will function properly. Here, a data transfer process flow has been outlined.

The goal of the study is to develop defenses against attacks at the app level, where users are in direct contact with the network as a whole. TELNET, HTTP, FTP, and others are utilized at the application layer. The primary aim of research is to create a more time-consuming but more effective application layer system. The emphasis of research has been on learning about various types of attacks, including as aggressive and passive attacks, and the use of cryptographic techniques to increase the security of networks at various stages. Another task proposed is the development and implementation of an effective data security system against active and passive application layer attacks. Using a splitter, this method splits data into two layers and protects it. Finally, studies are conducted to demonstrate that the suggested security model is superior to the current security paradigm.

11.5   Comparative Analysis

11.5.1   Time Comparison

Simulation has been made in MATLAB to present the time taken during data transmission. It has been observed that the time taken in the case of the proposed work is less as compare to time taken during data transmission of uncompressed data and data encrypted using RSA. In Table 11.2, x presents the number of packets and y coordinates are presenting time taken to transfer data.

Table 11.2 Comparison of time taken in different cases.

X	Time taken by uncompressed data	Time taken by advance RSA	Time taken by proposed work
10	1	0.9	0.7
20	1.8	1.7	1.4
30	2.4	2.2	1.9
40	3.2	3.0	2.6
50	4.0	3.9	3.1
60	5.0	4.9	3.7
70	5.5	5.0	4.0
80	6.0	5.2	4.3
90	6.3	5.6	4.8
100	6.5	6.0	5.0

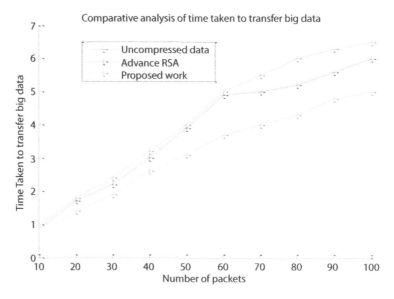

Figure 11.12 Comparative analysis of time taken.

11.5.2   Error Rate Comparison

Simulation has been made in MATLAB to present the error rate during data transmission. It has been observed that the error rate in the case of the proposed work is less as compare to error rate during data transmission of uncompressed data and data encrypted using RSA. In Table 11.3, x presents the number of packets and y coordinates are presenting error rate to transferred data.

11.5.3   Packet Size Comparison

Simulation has been made in MATLAB [35] to present the packet size during data transmission. It has been observed that the packet size in the case of the proposed work is less as compare to packet size during data transmission of uncompressed data. In Table 11.4, x presents the number of packets and y coordinates are presenting packet size of transferred data.

11.5.4   Packet Affected Due to Attack

Simulation has been made in MATLAB to present the packet affected due to attack during data transmission. It has been observed that the packet affected due to attack in the case of the proposed work is less as compare

Table 11.3 Comparison of error rate in different cases.

X	Time taken by uncompressed data	Time taken by advance RSA	Time taken by proposed work
10	0.9	0.8	0.7
20	1.5	1.4	1.0
30	2.4	2.2	1.8
40	2.7	2.3	2.0
50	4.0	3.1	2.6
60	4.4	4.0	3.8
70	4.8	4.3	4.0
80	5.0	4.5	4.2
90	5.2	4.8	4.4
100	5.6	5.0	4.8

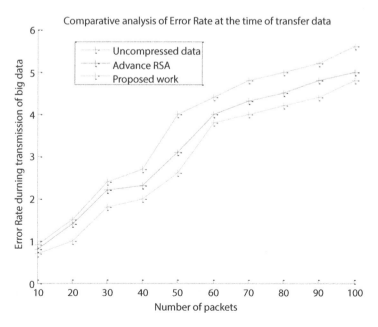

Figure 11.13 Comparative analysis of error rate.

Table 11.4 Comparison of packet size in different cases.

X	Time taken by uncompressed data	Time taken by proposed work
10	9	5
20	15	8
30	22	10
40	29	12
50	34	15
60	43	20
70	4.8	25
80	50	31
90	54	33
100	62	35

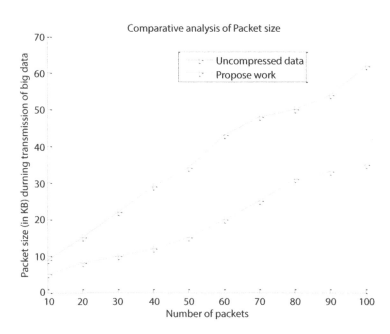

Figure 11.14 Comparative analysis of packet size.

Table 11.5 Comparison of security mechanism in different cases.

X	Time taken by uncompressed data	Time taken by advance RSA	Time taken by proposed work
10	9	7	5
20	14	10	8
30	21	14	10
40	27	18	14
50	30	23	17
60	35	30	20
70	37	32	22
80	40	35	25
90	43	38	28
100	45	40	30

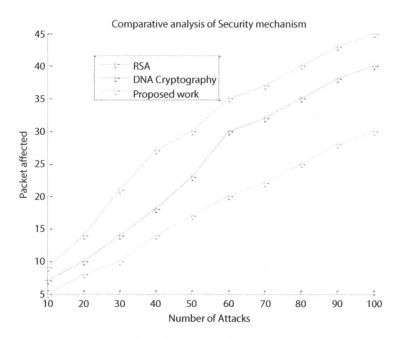

Figure 11.15 Comparative analysis of security mechanism.

to packet affected due to attack during data transmission of uncompressed data. In Table 11.5, x presents the number of packets and y coordinates are presenting packet affected due to attack.

11.6   Conclusion and Future Scope

11.6.1   Conclusion

The suggested approach guarantees big data security by isolating and encrypting big data using advanced cryptographic methods. Packet loss and congestion are less likely with this design. In order to provide network security at different levels, this research examined active and passive threats. A more secure solution has been provided at the application layer, which protects big data from both active and passive assaults. The proposed model was compared to an already existing network security model throughout the study process. Packet dropping was shown to be less common in the proposed work as compared to the usual approach. Traditionally implemented security solutions only provide protection at the application layer, according to this research. Packets in the proposed work are made secure by being divided into several parts. The limits of traditional security techniques have created a need for a new security system. Securing big data presents many difficulties. Therefore, strive to take nothing for granted when you host big data platform. In order to meet these difficulties with a solid security SLA, it is essential to collaborate with the Service Level Agreement. IT is in charge of security software, regulations, and procedures. Security software protects big data deployments against viruses and unauthorized access.

To ensure compliance, compliance officials should collaborate closely with the IT team, which means credit card information, is automatically secured. Database Administrators (DBA) should also be working in close collaboration with IT team to protect databases. Enabling your company to offer services in long term will help ensure big data platform from high and low risks.

Great data are analyzed for pieces of information, leading to improved choices and strategic actions for companies worldwide. However, only a tiny proportion of data gets analyzed. To find out if current data protection solutions are enough for processing big data, we looked at the problems of privacy in big data by first defining big data privacy standards. In every step of large data life cycle, privacy issues and benefits and drawbacks of current technology that protects privacy in connection with large data applications are discussed. This article also covers both classic and modern data protection methods. One example is to hide a needle in a haystack, in that protection of privacy is utilized by rules of association. Identity-based anonymization and differential privacy are also discussed, as is a comparative study of many existing big data techniques. MapReduce Framework provides scalable anonymization techniques. Number of mappers and reducers may simply be increased. In future, we need views to find effective solutions to privacy and security scalability issue in age of big data and, in particular, difficulty of combining security and privacy models by using framework to decrease map. More effective data protection methods must also be created in terms of healthcare services. Differential privacy is one area that has tremendous untapped potential to be further exploited. When IoT and big data are introduced, there is a lot to do with the rapid development of IoT; although data is plentiful, its quality is poor, and it comes from a variety of sources, with a wide range of representations, and it is heterogeneous in that it is both organized and unstructured in different ways. This brings with it new difficulties in terms of privacy and open research. In future, various ways of protecting privacy of mining may thus be examined and applied. As a result, a wide range of further study on protection of privacy in large data exists.

11.6.2   Future Scope

In conventional employment, big data security was limited to application layer. Packet security has been given in the proposed work. In light of the shortcomings of existing network security measures, a new network security system was required. It should be more difficult to decrypt data without first confirming your identity. As a result, decentralized network security is required in order to guard against attacks coming from different networks. Multilayer security would improve Advanced Encryption Standard. To offer a dependable transmission method, suggested work has split data into numerous pieces. This technique would make network security system impervious to hacker or cracker assaults. Decryption without authentication should become less likely. In order to avoid attackers, security on big data transmission was required. Big data transmission across several networks has improved Advanced Encryption Standard by adding security and dependability. This technique has rendered security system resistant to hacker or cracker assaults.

References

1. Sheng, J., Amankwah-Amoah, J., Wang, X., A multidisciplinary perspective of big data in management research, *International Journal of Production Economics*, 191, (C), 97–112, 2017.
2. Bansal, R., Obaid, A.J., Gupta, A., Singh, R., Pramanik, S., Impact of Big Data on Digital Transformation in 5G Era. *2nd International Conference on Physics and Applied Sciences (ICPAS 2021), Journal of Physics: Conference Series*, 2021.
3. Suthaharan, S., Big data classification: problems and challenges in network intrusion prediction with machine learning, in: *ACM SIGMETRICS Performance Evaluation Review*, vol. 41, pp. 70–73, 2014.
4. Shafaque, U. and Thakare, P.D., Foundation of Computer Science (FCS), 2014. *Algorithm and Approaches to Handle Big Data. IJCA Proceedings on National Level Technical Conference X-PLORE 2014*, vol. 1, 2014.
5. Pramanik, S. and Singh, R.P., Role of Steganography in Security Issues. *International Conference on Advance Studies in Engineering and Sciences*, pp. 1225–1230, 2017.
6. Gupta, A., Pramanik, S., Bui, H.T., Ibenu, N.M., Machine Learning and Deep Learning in Steganography and Steganalysis, in: *Multidisciplinary Approach to Modern Digital Steganography*, S. Pramanik, M. Ghonge, R.V. Ravi, K. Cengiz (Eds.), IGI Global, 2021, doi: DOI: 10.4018/978-1-7998-7160-6. ch004.
7. Bhattacharya, A., Ghosal, A., Obaid, A.J., Krit, S., Shukla, V.K., Mandal, K., Pramanik, S., Unsupervised Summarization Approach With Computational Statistics of Microblog Data, in: *Methodologies and Applications of Computational Statistics for Machine Intelligence*, D. Samanta, R.R. Althar, S. Pramanik, S. Dutta (Eds.), IGI Global, 2021, doi: DOI: 10.4018/978-1-7998-7701-1.ch002.
8. Danasingh, Asir A., Fernando, A., Leavline, E.J., Performance Analysis on Clustering Approaches for Gene Expression Data, 5, 196–200, 2016. doi: 10.17148/IJARCCE.2016.5242.
9. Verma, C. and Pandey, R., Big Data representation for grade analysis through Hadoop framework. *Proceedings of the 2016 6th International Conference - Cloud System and Big Data Engineering, Confluence 2016*, pp. 312–315, 2016.
10. Arora, M. and Bahuguna, Dr H., Big Data Security – The Big Challenge. *Int. J. Sci. Eng. Res.*, 7, 12, 2229–5518, 2016, December.
11. Rishishwar, N. and Vartika, Mr. K. T., Big Data: Security Issues and Challenges. *Int. J. Tech. Res. Appl.*, e-ISSN: 2320-8163, Special Issue 42 (AMBALIKA), 21–25, 2017, March.
12. Sivarajah, U., Kamal, M.M., Irani, Z., Weerakkody, V., Critical analysis of Big Data challenges and analytical methods. *J. Bus. Res.*, 70, 263–286, Jan 2017.

13. Bandyopadhyay, S., Dutta, S., Pramanik, S., Prediction of Weight Gain during COVID-19 for Avoiding Complication in Health. *Preprints*, 2021050177, 2021. doi: 10.20944/preprints202105.0177.v1

14. Bhogal, N. and Jain, S., A Review on Big Data Security and Handling. *Int. J. Res. Based*, 6, 1, 2348–1943, 2017, March.

15. Mohammed, S.A.-K., Security and Privacy in Big Data. *Int. J. Comput. Eng. Inf. Technol.*, 9, 2, 2412–8856, 2017, February.

16. Pathrabe, T.V., Survey on Security Issues of Growing Technology: Big Data. *IJIRST, National Conference on Latest Trends in Networking and Cyber Security*, 2017, march.

17. Kadam, Mr.S.R. and Patil, V., Review on Big Data Security in Hadoop. *Int. Res. J. Eng. Technol. (IRJET)*, 04, 01, 1362–1365, Jan 2017.

18. Patel, A., A Survey Paper on Security Issue with Big Data on Association Rule Mining. *IJIRST, National Conference on Latest Trends in Networking and Cyber Security*, March 2017.

19. Oussous, A., Benjelloun, F., Lahcen, A.A., Belfkih, S., Big Data technologies: A survey. J. King Saud Univ. *Comput. Inf. Sci.*, 30, 431–448, 2018.

20. Prasdika, P. and Sugiantoro, B., A Review Paper on Big Data and Data Mining Concepts and Techniques. *IJID (International J. Inf. Development)*, 7, 33, 36–38, 2018. 10.14421/ijid.2018.07107.

21. Hadi, M., Lawey, A., El-Gorashi, T., & Elmirghani, J., Big Data Analytics for Wireless and Wired Network Design: A Survey. *Computer Networks*, 132, 180–199, 2018. 10.1016/j.comnet.2018.01.016.

22. Pramanik, S., Sagayam, K.M., Jena, O.P., Machine Learning Frameworks, in: *Cancer Detection, ICCSRE 2021*, Morocco, 2021, https://doi.org/10.1051/e3sconf/202129701073.

23. Gupta, D. and Rani, R., Big Data Framework for Zero-Day Malware Detection. *Cybern. Syst.*, 49, 2, 103–121, 2018, doi: 10.1080/01969722.2018.1429835.

24. Jung, J., Kim, K., Park, J., Framework of Big data Analysis about IoT-Home-device for supporting a decision making an effective strategy about new product design, in: *2019 International Conference on Artificial Intelligence in Information and Communication (ICAIIC)*, pp. 582–584, Okinawa, Japan, 2019.

25. Tabary, M.Y., Memariani, A., Ebadati, E., Chapter 3 - Developing a decision support system for big data analysis and cost allocation in national healthcare, in: *Healthcare data analytics and management*, N. Dey, A.S. Ashour, C. Bhat, S.J. Fong (Eds.), pp. 89-109, Academic Press, Cambridge, MA, 2019.

26. Almansouri, H.T. and Masmoudi, Y., Hadoop Distributed File System for Big data analysis, *2019 4th World Conference on Complex Systems (WCCS)*, pp. 1–5, 2019.

27. Freeman, J.D., Blacker, B., Hatt, G., Tan, S., Ratcliff, J., Woolf, T.B. *et al.*, Use of big data and information and communications technology in disasters: an

integrative review. *Disaster Med. Public Health Prep.*, 13, 2, 353–367, 2019, Apr.

28. Kantarcioglu, M. and Ferrari, E., Research Challenges at the Intersection of Big Data, Security and Privacy, Specialty grand challenge article. *Front. Big Data*, 14, 2, 1, 2019, February. doi: 10.3389/fdata.2019.00001. PMID: 33693324; PMCID: PMC7931933.

29. Niveditha, V. R., Ananthan, T., Amudha, S., Sam, D., Srinidhi, S., Detect and Classify Zero Day Malware Efficiently In Big Data Platform. *Journal of Advanced Science*, 1947–1954, 2020.

30. Aburawi, Y., & Albaour, A., Big Data: Review Paper. *International Journal Of Advance Research And Innovative Ideas In Education*, 7, 2021, 2021.

31. Pramanik, S. and Raja, S.S., A Secured Image Steganography using Genetic Algorithm. *Adv. Math.: Sci. J.*, 9, 7, 4533–4541, 2020.

32. Pramanik, S. and Bandyopadhyay, S.K., Image Steganography Using Wavelet Transform and Genetic Algorithm. *Int. J. Innov. Res. Adv. Eng.*, 1, 1–4, 2014.

33. Pramanik, S. and Bandyopadhyay, S.K., An Innovative Approach in Steganography. *Scholars J. Eng. Technol.*, 9, 276–280, 2014.

34. Pramanik, S. and Bandyopadhyay, S.K., Application of Steganography in Symmetric Key Cryptography with Genetic Algorithm. *Int. J. Eng. Technol.*, 10, 1791–1799, 2013.

35. Pramanik, S., Singh, R.P., Ghosh, R., Application of Bi-orthogonal Wavelet Transform and Genetic Algorithm in Image Steganography. *Multimed. Tools Appl.*, 79, 17463–17482, 2020, https://doi.org/10.1007/s11042-020-08676-1.

36. Samanta, D., Dutta, S., Galety, M.G., Pramanik, S., A Novel Approach for Web Mining Taxonomy for High-Performance Computing, in: *Cyber Intelligence and Information Retrieval*, pp. 425–432, Springer, 2021, https://doi.org/10.1007/978-981-16-4284-5_37.

37. Pramanik, S., Ghosh, R., Ghonge, M., Narayan, V., Sinha, M., Pandey, D., Samanta, D., A Novel Approach using Steganography and Cryptography in Business Intelligence, in: *Integration Challenges for Analytics, Business Intelligence and Data Mining*, A. Azevedo and M.F. Santos (Eds.), pp. 192–217, IGI Global, 2020, DOI: 10.4018/978-1-7998-5781-5.ch010.

38. Mandal, A., Dutta, S., Pramanik, S., Machine Intelligence of Pi from Geometrical Figures with Variable Parameters using SCILab, in: *Methodologies and Applications of Computational Statistics for Machine Intelligence*, D. Samanta, R.R. Althar, S. Pramanik, S. Dutta (Eds.), IGI Global, 2021, DOI: 10.4018/978-1-7998-7701-1.ch003.

39. Ghosh, R., Mohanty, S., Pattnaik, P., Pramanik, S., Performance analysis based on probability of false alarm and miss detection in cognitive radio network. *Int. J. Wirel. Mob. Comput.*, 20, 4, 390–400, 2021.

40. Ghosh, R., Mohanty, S., Pattnaik, P., Pramanik, S., A Performance Assessment of Power-Efficient Variants of Distributed Energy-Efficient Clustering Protocols in WSN. *Int. J. Interact. Commun. Syst. Technol.*, 10, 2, 1–14, article 1, 2021.

41. Ghosh, R., Mohanty, S., Pattnaik, P., Pramanik, S., A Novel Performance Evaluation of Resourceful Energy Saving Protocols of Heterogeneous WSN to Maximize Network Stability and Lifetime, in: *International Journal of Interdisciplinary Telecommunications and Networking*, vol. 13, issue 2, 2021.

42. Ghosh, R., Mohanty, S., Pramanik, S., Low Energy Adaptive Clustering Hierarchy (LEACH) Protocol for Extending the Lifetime of the Wireless Sensor Network. *Int. J. Comput. Sci. Eng.*, 7, 6, 1118–1124, 2019.

43. Pramanik, S., Singh, R.P., Ghosh, R., Bandyopadhyay, S.K., A Unique Way to Generate Password at Random Basis and Sending it Using a New Steganography Technique. *Indones. J. Electr. Eng. Inform.*, 8, 3, 525–531, 2020.

44. Pramanik, S., Samanta, D., Ghosh, R., Bandyopadhyay, S.K., A New Combinational Technique in Image Steganography. *Int. J. Inf. Secur. Priv.*, 15, 3, article 4, IGI Global, 2021.

About the Editors

Sabyasachi Pramanik is an assistant professor in the Department of Computer Science and Engineering, Haldia Institute of Technology, India. After earned his PhD in computer science and engineering from the Sri Satya Sai University of Technology and Medical Sciences, Bhopal, India. He has more than 50 publications in various scientific and technical conferences, journals, and online book chapter contributions. He is also serving as the editorial board member on many scholarly journals and has authored one book. He is an editor of various books from a number of publishers, including Scrivener Publishing.

Debabrata Samanta, PhD, is an assistant professor in the Department of Computer Science, CHRIST (Deemed to be University), Bangalore, India. He obtained his PhD in from the National Institute of Technology, Durgapur, India, and he is the owner of 20 patents and two copyrights. He has authored or coauthored over 166 research papers in international journals and conferences and has received the "Scholastic Award" at the Second International Conference on Computer Science and IT application in Delhi, India. He is a co-author of 11 books and the co-editor of 7 books and has presented various papers at international conferences and received Best Paper awards. He has authored or co-authored 20 Book Chapters.

 **M. Vinay, PhD**, obtained his PhD at JJT University Rajasthan for Computer Science and is an assistant professor of computer science at CHRIST (Deemed to be University) Bengaluru, India. With over 14 years of teaching, he has received numerous prestigious teaching awards. He has given more than 30 invited talks, 35 guests lectures and conducted more than 25 workshops, he has also published over a dozen papers in distinguished scholarly journals.

 **Abhijit Guha** is pursuing a doctorate with the Department of Data Science, CHRIST (Deemed to be University), India. He is currently working as a research and development scientist with First American India Private Ltd. He received three consecutive "Innovation of the Year" awards, from 2015 to 2017, by First American India for his contribution towards his research.

Index

Also of Interest

Check out these other related titles from Scrivener Publishing

Also in the series, "Advances in Cyber Security"

CYBER SECURITY AND DIGITAL FORENSICS: Challenges and Future Trends, Edited by Mangesh M. Ghonge, Sabyasachi Pramanik, Ramchandra Mangrulkar, and Dac-Nhuong Le, ISBN: 9781119795636. Written and edited by a team of world renowned experts in the field, this groundbreaking new volume covers key technical topics and gives readers a comprehensive understanding of the latest research findings in cyber security and digital forensics. *NOW AVAILABLE!*

DEEP LEARNING APPROACHES TO CLOUD SECURITY, Edited by Pramod Singh Rathore, Vishal Dutt, Rashmi Agrawal, Satya Murthy Sasubilli, and Srinivasa Rao Swarna, ISBN 9781119760528. Covering one of the most important subjects to our society today, this editorial team delves into solutions taken from evolving deep learning approaches, solutions allow computers to learn from experience and understand the world in terms of a hierarchy of concepts. *NOW AVAILABLE!*

Other related titles

SECURITY ISSUES AND PRIVACY CONCERNS IN INDUSTRY 4.0 APPLICATIONS, Edited by Shibin David, R. S. Anand, V. Jeyakrishnan, and M. Niranjanamurthy, ISBN: 9781119775621. Written and edited by a team of international experts, this is the most comprehensive and up-to-date coverage of the security and privacy issues surrounding Industry 4.0 applications, a must-have for any library. *NOW AVAILABLE!*

MACHINE LEARNING TECHNIQUES AND ANALYTICS FOR CLOUD SECURITY, Edited by Rajdeep Chakraborty, Anupam Ghosh and Jyotsna Kumar Mandal, ISBN: 9781119762256. This book covers new methods, surveys, case studies, and policy with almost all machine learning techniques and analytics for cloud security solutions. *NOW AVAILABLE!*

ARTIFICIAL INTELLIGENCE AND DATA MINING IN SECURITY FRAMEWORKS, Edited by Neeraj Bhargava, Ritu Bhargava, Pramod Singh Rathore, and Rashmi Agrawal, ISBN 9781119760405. Written and edited by a team of experts in the field, this outstanding new volume offers solutions to the problems of security, outlining the concepts behind allowing computers to learn from experience and understand the world in terms of a hierarchy of concepts. *NOW AVAILABLE!*

SECURITY DESIGNS FOR THE CLOUD, IOT AND SOCIAL NETWORKING, Edited by Dac-Nhuong Le, Chintin Bhatt and Mani Madhukar, ISBN: 9781119592266. The book provides cutting-edge research that delivers insights into the tools, opportunities, novel strategies, techniques, and challenges for handling security issues in cloud computing, Internet of Things and social networking. *NOW AVAILABLE!*

DESIGN AND ANALYSIS OF SECURITY PROTOCOLS FOR COMMUNICATION, Edited by Dinesh Goyal, S. Balamurugan, Sheng-Lung Peng and O.P. Verma, ISBN: 9781119555643. The book combines analysis and comparison of various security protocols such as HTTP, SMTP, RTP, RTCP, FTP, UDP for mobile or multimedia streaming security protocol. *NOW AVAILABLE!*

Printed and bound by CPI Group (UK) Ltd, Croydon, CR0 4YY

27/10/2024

14580470-0003